HM
251
.C46
1998

SIXTH EDITION

P9-AQF-331

Symbolic Interactionism
An Introduction,
An Interpretation,
An Integration

Joel M. Charon

Moorhead State University
Moorhead, Minnesota

With a chapter on Erving Goffman
by Spencer Cahill

University of South Florida

Prentice Hall

Upper Saddle River, New Jersey 07458

GOSHEN COLLEGE LIBRARY
GOSHEN, INDIANA

Library of Congress Cataloging-in-Publication Data

CHARON, JOEL M.
  Symbolic interactionism: an introduction, an interpretation,
an integration / JOEL M. CHARON — 6th ed. / with a chapter
on Erving Goffman written by Spencer Cahill.
      p. cm.
  Includes bibliographical references and index.
  ISBN 0-13-671694-6 (pbk. : alk. paper)
  1. Symbolic interactionism I. Title.
  HM251.C46   1998
  302—dc21   97030940

Editorial director: *Charlyce Jones Owen*
Acquisitions editor: *Nancy Roberts*
Production editor: *Edie Riker*
Cover design: *Rosemarie Votta*
Buyer: *Mary Ann Gloriande*
Marketing manager: *Christopher DeJohn*

This book was set in 10/12 New Baskerville by East End Publishing Services
and was printed and bound by Courier Companies, Inc. The cover was
printed by Phoenix Color Corp.

© 1998, 1995, 1992, 1989, 1985, 1979 by Prentice-Hall, Inc.
Simon & Schuster / A Viacom Company
Upper Saddle River, New Jersey 07458

All rights reserved. No part of this book may be
reproduced, in any form or by any means,
without permission in writing from the publisher.

Printed in the United States of America

10   9   8   7   6   5   4   3

ISBN   0-13-671694-6

Prentice-Hall International (UK) Limited, *London*
Prentice-Hall of Australia Pty. Limited, *Sydney*
Prentice-Hall Canada Inc., *Toronto*
Prentice-Hall Hispanoamericana, S.A., *Mexico*
Prentice-Hall of India Private Limited, *New Delhi*
Prentice-Hall of Japan, Inc., *Tokyo*
Simon & Schuster Asia Pte. Ltd., *Singapore*
Editora Prentice-Hall do Brasil, Ltda., *Rio de Janeiro*

Contents

4   **The Meaning of the Symbol**   **41**

5   **The Importance of the Symbol**   **60**

9   Human Action   126

10   Social Interaction   151

11   Society   171

12   Erving Goffman (by Spencer Cahill)   191

Preface

The first edition of this book was an attempt to fulfill a promise I made to myself in graduate school: to write a clear, organized, and interesting introduction to symbolic interactionism. It was meant to integrate that perspective, to be as accurate as possible, and to help the reader apply the ideas to real life.

Since that first edition, symbolic interactionism has become increasingly important to the discipline of sociology. Its criticisms of traditional sociology have made an impact. Its research studies have increasingly become a part of sociology. Its practitioners are some of the leading officers, journal editors, and researchers in the discipline.

In the fourth edition I was very fortunate to include a chapter on Erving Goffman by Spencer Cahill, which proved to be a wonderful addition. Joel Powell's contribution to that fourth edition also proved significant.

Each time I attempt to improve on what I have written before, it brings a certain humility to my work. After revising each edition, I wonder how in the world I could ever have written what I had previously. In the fifth edition I thoroughly revised the chapter on social interaction and the last chapter on applications of the perspective. In this sixth edition, I tried to thoroughly revise the first three chapters, largely as a result of good comments made by reviewers and students from my classes.

I always go through every chapter carefully in order to update it and make the text clearer. Based on my teaching experience, I constantly ask myself how to best present this difficult material to students so they understand it and see its relevance for understanding themselves and their society. I try to be sensitive to other professors who use my books, since they know well what needs to be done. Of course, in the end, I have made the final decisions as to what ended up in this book, and I thank my editors at Prentice Hall for allowing me to do this.

I wish to thank the reviewers of my book: Jerry L. Johnson, Grand Valley State University; Norman Goodman, State University of New York; and Whitney Garcia, University of Maryland. Their comments were encouraging and helped me to be more critical of my own work.

Finally, I would also like to thank certain symbolic interactionists who have been very important to my thinking from afar. I read what they write; I listen to and watch them at meetings; they are important models to me, although they may not know it. They are Howard Becker, Lonnie Athens, Spencer Cahill, Norman Denzin, Gary Fine, Ruth Horowitz, Helena Lopata, John Lofland, Lyn Lofland, David Maines, Bernard Meltzer, and Tamotsu Shibutani. I also admired Carl Couch, and I will miss him.

I dedicate this book to my wife, Susan, who continues to be my best friend and greatest supporter.

Joel M. Charon
Moorhead State University

1

The Nature of "Perspective"

The O. J. Simpson trial was very hard for me to ignore. There were many issues that had real importance to me. Indeed, many of the values I give lip service to and try to pursue in my life were challenged, questioned, put at risk. As a sociologist and teacher I have tried very hard to care about people, to seek justice, truth, equality. The trial forced me to ask many questions about these values, their importance to me, and their importance to others. I experienced a lot of conflict, because the issues involved were very complex to me.

One of the issues, of course, had to do with truth. Who has truth, and how can we tell who has truth? Is there a real truth to be found? Do lawyers know the truth? Which jury does? Can the system of justice that we have ever find the truth? Is it supposed to? What does O.J. Simpson really believe? How much of what he says does he actually believe? Then there is the emphasis the media has placed on the division between the African-American community and the white community: Who has the truth? How can there be such a gulf between them? Is one of them wrong?

It occurred to me that many of my questions made much more sense by introducing the concept of "perspective" to my conflicting questions, especially the division between the two communities. If I bring in "perspective" in trying to unravel this mystery, everything begins to make a lot more sense. People interact over a period of time; out of that interaction they come to share a perspective; what they see will be interpreted through that perspective; often each perspective tells us something very important about what is really true.

The word "perspective" has a long history with me. Many years ago, I read the following story by A. Averchenko. It underscores the difficulty the human has in knowing what is really happening "out there." When I first read it, I thought that it illustrated well how people could be so closed-minded, narrow, and less than truthful. Eventually, it, like my questions about the Simpson trial, led me to see the importance of understanding the big role that "perspective" plays in all of our lives.

"Men are comic," she said, smiling dreamily. Not knowing whether this indicated praise or blame, I answered noncommittally: "Quite true."

"Really, my husband's a regular Othello. Sometimes I'm sorry I married him." I looked helplessly at her. "Until you explain—" I began.

"Oh, I forgot that you haven't heard. About three weeks ago, I was walking home with my husband through the square. I had a large black hat on, which suits me awfully well, and my cheeks were quite pink from walking. As we passed under a street light, a pale, dark-haired fellow standing nearby glanced at me and suddenly took my husband by his sleeve."

"'Would you oblige me with a light,' he says. Alexander pulled his arm away, stooped down, and quicker than lightning, banged him on the head with a brick. He fell like a log. Awful!"

"Why, what on earth made your husband get jealous all of a sudden?" She shrugged her shoulders. "I told you men are very comic."

Bidding her farewell, I went out, and at the corner came across her husband.

"Hello, old chap," I said. "They tell me you've been breaking people's heads."

He burst out laughing. "So, you've been talking to my wife. It was jolly lucky that brick came so pat into my hand. Otherwise, just think: I had about fifteen hundred rubles in my pocket, and my wife was wearing her diamond earrings."

"Do you think he wanted to rob you?"

"A man accosts you in a deserted spot, asks for a light and gets hold of your arm. What more do you want?"

Perplexed, I left him and walked on.

"There's no catching you today," I heard a voice from behind.

I looked around and saw a friend I hadn't set eyes upon for three weeks.

"Lord!" I exclaimed. "What on earth has happened to you?"

He smiled faintly and asked in turn: "Do you know whether any lunatics have been at large lately? I was attacked by one three weeks ago. I left the hospital only today."

With sudden interest, I asked: "Three weeks ago? Were you sitting in the square?"

"Yes, I was. The most absurd thing. I was sitting in the square, dying for a smoke. No matches! After ten minutes or so, a gentleman passes with some old hag. He was smoking. I go up to him, touch him on the sleeve and ask in my most polite manner: 'Can you oblige me with a light?' And what do you think? The madman stoops down, picks up something, and the next moment I am lying on the ground with a broken head, unconscious. You probably read about it in the newspapers."

I looked at him and asked earnestly: "Do you really believe you met up with a lunatic?"

"I am sure of it."

Anyhow, afterwards I was eagerly digging in old back numbers of the local paper. At last I found what I was looking for: A short note in the accident column.

UNDER THE INFLUENCE OF DRINK

"Yesterday morning, the keepers of the square found on a bench a young man whose papers show him to be of good family. He had evidently fallen to the ground while in a state of extreme intoxication, and had broken his head on a nearby brick. The distress of the prodigal's parents is indescribable."

The seeker of truth wants to know: "What really happened?" The police, of course, will investigate situations such as this one in order to determine who is telling the truth. Usually they conclude "someone must be lying" or "someone is twisting the truth to fit his or her own selfish needs." It is difficult for the police—and for most of the rest of us—to believe that all may be telling what they believe to be the "truth," and, indeed, each one may actually be capturing part of the truth. If we place ourselves in the positions of the people involved, however, and try very hard to imagine what they were seeing from their particular angle, we might begin to appreciate the powerful role that "perspective" plays as we try to see reality "as it really is." It actually may be that some of these perspectives bring the actor closer to reality than the others, but none of them is able to capture the whole of it. Not a single one of these is omniscient nor all-inclusive.

The story is called "Point of View," and in a sense, that is the very best definition of what a perspective is. A perspective is an angle on reality, a place where the individual stands as he or she looks at and tries to understand reality. An angle will always limit what one sees, since other angles—many of which may also be accurate—cannot be considered at the same time.

Human beings always see reality through perspectives. Once we begin to learn perspectives as children we are doomed—or blessed—to use them as our angle of vision. If we recognize this, then we must also admit there is no possible way that any individual can see all aspects of any situation simultaneously. Perspectives force us to pull out certain stimuli from our environment and to totally ignore other stimuli. Perspectives force us to make sense out of that stimuli in one way rather than another. Perspectives sensitize the individual to see parts of reality, they desensitize the individual to other parts, and they guide the individual to make sense of the reality to which he or she is sensitized. Seen in this light, a perspective is an absolutely basic part of everyone's existence, and it acts as a filter through which everything around us is perceived and interpreted. There is no possible way that the individual can encounter reality "in the raw," directly, as it really is, for whatever is seen can be only part of the real situation.

Whatever might have happened in the trial of O.J. Simpson, those involved are going to see it differently, and those observing it from the outside will inevitably disagree about what is and is not true about it. It becomes clearer to me why those in the African-American community will see it differently from me. What they see comes from a perspective that arose out of oppression. For hundreds of years there has been an ongoing discussion about events affecting people in that community. Learning about their own history and seeing how friends and neighbors are treated by many outside the community, including and especially the police and the courts, develop a perspective that causes many individuals who hold it to notice a racist system of justice, to be skeptical of police officers, to wonder about the good intentions of white judges, white middle-class jurors, and white reporters. Does their perspective allow them to see the truth? Sometimes a part of it—

never the full truth. And how about those who come from the perspective of whites outside of that community—will their perspective allow them to see the truth? Sometimes a part of it—never the full truth. Can those of us trying to understand reality benefit from the fact that there are many perspectives that people can use to see the reality of the O.J. Simpson trial? Of course we can. It is important for all of us who seek the truth to understand why some people, because of their perspective, will see the criminal justice system as unjust, while others will think of it as democratic and fair. It is probably both of these, and for the pursuer of truth to understand it well, both perspectives may be important to understand.

Perspectives are made up of words—it is these words that are used by the observer to make sense out of situations. In a way, the best definition of perspective is a *conceptual framework*, which emphasizes that perspectives are really interrelated sets of words used to order physical reality. The words we use cause us to make assumptions and value judgments about what we are seeing (and not seeing).

Reality, for the individual, depends on the words used to look at situations. If we examine the story by Averchenko in this light, it becomes obvious that the differences between actors' viewpoints depend on the words they used to *see*. The woman uses "Othello," "married," "black hat" ("which suits me"), "pale, dark-haired fellow," all of which reveal that in that situation she was "seeing" according to a perspective associated with a woman concerned with her attractiveness. Her husband, fearful of his money, uses these words: "fifteen hundred rubles," "diamond earrings," "accosts," "deserted," "gets hold of your arm." In both cases, and in other cases too, certain aspects of the situation were pulled out, emphasized, and integrated, according to each person's *perspective*, or conceptual framework. And in each case, the conceptual framework led to various value judgments and assumptions by the actor in the situation.

In this same way, whites who look at the O.J. trial might use words such as evidence, DNA, science, injustice, biased jurors, ruthless lawyers, and abuse to describe what took place in the first trial where he was found not guilty. In the African-American community words such as planted evidence, racist police, and discrimination might be words that were used when people saw the same reality. There is probably some truth in each perspective, and there may be ideas that are downright false. However, if we focus on people's personal life experiences as well as the words they use among one another, we can begin to see why people differ in how they see reality, and it is not simply that one side is correct and the other is wrong.

It is also a mistake to believe that individuals have simply one perspective that is important to them. There may have been nine African Americans on the jury, and that perspective may have been important to some of them, but other perspectives also came to be important to them, and sometimes even more important. Being on the jury became a perspective: Each had an occupational perspective he or she brought, each had a perspective associated with age and gender. It is, therefore, a mistake to claim that this jury was simply made up of nine African Americans and three others; perspectives are very complex, and being African American may not have been as important to people on the jury as it was for those people who were in the wider community and who did not have to see the situation from the perspective of jury member.

A college education, in many ways, is an introduction to a variety of perspectives, each telling us something about what is going on around us. Sociology, psychology, history, humanities, art, George Orwell, Machiavelli, Freud, James Joyce, and Malcolm X—each represents a perspective that we might adopt as our own, integrate with others we have, or forget entirely after our final exam. Each perspective is a different approach to "reality," and each, therefore, tells us something but cannot include everything.

It seems that the most difficult aspect of "perspective" to grasp is that perspectives cannot capture the whole physical reality. It is probably because we want so desperately to know that what we believe is true that we cannot face the fact that whatever we know must be seen only as a truth gained from a certain *perspective*. We cannot, for example, even agree totally on what a simple object is. One day in the middle of winter, I went outside and picked up something from the ground and brought it to class. I asked, "What is this?" The answers were snow, a snowball, ice crystals, frozen water, something you are showing us to make some point, something little boys use to frighten little girls, the beginning of the world's biggest snowman, molecules, dirty snow, a very interesting shape to draw, the symbol of cold weather. Of course, my response was, "What is this really?" And, of course, the response by them was that it is all of these things, and probably many, many more things. Indeed, whatever that physical reality was is interpreted by people in many ways, depending entirely on the perspective they use to see it. No one of these perspectives could ever claim to have grasped the true essence of that which was brought in from outside. And even if we might try to claim that all of these perspectives together capture the object completely, we would be missing the point: Perspectives are almost infinite; thus, we can never claim to have found all the possible perspectives we might use to see anything.

Human beings are limited by their perspectives; they cannot see outside of their perspectives. Yet perspectives are vitally important: They make it possible for human beings to make sense out of what is "out there."

It is important for me to emphasize that I am *not* saying here that there is no truth at all, or that every opinion about reality is equally correct. Unfortunately, many people do in fact believe this, and many will try to interpret my discussion as a way to support their position. Reality does in fact exist—that is, there is something actually happening out there in the world—but we cannot know it completely or in any perfectly accurate way, because we always see it through filters we are here calling perspectives.

NEW PERSPECTIVES MEAN NEW REALITIES

The Autobiography of Malcolm X is a fascinating book and movie about an important leader in the Civil Rights movement during the 1960s. Here is an individual whose life situations caused him to see the reality around him in very different ways. He changed because his truths changed, and his truth changed because each perspective he took on as he interacted with others opened up whole new worlds for him. In seventh grade, for instance, he was elected class president, and in looking back, he reports:

> And I was proud: I'm not going to say I wasn't. In fact, by then, I didn't really have much feeling about being a Negro, because I was trying so hard, in every way I could, to be white. . . . I remember one thing that marred this time for me: the movie "Gone With the Wind." When it played in Mason, I was the only Negro in the theater, and when Butterfly McQueen went into her act, I felt like crawling under the rug. (Malcolm X and Haley, 1965, 31-32)*

Malcolm remembers his perspective changing in school:

> It was then that I began to change—inside. I drew away from white people. I came to class, and I answered when called upon. It became a physical strain simply to sit in Mr. Ostrowski's class. Where "nigger" had slipped off my back before, wherever I heard it now, I stopped and looked at whoever said it. And they looked surprised that I did. (P. 37)

Then in New York:

> "Man, you can't tell him nothing!" they'd exclaim. And they couldn't. At home in Roxbury, they would see me parading with Sophia, dressed in my wild zoot suits. Then I'd come to work, loud and wild and half-high on liquor or reefers, and I'd stay that way, jamming sandwiches at people until we got to New York. Off the train, I'd go through the Grand Central Station afternoon rush-hour crowd, and many white people simply stopped in their tracks to watch me pass. The drape and the cut of a zoot suit showed to the best advantage if you were tall—and I was over six feet. My conk was fire-red. I was really a clown, but my ignorance made me think I was "sharp." My knob-toed, orange-colored "kick-up" shoes were nothing but Florsheims, the ghetto's Cadillac of shoes in those days. . . . And then, between Small's Paradise, the Braddock Hotel, and other places—as much as my twenty- or twenty-five dollar pay would allow, I drank liquor, smoked marijuana, painted the Big Apple red with increasing numbers of friends, and finally in Mrs. Fisher's rooming house I got a few hours of sleep before the "Yankee Clipper" rolled again. (P. 79)

Malcolm has been seeing the world from the perspective of zoot suits, reefers, conk, Cadillac of shoes, but he is suddenly exposed to a new perspective, which opens up a new world to him:

> When Reginald left, he left me rocking with some of the first serious thoughts I had ever had in my life: that the white man was fast losing his power to oppress and exploit the dark world; that the dark world was starting to rise to rule the world

again, as it had before; that the white man's world was on the way down, it was on the way out. (P. 162)

Because of this new perspective, Malcolm X becomes sensitive to things in his world he never really saw before. His past takes on a new meaning, and the many situations that took place between blacks and whites in his past are seen differently. He joins the Black Muslims, and he becomes a great leader in that movement. At the height of his activity in that movement, the words he preaches reflect his perspective:

> No *sane* black man really wants integration! No *sane* white man really wants integration. No *sane* black man really believes that the white man ever will give the black man anything more than token integration. No! The Honorable Elijah Muhammed teaches that for the black man in America the only solution is complete *separation* from the white man! (P. 248)

And, finally, Malcolm's perspective changes once more, as a result of a pilgrimage he makes to Mecca. As his perspective changes, the world around him becomes transformed:

> It was in the Holy World that my attitude was changed, by what I experienced there, and by what I witnessed there, in terms of brotherhood—not just brotherhood toward me, but brotherhood between all men, of all nationalities and complexions, who were there. And now that I am back in America, my attitude here concerning white people has to be governed by what my black brothers and I experience here, and what we witness here—in terms of brotherhood. The *problem* here in America is that we meet such a small minority of individual so-called "good," or "brotherly" white people. . . . (P. 368)

Malcolm X's autobiography is an excellent description of an individual undergoing profound changes in perspective. His story is not unique, but what is happening is probably more obvious to us in his story than it would be in many others.

Not only do we all undergo *basic* change in our perspectives many times throughout our lives, but our perspectives change from situation to situation, often many times during the same day. Few of us have one perspective that we can apply to every situation we encounter. Perspectives are situational: In the classroom my perspective is that of teacher/sociologist; in my home it becomes father or husband; on a fishing trip it changes to "seasoned fisherman." Each situation calls forth a different role, which means a different perspective. Some roles we play may have more than one perspective we can use (there are many different *student* perspectives we might draw on depending on the situation we encounter), and some perspectives may apply to more

*From *The Autobiography of Malcolm X* by Malcolm X, with the assistance of Alex Haley. Copyright © 1964 by Alex Haley and Malcolm X. Copyright © 1965 by Alex Haley and Betty Shabazz. Reprinted by permission of Random House, Inc., New York, and the Hutchinson Publishing, Random Century Group Ltd., London.

than one role we play (e.g., a Christian may apply his or her perspective as a Christian to a number of roles). Perspectives are a complex matter.

Perspectives are not perceptions but are guides to our perceptions; they influence what we see and how we interpret what we see. They are our "eyeglasses" we put on to see. Figure 1-1 summarizes the meaning of perspective.

A perspective, then, by its very nature, is a bias; it contains assumptions, value judgments, and ideas; it orders the world; it divides it up in a certain way; and as a result it influences our action in the world. A father and his son see each other from at least two perspectives (one the father's and the other the son's) and thus define a situation that affects them both (e.g., the use of the car) in two very different ways. Neither is necessarily wrong or in error, although they may certainly disagree. A candidate for president of the United States may see the society as in need of change and promise all kinds of possibilities, but once that person is in office, his or her perspective will change and his or her behavior will be affected. It is not, as may appear to us, that the new president is dishonest, but rather that the definition of the situation has changed because that person now sees the world from the perspective of president, not candidate.

PERSPECTIVES ARE SOCIALLY CREATED

The Autobiography of Malcolm X highlights another important quality of perspective. In every case his perspective changed as he entered into and out of various groups of people and took on new roles in life. As a junior high student he had one perspective, as an African American in a junior high with mostly whites he had another, then as a young man on the make in the big city another, then as a Black Muslim still another. In each case here we see someone changing as he or she changes groups or roles, and that is true of almost all our perspectives. Examine the points of view we take on the world. Examine why we believe them: "Because they are true?" Maybe. But are we encouraged to believe them by our particular place in society? Definitely. Groups and roles are what give most of us the filters through which we see reality. Not only do our biases come from our perspectives, but our perspectives in turn are not simply chosen by each of us; they are products in large part of the social worlds within which we move.

FIGURE 1–1

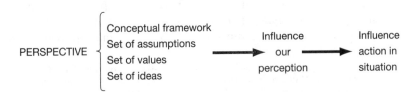

IS THERE A "BEST" PERSPECTIVE?

If we are honest and careful in our analysis of the perspectives we learn and take on as our own, we will discover that some of these are in fact more accurate than others, some will allow us to come closer to reality than others, and some will actually stand in the way of our understanding reality. We normally believe in the perspectives we hold, but it is important to recognize that we can be too easily fooled to use perspectives that lead us far from reality as it really is. Except for the serious scholar who is bothered by the difficulties of finding truth, most of us come to believe that "my perspective is better than yours."

Comparing perspectives is very difficult to do. To begin with, whenever we try to compare any two things (such as perspectives or instructors or pictures), we must decide on some criteria for comparison. If more than one of us are comparing, we must agree on the criteria. So, for example, Martha is "better" than Marsha if we can agree that the criterion is IQ score and we can agree on how it should be measured. One painting is "better" than another if we use "capturing physical reality" as a criterion for comparison and can agree on how to measure "capture physical reality." Of course, if "beauty" becomes the criterion, the other "painting" could be judged better.

All perspectives are not equal. Some are "better than others." To judge which is better, however, a standard of comparison must be established. Some people, for example, would argue that the better perspective is the one that is closest to Holy Scripture or the one that comes closest to the American creed. Thus, atheism is not a good perspective in the first case, and for most of us, a racist perspective is not good in the second case.

Most of us are probably interested in using perspectives that *accurately describe* what is "really" happening in the world around us. Certainly, in the world of scholarship accurate description is one of the most important measurements of a "good perspective." A good perspective gives us insight, clearly describes reality, helps us find the truth. Most scientists, natural and social, make a claim that their perspectives are better than common-sense ones because there is a disciplined control of personal bias. The fruits of science do indeed support the fact that the scientific perspective is superior to the vast majority of perspectives that deal with the natural and social worlds. If given a choice between a scientific perspective and a nonscientific perspective examining exactly the same question, it would be unusual for me to opt for the latter, because it is clear to me that scientific perspectives are usually more reliable than nonscientific ones in accurately answering questions about the natural and social world. It depends a great deal, however, on the nature of the question asked.

Science is far from accurate in answering a number of important questions, and scientists are unable to deal with whole layers of reality that other perspectives deal with. Even in the natural and social worlds that the scientist does examine, there are realities that go unnoticed and are not even looked for, realities too difficult to examine scientifically. To claim that the perspective of science is better than any other because it is more accurate is not a just claim for all questions.

The problem of the "best" perspective is confounded when we try to determine the most accurate scientific perspective. Although scientists share a scientific perspective, they differ in what they focus on in reality, and it would be very difficult to establish criteria for judging which one of the sciences captures reality the best. This could be done, but probably to no good purpose. It is best to understand scientific perspectives as each focusing on a different aspect of the natural and social world, each helping us more clearly understand that aspect. Comparing scientific perspectives—indeed, comparing all perspectives—is a difficult task, but it is not impossible if criteria are *carefully* established.

SUMMARY

It may be beneficial to summarize this chapter by simply restating the basic points and by listing some examples of perspectives:

1. Perspectives are points of view—eyeglasses, sensitizers—that guide our perceptions of reality.
2. Perspectives can further be described as conceptual frameworks—a set of assumptions, values, and beliefs used to organize our perceptions and control our behavior.
3. The individual has many perspectives. Each acts as a filter and therefore does not allow the individual to see all of reality. Each perspective is created in the individual's social life. Each also changes as the individual's groups and roles change.
4. No object can simply be understood from only one perspective. Many perspectives can be used to see the same object, and each might tell us something important about that object.
5. Some perspectives can be considered better than other perspectives if we can agree that "better" means more accurate and if we can measure accuracy—a difficult task. In science some may be more accurate than others, but it is probably more correct to argue that each *focuses* on a different aspect of reality.

SOME EXAMPLES OF PERSPECTIVES: INFORMAL AND FORMAL PERSPECTIVES

One way of understanding how important perspectives are is to list many examples. We might divide all perspectives into informal everyday perspectives and formal written ones. In a given day I might use many informal perspectives: male, instructor, husband, consumer, opera fan, friend, poker player, homeowner, amateur counselor, and employee of Moorhead State University. There are other more formal perspectives I may use, however: sociologist, scientist, and existentialist, for example. Furthermore, we might also divide up sociology, scientist, and existentialist into several subperspectives, each one causing us to see a slightly different focus on reality. We might briefly illustrate the diversity of perspectives an individual might use. Of course, this is not meant to be all-inclusive, only suggestive of the diversity of perspectives available.

1. Some informal everyday perspectives:
   student
   daughter
   mother
2. Some formal perspectives—nonscientific:
   stamp collector
   artist
   poet
   Asian
   American
   Jewish
3. Some formal perspectives—scientific:
   biologist
   physicist
   chemist
   astronomer
   psychologist
   anthropologist
   economist
   sociologist
4. Some perspectives within sociology:
   Marxist
   Parsonian
   Symbolic interactionist
   Weberian
   Durkheimian
   Systems theory
   Exchange

Any one individual is made up of several of these kinds of perspectives and may enter any one of them in a situation. Indeed, once in the situation, the individual can change perspectives or even find that the initial perspective is being transformed as he or she interacts with others. A person may in a single day be student, daughter, mother, artist, Asian, American, Jewish, biologist, sociologist, Marxist, and Parsonian. In each perspective a different world will be seen, and perhaps a new way of looking at old things will be revealed.

Perspective is a wonderful word to understand. It is also, I believe, a wonderful way to introduce this book. The title of this Book is *Symbolic Interactionism,* and its purpose is to focus on one perspective within social psychology. Symbolic interactionism—like physics, chemistry, sociology, existentialism, psychology—is a perspective, and that means it is *one way of understanding reality.* Since it is part of social science, it focuses on the human being and tries to understand human behavior. Since it is part of sociology, it attempts to uncover the significance of our social life. Yet, it is incomplete, it exaggerates certain qualities of the human being, and it ignores other qualities. It is therefore limited, but so are all other perspectives. The real question we need to ponder is how much does it tell us about the human being, and how much does it ignore?

Symbolic interactionism is a very unusual perspective, in my opinion. It is unlike psychology and much of sociology. For some people it may seem like common sense because we recognize that its ideas explain so well what we all do in the situations we encounter. Yet, to most of us the ideas here will be new and sometimes seem strange. After all, we have been exposed to other social sciences in our search for truth: psychology, sociology, anthropology, for example, and these have become more familiar to us. Symbolic interactionism will often cause us to question some of the assumptions we have come to accept from these other perspectives, and it is difficult to break away, even temporarily, from them. You are, however, invited to give this perspective a chance. It is far from perfect, but it promises much, as you will undoubtedly recognize. We will begin to look at it in Chapter 3. Before that, however, it is important to examine briefly some other perspectives in social science in order to see symbolic interactionism in a larger context and to better recognize its uniqueness as we describe it through the rest of the chapters.

REFERENCES

MALCOLM X AND ALEX HALEY
   1965   *The Autobiography of Malcolm X.* New York: Grove Press. Copyright © 1965 by Alex Haley and Betty Shabazz. Reprinted by permission of Random House, Inc., New York, and the Hutchinson Publishing, Random Century Group Ltd., London.

2

The Perspective of Social Science

Social science is a perspective. That means it is one way of understanding the human being. Because it is a science, it has much in common with natural sciences. Yet, it is to some extent distinct from natural science, and it is important to recognize that there are several perspectives within social science, each unique to some extent, yet sharing some qualities with one another. This chapter is an attempt to introduce social science as a perspective and to lay out in very rough form some of the various perspectives within social science, especially sociology, psychology, and social psychology.

It is probably best to start with an important philosopher who lived at about the same time as the development of social science. His name was Immanuel Kant (1724–1804). Kant was a believer in God, a Christian who was very concerned about the assault of reason and science on traditional religious belief as well as the feeble attempts of religious thinkers to defend their grounds through the tools of rational argument. Kant wanted to understand the limits of reason and science. He was critical of attempts by religious people to defend the metaphysical world through reason, for he felt it was an impossible task and therefore a waste of time. And, after all, he argued, reason is not everything, and we need to understand certain aspects of the universe through something other than reason and science.

He argued that there are two worlds of reality: a world of *phenomena* and a world of the *noumena*. The world of phenomena is the world we can experience with our senses; it is open to scientific and rational investigation. Science observes the world of phenomena—the natural world—and reason orders these observations. The world of noumena is above scientific investigation; it cannot be approached by empirical observation, because it is not physical/empirical. Although many people have attempted to approach this world through reason, they have failed. Kant (1781–1952) stated in the Preface to the second edition of *The Critique of Pure Reason*::

> We find, too, that those who are engaged in metaphysical pursuits are far from being able to agree among themselves, but that, on the contrary, this science appears to furnish an arena specially adapted for the display of skill or the exer-

cise of strength in mock-contests—a field in which no combatant ever yet succeeded in gaining an inch of ground, in which, at least, no victory was ever yet crowned with permanent possession. (P. 6)

Those who use reason or science, or both, to understand some things are engaged in "mock-contests," never "gaining an inch of ground." Further he stated, "Now there are objects which reason *thinks*. . . but which cannot be given in experience, or, at least, cannot be given so as reason thinks them" (p. 7). Kant is saying that although we can imagine the world of the noumena, reason and science, limited to the world of phenomena, cannot be used to investigate it. In a sense, Kant then is arguing that science is a *perspective* sensitizing the investigator to part of the world, the natural, phenomenal world, but that science is unable to sensitize us to another world, nor should we use it to try.

One of the reasons that Kant is important to us here relates to how he applied this philosophy to an understanding of the human being. Physical objects such as plants, livers, wastepaper baskets, dogs, and tape recorders are clearly in the world of phenomena and therefore subject to scientific investigation, and God, heavenly angels, and the Devil are clearly noumena. But in which world does the human being belong? If we are in the world of phenomena, we are physical, we are part of the natural universe, we can be investigated and fully understood through the tools of science. If we are noumena, however, then we are beyond science, not understandable as part of the natural physical universe. Kant argued that we are both; we are phenomena, subject to the laws of nature, open to science, and "subject to natural necessity"; that is, our behavior is subject to natural cause. On the other hand, we are also noumena, the "human soul," at least in part, containing a will that is *free*. The human being is conceptualized here as both *passive* in that individuals are caused, shaped, and driven by forces beyond their control, and *active* in that individuals are also controlling, shaping, acting, free.

We will not describe here Kant's other insights in relation to this issue, but it is important to underline the fact that science, by its very nature, is empirical and investigates the phenomenal world and, at least according to Kant's framework, cannot deal with part of that which we call *human*. For social *scientists*, the investigation of the human being takes the form of proving whatever information we can gather about those aspects of the human being that are subject to natural causation. And the greater our attempt to be scientific, the greater will be our focus on those aspects of the human being to which Kant referred as phenomenal—those qualities of the human being that lend themselves to scientific measurement. We *risk*, however, the danger of concluding that all of the human being can be, at least theoretically, captured or measured scientifically and that what we have already been able to learn gives us a good representation of the human being rather than a selective biased one.

SOCIAL SCIENCE AS A PERSPECTIVE

It is maintained here that social science is a *perspective*. Since its beginning it has attempted to apply the tools of science to understanding the human being. As a perspective, it has made certain assumptions, the most important being that the human being is phenomenal, caused, open to scientific measurement, and not an active agent in relation to his or her environment—not self-determining or free. As social scientists, we assume causality in social life, and our goal is (perhaps must be) to uncover that causality.

Peter Berger (1963) clearly presents the problem of finding a place for freedom in social science. After showing vividly how human beings are controlled, imprisoned, caused, shaped, and molded by a multitude of social forces, he turns the argument around and attempts to eke out some room for human freedom. Before trying to determine how that freedom is possible, however, he discusses freedom and science, and in so doing develops an argument almost identical with Kant's:

> Freedom is not empirically available. More precisely, while freedom may be experienced by us as a certainty along with other empirical certainties, it is not open to demonstration by any scientific methods. If we wish to follow Kant, freedom is also not available rationally, that is, cannot be demonstrated by philosophical methods based on the operations of pure reason. . . the elusiveness of freedom with regard to scientific comprehension does not lie so much in the unspeakable mysteriousness of the phenomenon. . . as in the *strictly limited scope of scientific methods*. An empirical science must operate within certain assumptions, one of which is that of universal causality. Every object of scientific scrutiny is presumed to have an anterior cause. An object, or an event, that is its own cause lies outside the scientific universe of discourse. Yet freedom has precisely that character. For this reason, no amount of scientific research will ever uncover a phenomenon that can be designated as free. Whatever may appear as free within the subjective consciousness of an individual will find its place in the scientific scheme as a link in some chain of causation. . . .
>
> In terms of social-scientific method, one is faced with a way of thinking that assumes a priori that the human world is a causally closed system. The method would not be scientific if it thought otherwise. Freedom as a special kind of cause is excluded from this system a priori. In terms of social phenomena, the social scientist must assume an infinite regress of causes, none of them holding a privileged ontological status. If he cannot explain a phenomenon causally by one set of sociological categories, he will try another one. If political causes do not seem satisfactory, he will try economic ones. And if the entire conceptual apparatus of sociology seems inadequate to explain a given phenomenon, he may switch to a different apparatus, such as the psychological or the biological one. But in doing so, he will still move within the scientific cosmos—that is, he will discover new orders of causes, but he will not encounter freedom. There is no way of perceiving freedom, either in oneself or another human being, except through a subjective inner certainty that dissolves as soon as it is attacked with the tools of scientific analysis. (Pp. 122-24)*

*From *Invitation to Sociology,* copyright © 1963 by Peter L. Berger. Used by permission of Doubleday, a Division of Bantam, Doubleday, Dell Publishing Group, Inc., and Penguin Books Ltd.

One is reminded of the cocktail party where the bright new college graduate with one sociology course and one psychology course under his belt is impressing everyone with how much he understands about human behavior. The conversation goes something like this:

> "That's silly. You're not free to do anything," he brags.
>
> "Of course, I am. I decided what I believe and where I go," the innocent citizen responds.
>
> "Take the girl you're with here tonight. Did you freely choose to bring her?"
>
> "Of course."
>
> "Aha." (I've got you, he says to himself.) "You are attracted to her because she is in the 'right' social class. She reminds you of your mother. She is approximately at your own level of physical attractiveness." Etc., etc., etc., etc.
>
> "Wow!"

Most of us are amazed at the predictability of human behavior and at all the social and psychological causes of behavior that social scientists have been able to amass. But Berger's point must be reiterated: "Freedom as a special kind of cause is *excluded* from this system." It is one of science's central assumptions. The purpose of science is to isolate cause, not freedom, so it must, in the end, be considered as excluding some things about the human being. This is not, of course, to criticize science; it is merely to try to isolate its limits as a perspective.

Social scientists seem to be becoming increasingly aware of the fact that social science is a *perspective*, that it makes certain assumptions, that it sensitizes and desensitizes the investigator, that it has a certain conceptual framework (e.g., "empirical," "cause," "independent variable," "dependent variable," "measurement," etc.), and that it can never reveal the whole truth about the human being.

Indeed, social science might even lead us to a misleading or even false picture of the human being. Charles Hampden-Turner (1970) argues this in his thoughtful book *Radical Man*. He describes social science as a *perspective* and then concludes that it is clearly a biased one by its very nature: It is consistently a politically *conservative* one, and it must inevitably lead the social scientist to take a conservative view of the human being, systematically ignoring a host of important human qualities. Hampden-Turner (pp. 1–15) takes the position that the social-scientific perspective by its very nature:

1. *Concentrates on the repetitive, predictable, unvariable aspects of the human.* In a sense, social science assures a "compulsive, obsessive, and ritualistic" human subject, rather than recognizing the centrality of creativity and novelty to human life.

2. *Concentrates on "visible externalities,"* that which is "exposed to the general gaze," rather than the subjective world of dreams, philosophies, and the whole mental life of those whose physical movements we observe.

3. *Concentrates on the various parts of the person*, analyzing the parts in order to understand the whole. In a sense, "the human is indivisible" and "we are left with the same problems as all the king's horses and all the king's men."

Hampden-Turner criticizes the scientific perspective on other grounds, too, but the point that he makes for our discussion here is that social science is a perspective, and what emerges from it is a picture of the human being that is far from objective and "value free." That perspective may indeed be as conservative and biased as Hampden-Turner describes it, or it may be less so—on the other hand, it may be even more biased than any of us realize. The treatment of social science as a perspective has only recently been investigated seriously, so it is difficult to know the nature of its bias. But it does indeed appear that in order to be scientific we have to focus on those aspects of the human that are more open to measurement. It is important to recognize that there are qualities left untouched because of our scientific search, even qualities that are measurable but not perfectly open to our contemporary instruments of investigation.

Social science is a perspective; it is an important approach to understanding the human being; it has produced much that has helped us predict, control, improve, and even mess up the condition of the human being. It is not complete, for no perspective can be complete, and it is a bias, but it is a most important perspective for understanding, as witnessed by its results over the past two hundred or more years.

Within social science there are, of course, many perspectives (we might call these subperspectives), and each one is thought unique in its approach to the human being. Each one pulls out some aspects of reality, emphasizing those, and in a sense ignores other aspects of reality picked up by other social sciences.

Sociology as a Perspective

Sociology is the study of society. It is the study of how society works and how society is an important cause of human action. In fact, it is not just the study of society, but the study of all organized life, from small groups and formal organizations to communities and society. It begins with the assumption that humans have always existed within society, that society is the source of our qualities as a species (for example, conscience, language, mind, self), and it is the source of our qualities as individuals (interests, values, talents, rules, ideas, and so on).

Sociology is the study of the human being in society as well as how society gets inside the human being. Society is external to the human being, yet through socialization society is internalized and becomes part of each person. Society is made up of social patterns, developed in the past and important to each of us living in society.

For example, social structure is a social pattern in society. Social structure was formed in the past and we are all placed in it at birth and as we go through life. We are placed in a class position in social structure, and gender and ethnic group membership are also positions. We live within a political structure and in every organization we encounter an authority structure. Even the small groups we exist in develop structures that we are influenced by.

Another social pattern that exists in society is culture. Culture is the consensus developed by people over a long history. It is their shared view of reality, the basic ideas, values, and rules they have come to believe in. That culture is something we are born into and are socialized to accept. Its ideas become our truths, its rules become our morals, its values become what we regard as important in life.

We are also born into a society that has developed a particular set of social institutions. These are the grooves that are there for us to follow and participate in. We live within hundreds of institutions, some, for example, are political institutions, while others might be economic, familial, religious, military, criminal justice, educational, health care, or recreational. So, in American society the corporation, private health insurance, a volunteer army, and public education exist as social institutions. How the individual acts in society is shaped by such grooves. In *Invitation to Sociology*, Peter Berger describes the power of society in his conclusion to Chapter 4:

> We are located in society not only in space but in time. Our society is a historical entity that extends temporally beyond any individual biography. Society antedates us and it will survive us. It was there before we were born and it will be there after we are dead. Our lives are but episodes in its majestic march through time. In sum, society is the walls of our imprisonment in history. (P. 92)

To the sociologist, therefore, humans exist within a massive reality—society—developed historically, regarded by us as legitimate, telling us what to do and what to think, and shaping our behavior through a variety of mechanisms.

But society also exists within all of us. In a sense we agree to this imprisonment precisely because the society has penetrated us through socialization; we have, in a real sense, become what society has demanded. This is the role of socialization, and it is an important part of what sociology examines. Berger continues:

> Society not only controls our movements, but shapes our identity, our thought and our emotions. The structures of society become the structures of our own consciousness. Society does not stop at the surface of our skins. Society penetrates us as much as it envelopes us. Our bondage to society is not so much established by conquest as by collusion. . . . The walls of our imprisonment were there before we appeared on the scene, but they are ever rebuilt by ourselves. We are betrayed into captivity with our own cooperation. (P. 121)

Sociology is a perspective that thinks of the human being as an actor. We act out roles. Think of roles as scripts handed out to us in the positions we fill in organization. A male in society, a student, a sociology major, an employee at a department store, and an unemployed shoe salesman are all positions in society, and all of them direct what the actor does in organization. This is significant here because sociologists tend to see actors changing all through life, from situation to situation, because we change our roles in society and because society itself changes. How we act in life then, is tied, once again to society.

There is, in this perspective, a lot of determinism. That is, humans are thought to be linked to society, products of society, controlled by society. The purpose of sociology is to understand this and to understand also how society itself works. Many sociologists will claim that I am exaggerating the determinism of sociology, and perhaps I am, but it is important to see this determinism as central to any social scientific perspective that seeks to understand *why* humans act the way they do. Sociology describes society as an important cause of human action. Its whole conceptual framework aims at this, as do its studies. It is different from other perspectives in social science, such as psychology, since its focus is society. Sociology is a useful perspective because it does help explain a great deal about human behavior. As a perspective, however, it can only sensitize us to part of the picture, and it is really up to other social-scientific perspectives to help us understand the other parts.

Psychology as a Perspective

If sociology is most easily defined as the study of society, then psychology is most easily defined as the study of the person. It is an understanding of how the person works, and how the characteristics of the person influence what he or she does.

Psychology is similar to sociology in some ways. It is a perspective, and it is a social science. As a science it attempts to apply the tools developed in natural science. More than sociology, it has relied heavily on the controlled laboratory experiment (indeed, some psychologists will define a perspective as scientific only if the controlled laboratory experiment is the norm), and it has usually considered the human being as part of nature, in the world of phenomena, moved by natural laws, created, shaped.

Because there are many schools of psychology (each can be called a perspective), there are differences among psychologists. Psychologists, however, like sociologists, seem to share certain assumptions, ideas, and concepts, sensitizing the investigator to certain aspects of the human being while neglecting others. Let us emphasize again that it is not a fault; it is a limitation of every perspective, and there seems to be no way to escape it: Perspectives are absolutely essential for understanding, but by their very nature they do not capture the whole of reality.

The threads of the psychological perspective are not always clear, and there is always a danger that someone who is not a psychologist will mistake the perspective. However, it seems that all schools of psychology emphasize the following:

1. The *individual* organism, shaped by various combinations of heredity and environment, social and nonsocial.
2. An underlying belief that a person's performance at any point is tied to previous experience. This can be labeled a *predispositional* orientation. For example, in psychoanalysis this means that very early childhood training causes one to act later on in a certain manner; in learning theory previous conditioning causes behavior; in Gestalt psychology it may be the person's conceptual framework or cognitive structure developed in the past that is all-important.
3. An attempt to explain behavior in relation to the *organism:* Change is explained in relation to change *in* the organism; stability of behavior is due the to the stability *in the organism.*
4. A focus on personality traits, qualities of the person, developed over time, such as aggressiveness, shyness, lack of self-confidence, and compulsiveness. Some would call a person's attitude a trait, intelligence, even a habit. These are the qualities the person brings to the situation, and these are the qualities that are thought to cause behavior in the situation. The term "personality" or "person" implies that these traits form a system, a network, an interrelated set. There is thought to be a stability of behavior from past to present and from situation to situation.
5. Behavior is not thought to be situational or structural but personal and trait related, even though social situations might influence traits over the long run. Roles and social patterns such as structure, culture, and institutions are not the focus of investigation.
6. Because psychology studies the traits of the individual, cause is located originating in the individual's past. That is where traits come from. What we do now has roots in our past. We act the way we do because that is the way we developed as a person.

It should be emphasized here that the psychological perspective differs significantly from the sociological. Although both emphasize studying human behavior, one (psychology) focuses on how the person develops, how the person works, and how the person's qualities influence behavior from situation to situation. The other (sociology) focuses on how society develops, how society works, and how society's qualities influence the individual in different situations. In psychology change happens to or within the organism, whereas in sociology change occurs in society, in the individual's roles in society, in different organizations one belongs to.

In both cases, the focus is on the human being's behavior being caused by forces beyond the individual's own will. The individual is conceptualized as passive in relation to these forces; that is, we are shaped, we are not actively shaping our behavior or our environment as individuals. By taking a scientific perspecitve, social science has focused on those aspects of the human being molded by the biological, physical, and social world. The purpose of social science has been to try to identify those forces.

Erich Fromm (1973) is critical of some scientists for creating this passive human organism who responds to stimuli, is driven by unconscious forces, and is shaped by animalistic instincts. He writes:

> In spite of the great differences between instinctivistic and behavioristic theory, they have a common basic orientation. They both exclude the *person*, the behaving man, from their field of vision. Whether man is the product of conditioning, or the product of animal evolution, he is exclusively determined by conditions outside himself; he has no part in his own life, no responsibiblity, and not even a trace of freedom. Man is a puppet, controlled by strings—instinct or conditioning. (Pp. 70–71)

There are, of course, exceptions to a deterministic and passive view of human beings in both sociology and psychology. Fromm is one such example in psychology, as are perhaps psychologists such as Carl Rogers and Abraham Maslow. Indeed, clinical psychology tends to emphasize the active human more than academic psychology does. Cognitive psychology in recent years has taken psychology more in the direction of a more active conception of the human being. In sociology, Max Weber is a fine example of a more active conception, as are phenomenology and dramaturgical sociology.

It is, in my opinion, the passive, determined, and nonreflective human being who has been portrayed in both psychology and sociology for the past two hundred years. We sometimes claim humans are really active, but in our work determinism is usually at work. This seems perfectly understandable since the goals have always been to examine the human as part of the natural universe, governed by laws that can be discovered through careful research. A liberal education in social science tends to create an image of the human caused by factors in the natural world, as are all other living organisms. Indeed, other social science perspectives (such as anthropology, economics, geography) do not seem to question this image but, on the contrary, to reinforce it.

The Perspective of Social Psychology in Psychology

Of all perspectives in social science, social psychology is the most difficult to describe. Some would argue that it is not a perspective at all, but a conglomeration of topics and studies with little unity. Others will argue that it is a discipline in its own right, with roots in both psychology and sociology, but with its own distinct history and subject matter.

It is useful to realize that two social psychologies have developed, sometimes influencing each other, but often developing as parallel and without overlap. We might call one "psychological social psychology" and the other "sociological social psychology."

Psychological social psychology has its roots, to a large extent, in Gestalt psychology, an important perspective in psychology first developed in the late nineteenth and early twentieth centuries. Gestalt psychology emphasizes the central importance of *perception* in human behavior: The human being acts according to how the situation is perceived. Gestalt psychologists have attempted to isolate various principles of perception in order to better understand how the individual organizes the stimuli he or she confronts. Gestalt psychology as such is entirely psychological in its orientation, but because of the work of some Gestaltists—especially Solomon Asch and Kurt Lewin—a social dimension was added to the framework, which greatly influenced the direction of social psychology.

The social psychology that developed out of Gestalt psychology focuses on interpersonal influence. "Social psychology," writes Elliot Aronson (1992), is the study of social influence, "the influences that people have upon the beliefs and behavior of others" (p. 6). The basic question to be answered is how other people around us influence our thoughts, feelings, and behaviors. The focus is on the social situation, and the most important idea is that human beings—whatever else they may bring to a situation—are influenced by what goes on in that situation. What I do influences you; what you do influences me. The study of social influence includes how speakers influence our thoughts, how groups form our attitudes, and how people influence us to like them. In this social-psychological perspective, human thought and behavior are thought to change according to the influence of others.

By far the most important concept investigated in social psychology has been attitudes and attitude change. An attitude is usually conceptualized as a person's set of beliefs and feelings toward an object that predisposes the person to act in a certain manner when confronted by that object (or class of objects). Studies have usually attempted to examine how attitudes are formed and changed through the influence of other individuals. Attitudes, it has been assumed, are useful traits to study because they lead to behavior. To change behavior, therefore, the strategy implied in social psychology has been to change one's attitudes. Although the usefulness of studying attitudes as predictors of behavior is increasingly being questioned by critics, it is still seen by most social scientists as one of social psychology's most useful concepts. For most people, attitudes are fascinating to study, and they seem to most of us to be basic to our action in real situations. Nothing seems so important to many people as knowing how to change such attitudes as prejudice toward nonwhites, sexist attitudes toward women, or narrow-minded attitudes toward cultures different from our own. Many, especially social psychologists, believe that attitudes are important and that attitude change is possible. It is, in a sense, an optimistic view of the future, implying that we can improve the world simply by changing people's attitudes. And nothing seems to be more appropriate to this view than an understanding of social psychology, which has focused much of its efforts on attitudes and attitude change.

Social psychology is also the study of how other people influence our *behavior.* Conformity, obedience, power, leadership, and attraction are some of the exciting topics covered in the field of social psychology. Interpersonal communication, group decision making, and propaganda are also important. The key to the perspective seems to be, as Aronson states, interpersonal influence, the importance of the social situation in influencing attitudes and/or behavior. The human being is conceptualized as a "social animal" in the sense that he or she adjusts his or her action to the action of others in the social situation.

There is a great similarity between the perspective described here as psychological social psychology and the sociological and psychological perspectives discussed earlier. That similarity is that there is a continuing focus on cause, the assumption being that something inside or outside the actor influences what he or she does. The purpose of all three perspectives is to uncover that cause. Social psychology looks at other people in the situations we act in. Others influence us through what they say and how they say it, by persuading us and manipulating us, by acting as models or teaching us directly. Others form our attitudes and influence our behavior in spite of our attitudes. Whatever we bring to the situation (our traits) must be balanced with the social situation itself if we are going to understand human behavior. Whatever social patterns of society play themselves out in what we do, the social situation will still matter. Together these three perspectives explain a lot of why human beings act as they do. Together they tell us to look at the social situation, who the person is, and the society within which the person exists. There is overlap among them, but each has a different focus, and whichever one we study or focus on will lead us down a path that emphasizes one of these three aspects rather than the others. That seems to be the nature of what a perspective is.

The Perspective of Social Psychology in Sociology

The world of social science is far more complex, unfortunately. Another approach to social psychology also exists within the discipline of sociology. Sociologists study the social psychology described above, and they borrow heavily from it in their work, and they make contributions to it. This social psychology can be thought to be a link of sorts between sociology and psychology. It is psychology in its focus on the person within a social situation where other individuals influence what we do; it is sociology in its focus on the social situation. It is distinct from much of psychology by de-emphasizing the person as cause; it is distinct from much of sociology by de-emphasizing the power of social patterns and society at large.

There are many other perspectives—or schools—of social psychology within sociology, and each has a distinct focus. Some sociologists focus on group dynamics and attempt to uncover the patterns that emerge in small groups. There is an exchange perspective also—very important to the study of family and gender interaction—emphasizing power relationships in face-to-face interaction.

Part of the distinction between the sociological approach to social psychology and the psychological is that the real focus of the sociological is on the concept "social interaction." Morris Rosenberg and Ralph Turner (1981) see this as central: Social interaction is ongoing action that actors take back and forth. It is not influence of others or groups on the individual as much as what takes place between and among people as they interact; for example the negotiation of identity or culture or the development of social structure. Rosenberg and Turner also draw attention to the fact that the sociological tends to place much greater emphasis on research of real-life events, such as interaction at a bar or in a kindergarten class. Psychological social psychologists, on the other hand, are far more likely to use surveys or laboratory experiments. Related to this distinction is the fact that sociology emphasizes "socialization," the way that people become members of society—learn the patterns of society in face-to-face interaction. Thus, for example, "identity" is a central concept here: Identity is tied to social interaction, it arises in social interaction, it changes in social interaction. We come to identify who we are through the interaction we have with others, and in that we become socialized into society.

The most important way of understanding the distinction between the psychological and sociological approach to social psychology is to recognize the tremendous importance that a perspective called "symbolic interactionism" has within sociology. No perspective in sociology has influenced our understanding of social interaction, socialization, and the social nature of the human being as much as this perspective. It is quite different from sociology, psychology, and psychological social psychology. It influences mainstream sociology when it comes to "socialization," and it is almost always an integral part of all approaches to social psychology within sociology.

The purpose of this book is to introduce this perspective of "symbolic interactionism." Its roots are different from other social-scientific perspectives, and its insights are also different. It is limited because it is a perspective, and whether or not it is useful depends on whether or not it helps us understand the human being. It is part of the social-scientific tradition, yet it also tries to stand apart from the determinism that characterizes most social science perspectives. What you will find is that there is a logic to the following chapters. Here I introduce the ideas that will unfold chapter by chapter.

1. *The perspective of symbolic interactionism grows out of pragmatism,* and is also heavily influenced by Charles Darwin's work. It emphasizes the uniqueness of the human being in nature, especially the fact that human beings act back on their environment rather than passively respond to that environment. The phrase "symbolic interactionism" gives away the focus of this perspective: To understand the human being we need to study interaction, and interaction of human beings is symbolic. (Chapter 3)

2. *Human beings are symbol users.* To George Herbert Mead, this is our essence. Symbols have a distinct meaning to the symbolic interactionist, and they contribute a great deal to the nature of our reality, the nature of our society, and they are the key to our uniqueness. (Chapters 4 and 5)

3. *Human beings possess a self.* This means that we are able to act back on our-selves in situations. We are not only actors in the world but we are also the object of our own actions.This quality, like symbols, is part of our essence and makes possible a whole number of actions we are capable of in situations. (Chapter 6)

4. *Human beings engage in mind action.* That is, we talk to ourselves about our environment. We understand our environment, we make decisions about how to act in the environment, we problem solve and organize our action according to goals we determine for ourselves as we engage in mind action. (Chapter 7)

5. *Human beings regularly take the role of the other.* As we act in the world, we constantly take account of other people around us, and we direct our actions accordingly. This ability is part of what we do when we engage in mind action, and it changes considerably the nature of how we act in relation to others. (Chapter 8)

6. *Human beings act along a continuous stream of action,* interacting with oth-ers and engaging in mind action, determining goals, and seeing objects in relation to goals. We have to understand action as continuous, direc-tional, and determined by decisions we make along the way. (Chapter 9)

7. *Human beings interact with one another.* Social interaction is different from simple social influence, and it is difficult dissect. It should be seen as the source of what we all are as individuals, and also as the source of society. (Chapter10)

8. *Society is any instance of (a) social interaction where actors (b) cooperate over time and (c) develop culture.* Two people, a small group, a community, or thou-sands of people interacting, is a society. Individuals exist in many soci-eties. Instead of society being an entity created in the past and imprison-ing the actor, society is dynamic, continuously being created and recreated, continuously shaped by actors in interaction, and held together not by force but by the voluntary commitment of the actors involved. (Chapter 11)

9. *Erving Goffman is one of the most important theorists in sociology whose ideas are built on the principles outlined in this perspective.* Goffman's ideas are central to understanding human interaction and human society. (Chapter 12)

10. The perspective described in this book—symbolic interactionism—is guided by certain scientific principles in its search for understanding and is applicable to many issues and situations—everyday and aca-demic—that we will encounter. (Chapter 13)

The purpose of this book is to present this perspective in an organized and understandable manner. Chapter 3 should give you a broad idea of what it is all about, and each chapter after that will take a part of that broad idea and bring in details that give a more basic understanding.

SUMMARY

This chapter is about social science and its view of the human being. It emphasizes that social science itself is a perspective and that within social science there are several somewhat unique perspectives. Each one of these is an example of how some scholars attempt to understand the human being. Each is a focus and makes assumptions about reality, each is limited, yet useful for examining reality.

Kant is used as a reminder to us that science itself assumes certain things about the universe. It does not study everything because it too is limited. Social science, in its acceptance of a scientifc approach to understanding the human being, is therefore also limited. One of the very basic elements of science examined here is the assumption of natural cause which tends to lead social science to take a deterministic perspective in attempting to understand the human being.

Chapter 2 briefly examined sociology, psychology, and social psychology to underline the tendency for social science to isolate the reasons for or causes of human behavior. Although each emphasizes a different set of causal factors, all tend to take a deterministic stance. Sociology focuses on society, psychology on the person's development resulting from heredity and environment, and social psychology on the social situations we encounter.

This chapter also introduces the rest of the book by highlighting a unique perspective in social psychology called symbolic interactionism. We now turn to a more detailed introduction to that perspective.

REFERENCES

ARONSON, ELLIOT
      1992   *The Social Animal*, 6th ed. San Francisco: Freeman.
BERGER, PETER
      1963   *Invitation to Sociology*. Garden City, N.Y.: Doubleday. Copyright © 1963 by
             Peter L. Berger. Used by permission of Doubleday & Company, Inc.,
             New York, and Penguin Books Ltd.
FROMM, ERICH
      1973   *The Anatomy of Human Destructiveness*. New York: Holt, Rinehart & Winston. Reprinted by permission of Holt, Rinehart & Winston.
HAMPDEN-TURNER, CHARLES
      1970   *Radical Man*. Cambridge, Mass.: Schenkman.
KANT, IMMANUEL
      1952   *The Critique of Pure Reason*. (1781) Trans. J.M.D. Meiklejohn. *The Great
             Books of the Western World*. Ed. Robert Hutchins. Chicago: Encyclopaedia
             Britannica.
ROSENBERG, MORRIS, AND RALPH TURNER
      1981   *Social Psychology*. New York: Basic Books.

3

Symbolic Interactionism as a Perspective

INTRODUCTION: FIVE CENTRAL IDEAS

Symbolic interactionism is a perspective in social psychology that is especially relevant to the concerns of sociology. Before we go into the details of this perspective, it might be best to look at the core ideas. There are five.

First, instead of focusing on the individual and his or her personality characteristics, or how the society or social situation causes human behavior, *symbolic interactionism focuses on the nature of social interaction, the dynamic social activities taking place among persons.* In focusing on the interaction itself as the unit of study, the symbolic interactionist creates a more active image of the human being and rejects the image of the passive, determined organism. Individuals interact; societies are made up of interacting individuals. People are constantly undergoing change in this interaction, and society arises and changes through this social interaction. Interaction is an ongoing activity; it means that human actors act in relation to the acts of one another; they take one another's acts into account as they act. Interaction means that the acts of each individual are built up over time depending in part on what the others do in the situation in relation to them. Interaction means that individuals are not simply influenced by others; it means that actors constantly influence one another as they act back and forth; hence, a more dynamic and active human being emerges, rather than an actor merely responding to others in the environment.

The second important idea is that *human action is caused not only by social interaction but also results from interaction within the individual.* Our ideas or attitudes or values are not as important to us as the active ongoing process of thinking. We act according to how we are thinking in the specific situation we are in, and although that thinking may be influenced to some extent by others with whom we interact, our own thinking within ourselves always matters.

The third idea was described briefly in Chapter 2. It has to do with the fact that *humans do not sense their environment directly but instead define their situation as they go along in their action.* We act according to this definition. I do not therefore respond to you, your words, your acts, your clothes—I define these things in the situation and I act according to whatever definition I give them at the time. Of course, definition does not simply happen; instead, it results from both social interaction and interaction with ourselves. As we interact with others and self, we develop our definitions of what is taking place in our situation, and we decide on how to act in that situation. The stimuli do not affect us directly; we do not respond to reality as it really is, but to reality as we define it.

Social interaction, interaction with self, and definition of the situation are three central concepts in the symbolic interactionist perspective. What does this do to understanding why we act as we do? In a very basic sense it places us into an immediate situation to look for cause. It is what I define right now that matters. It is social interaction right now that matters. It is thinking right now that matters. The fourth idea is exactly this: *We are not controlled by what happened to us in the past; we are not simply playing out personality traits we developed early in our lives. Our actions are always caused by what happens in the present situation, more specifically, how we are defining what is happening there.* It is also not society's past that matters to us, nor is it simply the qualities of that society developed in the past. It is what is unfolding right now that matters to what we end up doing. The past may play some role, but as a cause of present action it is not nearly as significant as the present. Indeed, the most important way it enters our action is how we define it and apply it to our present. Like everything else in our environment, our past is defined by us and it is applied to the situation at hand.

It has probably become obvious by now that the words used to describe the human being now take an active form. In contrast to other social-scientific perspectives that emphasize how passive and caused we all are, symbolic interactionism describes the actor as a being who thinks, defines, applies his or her past, imagines the future, and selects objects in the environment for his or her own use. The fifth idea is that *humans, unlike other animals in nature, are able to take an active part in the cause of their own action.* Perhaps the human being is now conceived to be "free," at least to some extent.

These ideas are not difficult to understand. You have no reason to believe them at this point, because the perspective has not yet been explained. However, here is the broad outline, and we will go back to these ideas again and again in the chapters that follow.

GENERAL HISTORICAL BACKGROUND OF SYMBOLIC INTERACTIONISM

Symbolic interactionism is usually traced back to the work of George Herbert Mead (1863–1931), who was a professor of philosophy at the University of Chicago. Mead wrote many articles, but much of his influence on symbolic interactionists comes through the publishing of his lectures and notes by his students, as well as through interpretation of his work by various other sociologists, especially one of his students, Herbert Blumer.

Blumer draws not only from Mead but also from others who pioneered symbolic interactionism. The perspective goes back to the work of John Dewey,

William James, Charles Peirce, William Thomas, and Charles Cooley, to name a few. Blumer, writing primarily in the 1950s and 1960s, integrated much of their work. Many others have drawn from these early interactionists, and the 1980s and 1990s brought new leaders to the perspective, such as Norman Denzin, Alfred Lindesmith, Anselm Strauss, Sheldon Stryker, Gary Fine, David Maines, Tamotsu Shibutani, Howard Becker, John Lofland, and Carl Couch, among others. With these, new directions and criticisms of Blumer's work have emerged. The 1980s and 1990s have also seen the growing importance of Erving Goffman and dramaturgical sociology, which has been influenced by and is influencing traditional symbolic interactionism.

One way of understanding the general position of the symbolic interactionist perspective is to summarize the major influences on Mead, its principal founder. [The following draws from Strauss (1964), and Desmonde (1957).] There were three such influences, each one being central to all the symbolic interactionists since.

1. The philosophy of pragmatism
2. The work of Charles Darwin
3. Behaviorism

Mead and Pragmatism

Mead is part of that school of philosophy known as *pragmatism*. The ideas of this school are especially important to Mead's approach to understanding the nature of truth. As we shall see, this becomes a very important foundation for the whole perspective of symbolic interactionism. Basically, four ideas are important here.

First, pragmatists examine the human's relationship to the environment, contrasting it with the relationship of other animals. What is real for human beings, it is proposed, always depends on our own active intervention, our own interpretation or definition. The world does not tell us what it is; we actively reach out and understand it and decide what to do with it. Reality does not impose itself on us without our taking a role in interpreting it. A fish is not a fish is not a fish to the human being; it is not a physical stimulus that we simply respond to. Instead, in looking at a fish we must engage in an interpretive process. We might call it a fish, a dead fish, a pike, something to eat, or set free, or put up on our wall. Objects that exist in our environment do not simply reveal themselves to us; we ourselves must make decisions as to what they are. We see nothing "in the raw": Nothing for humans ever "speaks for itself."

Second, pragmatists try to explain what knowledge is for the human being. What do we end up believing and remembering? *To the pragmatist knowledge is judged by how useful it is in defining the situations we enter.* The more we can apply it to what we encounter in our world, the more we come to believe it. Every situation tests our knowledge and beliefs; if we apply something and it does not work, we don't use it again and forget it. You may be familiar with the pronouncement "People see what they want to see and remember what they want to remember." The pragmatist is not disagreeing but is trying to explain why this is so: We remember that which works for us. Perspectives, facts, definitions, experiences, ideas—all are judged by the individual in terms of applicability. Right now whatever we believe may or may not actually be true—in fact, it may be completely wrong. Our ideas are not judged by truth or falsehood, nor are they judged by how carefully we learned them. They work and so we use and remember them. What is learned in college may or may not stay with us, not because what was learned is true or untrue, but simply because we are or are not able to actually apply it to real situations and achieve our goals there.

Third, pragmatism tries to explain how we actually see objects in the environment. What is it that we actually notice? Why do we notice some things and not others? Beyond the fact that we apply what we know to the situation, what exactly do we apply from all the knowledge we have? The answer is that *things in situations are defined according to the use they have for us at the time.* My office, for example, changes because its use for me changes as the day goes on. A scrap of paper on the floor is not even noticed by me until I find out that visitors are coming and I need to present my room in good order. The meaning of things to the actor depends on how the actor intends to use them. We have goals in situations, and we organize objects around us according to those particular goals. A given object has a multitude of uses, and it changes for us as our goals change. A wastebasket is something to throw trash in, something we use to store corn in, something to practice our basketball skills with—the definition depends entirely on the actor's goals. Objects probably in fact exist out there in the situation, but we humans always place them into a context related to our goals at the time. They are perceived according to how we are going to use them.

Fourth, pragmatism also tells us something about how philosophers and social scientists should study the human being. *Start with action. It is what human beings do in real situations that matters.* Ask: What exactly are people doing in that particular situation? What causes that particular action? The actor acts; actors act together in what we might call a society. We are examining acting units, not stable persons or societies, acting units that constantly form their actions as they go along. There are chapters in this book on what people *do* in their worlds, rather than what makes up their personality or what makes up the qualities of society. What social scientists can actually see in situations is action, movement by an organism toward the environment. Here is where we must begin our study—the understanding of individual persons or societies can come only after we come to understand what people are doing.

Notice what was introduced here. There are five ideas that are central to the whole perspective: social interaction, interaction with self, definition of the situation, cause in the present, and an active relationship humans have with their environment. On top of this, the pragmatist influence includes four more ideas: Humans define and do not respond; they believe what is useful to them; they see and define objects according to their use; and they can be understood primarily by focusing on what they do. Let us take one further step and see what the ideas of Charles Darwin tell us about the symbolic interactionist perspective.

Mead and Darwin

Mead was inspired and influenced by the work of Charles Darwin. Darwin's work, of course, helped to revolutionize the study of life through its contribution to the theory of evolution. For most scientists—natural and social—Darwin's work has had a tremendous impact. He was respected by Mead and influenced the direction that symbolic interactionism takes in studying the human being.

Darwin was a naturalist. He believed that we must try to understand the world we live in without appealing to supernatural explanation. God may, of course, exist, but nature should be understood on its own terms, as subject to natural laws. *So too, Mead argued, should we regard the human being in naturalistic terms.* If we are at all free, if we are unique in nature, if we possess qualities different from other animals, then these must be understood in natural rather than supernatural terms. Instead of examining the human in spiritual, metaphysical terms, possessing qualities such as soul, we need to identify the natural qualities that characterize what we are. Instead of claiming freedom for humans simply by assuming it, we need to examine those natural qualities that make freedom a possibility. Mead's whole approach to truth, self, mind, symbols, and other quite difficult and abstract concepts is meant to be naturalistic: It tries to understand them as part of the qualities developed by the human being as part of the natural world, as part of our heritage in the animal kingdom. Freedom, then, if it is important and unique, needs to be examined as something that develops in nature as we become active in relation to our environment, rather than accepted by faith alone.

Mead, by regarding the human in naturalistic terms, borrowed heavily from Darwin's theory of evolution, a theory that focused on the development of the various species of animals in the animal kingdom. Mead, like Darwin, saw human development as part of this evolutionary process. Humans are animals, social animals, evolved from other forms, and they are like all other animals in some ways, but because of their development, certain qualities make them unique. Mead, more than Darwin, tried to identify these unique qualities more carefully and concluded that they are not to be understood as single isolated qualities, but a unique combination of several qualities that together form a qualitative difference between the human species and other animals in nature. This uniqueness relates to physical traits such as a highly developed brain, a helplessness in childhood that makes it essential to rely heavily on society and socialization, and highly developed vocal chords and facial muscles making it possible to create many subtle and sophisticated sounds. Such qualities, when combined, make humans able to use language, and this, in turn, allows them to reason.

Mead went further, however. To Darwin, evolution for animals is really a passive process. This means that nature plays itself out on various living things, and whatever survives depends on these natural forces acting out on the organism. Changes in the environment and changes in genetic makeup together influence the changes in the animal kingdom. Mead accepts this idea, but only until the human being is formed. Once language and the ability to reason arise in nature, the resulting being is able to turn back on nature itself, actively controlling how the natural forces act. The human is no longer passive, simply shaped by nature, but can now learn about it, understand it, act back on it. Evolution does not have the same affect any more, since humans are able to adjust and alter the environment and even their heredity. We are still controlled to some extent, but we exercise more control than we would otherwise, and to some extent we turn around on that which formed us. We can understand the forces in nature, and we can build, invent, discover, shape what affects us.

Finally, Darwin also influenced Mead in his thinking about what the universe actually is. Darwin helped shape people's thinking that the universe is dynamic rather than static. Instead of everything in the universe being the same as it was millions of years ago, Darwin emphasized that everything has changed, and that there is a constant dynamic process rather than a static one that describes nature. Mead is interested in the human being and society, so the impact of Darwin was that Mead came to see everything about the human being as process, rather than as stable and fixed. Thus, instead of the individual being a consistent, structured personality, the individual is a dynamic changing actor, never becoming anything, but always in the state of becoming, unfolding, acting. Instead of being socialized, the actor is always in the process of being socialized. Society is not thought to be an static entity out there, influencing us, but entirely a developing process, characterized by ongoing continuous social interaction. Mind to Mead is action, and whatever self we have is a process, not a static entity. We converse with ourselves, we make decisions along a continuous stream of action. Truth for us always changes, our symbols do, rules change, our use for our environment changes. What we are today is different from what we were yesterday or even a moment ago. Our past changes, as do our views of the future. People are not thought to be brainwashed and conditioned so much as actively involved in testing and reassessing their truths. This dynamic approach to the human being is found throughout Mead's thinking, and it was shaped by Darwin's view of nature.

Thus, Darwin and his theory of evolution combined with the ideas of pragmatism to form the basis for Mead's ideas. Darwin influenced Mead to look for human qualities in natural terms, to understand the development of our most important qualities as arising from our physical evolution, but, Mead adds, once developed, combining to make humans active participants in their environment and their own evolution. Finally, Darwin influenced Mead to see humans as part of a changing universe rather than a static one, and Mead applied this idea to all human qualities. Some have even pointed out that Mead was uncomfortable with the word "society" since it seemed so static a term, and preferred more active terms to describe it.

Mead and Behaviorism

There is one more influence on Mead worth discussing. It is the school in psychology called behaviorism. Mead is a behaviorist, but he also breaks sharply with behaviorism on some very basic issues.

Mead was a behaviorist because he agreed that humans must be understood in terms of what they do, rather than who they are. As mentioned earlier, this idea is also central to pragmatism. The behaviorist argues that the only scientifically legitimate way to understand all animals, including humans, is by carefully observing their behavior. Concepts such as personality, attitudes, and society have little place in behaviorism.

However, Mead was also influenced in a negative way by behaviorism. John B. Watson, a psychologist who became one of the important founders of behaviorism in the United States, was actually a student of Mead's and Dewey's at the University of Chicago, but he rejected the pragmatists in favor of a behaviorism that ignored all behavior except that which can be directly observed. Minded behavior, so central to Mead and the other pragmatists, was not included in the study of human action.

Mead reacted to this kind of behaviorist science, believing always that without an understanding of mind, symbols, self, and so on, human behavior cannot be understood for what it actually is. To measure overt behavior alone without trying to understand covert, "minded" behavior was to ignore the central qualities of the human being; it was to ignore our uniqueness as a species; it was to treat humans identically with all other things in nature, as physical organisms. Mead was a behaviorist, but he called himself a social behaviorist and taught that in human behavior there is an interpretation to be included, an understanding of the acts of others and one's own acts, and that as we observe human overt action we must always consider what is going on in terms of understanding, definition, interpretation, meaning.

Pragmatism, Darwin, and behaviorism each has a place in Mead's work. They are his roots, and out of these Mead developed a unique perspective, one that regards the human being as an active being, a thinking, creative, self-directing, defining dynamic actor, one whose ability to use symbols, define, and alter the environment results in a unique being in nature.

A CONTRAST WITH OTHER PERSPECTIVES: WARRINER

Thus far we have examined the general outline of symbolic interactionism by looking at its key ideas and by highlighting some of the influences on George Herbert Mead's thinking. To go further in this analysis, I would like to introduce the ideas of two more people—Charles K. Warriner and Tamotsu Shibu-tani—both of whom expertly contrast symbolic interactionism with more tra-ditional social-scientific perspectives.

Warriner (1970, 1–13) explains that the issue of humans having an active or passive nature has traditionally been a very emotional issue in society, that society's idea system, its ideology, simply makes assumptions about human freedom and these assumptions are applied to many of the key social issues. Because this is assumed, the question of human freedom has rarely been tack-led from an objective perspective. Yet the real relation of the individual to soci-ety and society to the individual is probably "the most fundamental, the most frequently recurring" question we have ever dealt with, and the answer to this has had the "most extended implication" for our history. Do humans create society, or are we simply created by it? Do humans have an important role to play in the direction of their society, or is it a one-way influence where society is the shaper?

Traditional social science, in its attempt to take the lead from natural science, has built the human within the walls of society. Together with the bio-logical perspective, Warriner sees what he calls a "stable-man" view, the human having a "permanent nature," "inborn or learned." The human is born, is shaped, and, as an adult, is directed. According to stable-man views, human action is caused by human nature or nurture, the individual always acting according to earlier influences. Warriner's diagram of this sequence is shown in Figure 3–1. The cause of human behavior is found in earlier influ-ences, and stability is assumed within the human personality. This stable-man point of view, Warriner argues, is tied to a "physicalist," "deterministic and mechanistictic," nonmentalist view of the world that has dominated science and philosophy.

In reaction, Warriner describes another view that he calls "the emergent-human view," which in fact is the symbolic interactionist view we are describ-ing here. It is different from the stable-man view, emphasizing "immediate sit-uational factors" as cause, "examining the social and 'spiritual' characteristics

FIGURE 3–1

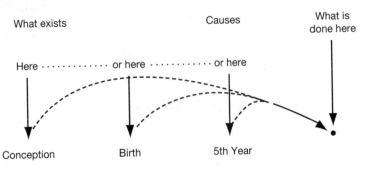

of human beings, and accepting "indeterminacy and probability" in dealing with causes of human action. This theory regards the human as an

> actor rather than as a being, treats [the human being's] acts as symbolic in character rather than primarily physical, and views interaction as the basic social and psychological process from which personalities and societies emerge, through which they are expressed, and by which they are maintained as continuities. (Warriner, 1970, 9)

Human beings are now to be understood as social, interactional, and symbolic by their very nature. Those who see only the physical, who measure only that which is directly observable, miss the whole essence of the human being. Our uniqueness is in

> the symboling process, in the capacity of [the human being] to see things not as they are but as they have been or might be in the future, in the capacity of [the human being] to use sound and marks on paper as conventional signs and thus to communicate with others, in the capacity of [the human being] through these functions to create worlds that never existed in physical reality. (Warriner, 1970, 9–10)

Warriner captures well the spirit of the perspective being described in this book.

SHIBUTANI: REFERENCE GROUPS AS PERSPECTIVES

Tamotsu Shibutani (1955) in "Reference Groups as Perspectives" also highlights the differences between the symbolic interactionist approach to the human being and traditional social science.

Human beings, he points out, use *perspectives* when they look at reality as it is. Perspectives filter what we see. Shibutani describes perspectives in much the same way they were described in Chapter 1 of this book. *They are points of view the actor uses to make sense out of his or her world.*

> A perspective is an ordered view of one's world—what is taken for granted about the attributes of various objects, events, and human nature. It is an order of things remembered and expected as well as things actually perceived, an organized conception of what is plausible and what is possible; it constitutes the matrix through which one perceives his [or her] environment. (P. 564)

It is necessary for us to have perspectives in order to put objects in place as we look at reality. A perspective is an "outline scheme defining and guiding experience." Shibutani likens a group's perspective to culture (as Robert Redfield [1941, p. 132] defines it), consisting of the "conventional understandings, manifest in act and artifact, that characterize societies." Culture is a social creation, influences what we do and make, and characterizes every society. Culture is a product of communication and acts as a guide for individuals who take part in that ongoing communication.

Shibutani links perspectives to reference groups. *A reference group is the society whose perspective the individual uses.* It is the group within which the individual communicates and whose perspective is applied to situations. Shibutani defines reference groups as simply those groups whose perspectives the individual borrows to see reality. Each individual has several reference groups. They can be groups the individual may belong to ("membership groups"), but social categories such as social class, ethnic group, community, or society may also act as reference groups. Reference groups can even be future groups—for instance, philanthropists may give for "posterity" or environmentalists may take on the perspective of unborn generations. Reference groups can be societies or groups from our distant past, as evidenced by many people's interest in the ancient Greeks or the American revolutionaries or the early Christians.

What Shibutani is telling us is that *what we see as reality is really a result of perspectives we take on through social interaction, and the groups whose perspective we use are called our reference groups.* Another word for reference group is "society" and another is "social world." A reference group is an individual's society, and its significance is not membership but the fact that its culture—or perspective—is used by the actor. Each individual uses many such societies, each one held together through communication, each one linked to the individual through communication. In a sense sociologists form a society as they interact, and those who use its perspective use the society of sociology as a reference group. The United States constitutes a society and it too is held together through ongoing communication through television, newspapers, economic and political activities, advertising, travel, and geographic mobility. African Americans also constitute a society within America to the extent that they interact on a continuous basis and develop a shared perspective that matters to people.

Shibutani also uses the term "social world" to define reference group. It is a less formal and structured concept and emphasizes the role of communication in forming and maintaining our reference groups. We live in modern mass societies, each one made up of several smaller social worlds. He writes:

> One of the characteristics of life in modern mass societies is simultaneous participation in a variety of social worlds. Because of the ease with which the individual may expose himself to a number of communication channels, he may lead a segmentalized life, participating successively in a number of unrelated activities. Furthermore, the particular combination of social worlds differs from person to person; this is what led Simmel to declare that each stands at that point at which a unique combination of social circles intersects. The geometric analogy is a happy one, for it enables us to conceive the numerous possibilities of combinations and the different degrees of participation in each circle. To understand what a man does, we must get at his unique perspectives—what he takes for granted and how he defines the situation—but in mass societies we must learn in addition the social world in which he is participating in a given act. (P. 567)

In Shibutani's description, what causes what we do? It is not our personalities developed in the past. It is not attitudes that are inside of us. It is not society itself or culture. In fact, it is not even our perspective. Instead, as soon as we focus on perspective we must recognize the importance of definition—a perspective is only something we borrow to help us define reality. Our interaction in a particular social world may lead us to take on a particular perspective, but that perspective becomes a tool in the hands of an active defining actor. The perspective is our guide. And what is the stability or permanence in all of this? It is not society, nor is it our continuous membership in society. It is not our interaction, nor is it culture or perspective. It is not our definition of reality nor our action in the world that results from our definition. Everything changes; humans are dynamic in everything that happens—action flows, it is ongoing, and all that enters into it is dynamic.

ATTITUDES VERSUS PERSPECTIVES

Perspectives are different from attitudes. When we use the term perspective to describe the human being, we enter the world of definition; when we use the term attitude we enter the world of response. That is why symbolic interactionism is an examination of perspectives and reference groups, while traditional social psychology is an examination of attitudes and social influence. The distinction here is a subtle one, but very important.

To focus on attitude is to focus on the individual, because an attitude is part of the individual. It is similar to a trait that is developed socially but carried around from situation to situation. An attitude is an internal response to an object or class of objects. The external environment acts as a stimulus; the person responds internally; the person responds externally following that internal response. When we have an attitude toward other people who are women or African Americans or poets, and an individual in one of these categories enters our presence, our attitude is thought to be activated, leading us to act in a certain direction. The attitude is a predisposition; it predisposes us to act a certain way. The actor is not thought to be in charge of his or her own action; *the actor does not use the attitude,* but instead the attitude directs the actor. To use the term "attitude" to describe the human being is to describe a passive being and to ignore the importance of active definition of the situation.

A perspective, on the other hand, is not a response to a stimulus, but something used as a guide to definition. It is not an internal trait, but something belonging to, arising in, shared in, and changing in social interaction. The individual uses it; it does not cause behavior. Because the individual interacts with many others and exists in many social worlds, he or she will have many perspectives, and therefore, any given object is not a simple stimulus; instead it can be defined in a number of ways depending on the actor's goals in the situation. A person I see in a situation may be Chinese, a teacher, a male, an artist, a scholar, a liberal, and a member of the upper class, but whatever I focus on and how I decide to act will depend on how I define him or her in the situation; and my definition, in turn, will be influenced by the perspective I use to define the situation. Any one of the individual's characteristics may or may not be important to me. For example, although I may be prejudiced against artists (an attitude), that may nor be an important influence on my action because I am seeing the individual as a teacher because of the perspective I am using.

An attitude is usually defined as a quality of the individual, so it is thought to be fairly fixed and stable over time. An attitude is generally seen to be tied to other qualities of the person, including other attitudes. The image of the human being described is one of a consistent, whole organism, responding to stimuli in situations according to this attitude brought to the situation. "He has an attitude toward women that causes him to treat them as property whenever he encounters them." That is the way he is. Perspectives, on the other hand, are conceptualized as dynamic and changing, guides to interpretation and then to action, undergoing change during interaction, and not necessarily consistent within the actor. Action can therefore never be perfectly predictable: Even if we know the actor's perspectives carried into a situation, we do not know beforehand which one will be chosen by the actor, nor can we predict how it will change in that situation. And even if we know the perspective that will be used, we still cannot know exactly how the individual will use it to define the situation. Finally, we must also recognize that whatever perspectives the actor brings to a situation may, over time, be put aside in favor of one that arises in the actual situation. The selection of juries that favor our side in a courtroom will depend on knowing what groups they interact with on an ongoing basis, and therefore which perspectives they might use to define the trial, but it is central to recognize that the perspective that emerges from the interaction of the jurors may become the most important one by far. Knowing the attitude an individual may have, according to symbolic interactionism, will give us much less information as how the jury member will vote.

Clearly a different type of actor is conceptualized when we use the concept "perspective" rather than "attitude." The human being interacts, uses perspectives, defines situations, acts according to the present, and is active. A dynamic actor is perceived. Figure 3–2 shows the view of the human being that is slowly being developed in this book. It conceptualizes the human as more complex, contradictory, situational, and dynamic, and less predictable and passive than almost all other social-scientific perspectives.

FIGURE 3–2

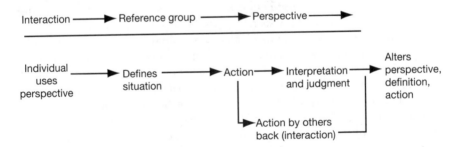

SUMMARY

This chapter has introduced the perspective of symbolic interactionism. Its real purpose is to give an overview of the central ideas of this perspective and to contrast it with several other perspectives that you might be more familiar with. The theme is to alert you to the basic assumptions so you have a context within which to place the following chapters, and, at the same time, to highlight the uniqueness of these assumptions.

1. Symbolic interactionism focuses on interaction in its understanding of the human being, rather than on personality, society, or the influence of others. Interaction includes social interaction and interaction with oneself. It emphasizes that human beings define their environment rather than simply respond to it, that a focus on interaction and definition focuses our attention on the present situation as the cause of what we do. Humans are seen as forever dynamic and active rather than static and passive.

2. Symbolic interactionism is heavily influenced by the work of George Herbert Mead, a philosopher and psychologist who worked at the University of Chicago during the first third of the twentieth century. Mead's work was heavily influenced by pragmatism, Charles Darwin, and behaviorism.

3. Pragmatism is very important to symbolic interactionism primarily in its approach to how humans relate to their environment. It teaches that we always intervene in determining what is real, that knowledge is believed and remembered because it is useful to us, that objects are defined in our environment according to their use to us, and humans must be understood primarily by what they do in their situations.

4. Darwin influences Mead to understand human uniqueness in naturalistic terms and to recognize that humans should be understood in dynamic terms, that the species, society, and the individual are constantly undergoing change. Mead goes further than Darwin in understanding humans by emphasizing our ability to be active in nature, even active participants in our own evolution.

5. Mead was a behaviorist in believing that we must always focus on human behavior in understanding the human being, but he is also critical of other behaviorists for not recognizing the importance of human uniqueness that includes our ability to engage in mind behavior as well as physical overt behavior.

6. Charles Warriner contrasts symbolic interactionism with other natural and social-scientific perspectives. The human is "emergent," always changing as he or she deals with situations encountered. We are not simply products of our past or society's past. What we do in a particular situation depends on our definition of that particular situation and makes it important to recognize that we must be understood as primarily social, symbolic, and mental, rather than simply physical.

7. Tamotsu Shibutani shows the central importance of perspective in understanding how we act in situations. We use perspectives to define our world, and these are always social, dynamic, and guiding, rather than determining agents. Attitudes are not central to symbolic interactionism because they imply a much more passive being, carrying qualities into situations that lead to response. The word "perspective" implies definition rather than response.

REFERENCES

DESMONDE, WILLIAM H.
  1957   "George Herbert Mead and Freud: American Society Psychology and Psychoanalysis." In Benjamin Nelson, ed., *Psychoanalysis and the Future*, pp. 31–50. New York: Psychological Association for Psychoanalysis.

REDFIELD, ROBERT
  1941   *The Folk Culture of YOucatan*, Chicago, University of Chicago Press.

SHIBUTANI, TAMOTSU
  1955   "Reference Groups as Perspectives." *American Journal of Sociology*, 60:562–69.

STRAUSS, ANSELM
  1964   "Introduction" to *On Social Psychology* by George Herbert Mead. Chicago: University of Chicago Press.

WARRINER, CHARLES K.
  1970   *The Emergence of Society*. Homewood, Ill.: Dorsey Press.

4

The Meaning of the Symbol

We walked down the path to the well-house, attracted by the fragrance of the honeysuckle with which it was covered. Someone was drawing water and my teacher placed my hand under the spout. As the cool stream gushed over one hand she spelled into the other the word water, first slowly, then rapidly. I stood still, my whole attention fixed upon the motions of her fingers. Suddenly I felt a misty consciousness as of something forgotten—a thrill of returning thought; and somehow the mystery of language was revealed to me. I knew then that "w-a-t-e-r" meant the wonderful cool something that was flowing over my hand. That living word awakened my soul, gave it light, hope, joy, set it free! There were barriers still, it is true, but barriers that could in time be swept away.

I left the well-house eager to learn. Everything had a name, and each name gave birth to a new thought. As we returned to the house every object which I touched seemed to quiver with life. That was because I saw everything with the strange, new sight that had come to me. . . .

I learned a great many new words that day. I do not remember what they all were; but I do know that *mother, father, sister, teacher* were among them—words that were to make the world blossom for me, "like Aaron's rod, with flowers." It would have been difficult to find a happier child than I was as I lay in my crib at the close of that eventful day and lived over the joys it had brought me, and for the first time longed for a new day to come. (Keller, 1954, 36–37)[*]

We take for granted the fact that we use language. We rarely think about what it would be like without language. Only when we consciously attempt to examine language objectively do we realize how central it is to what the human being is. Helen Keller, both blind and deaf, was not able to use language for a good part of her childhood, because she was unaware of words, unaware that humans can respond to a reality outside the physical reality, to a reality uniquely human—a social/symbolic reality that opens up for human beings behavioral possibilities that other organisms do not have. Indeed, it is due to the world of symbols and language that the human is not passive in nature and does not respond to physical stimuli as other organisms do. The symbolic interactionist perspective takes the use of symbols and relates it to all that is human. The symbol is, in a way, the central concept of the whole perspective.

[*]Excerpt from *The Story of My Life* by Helen Keller.

What is the nature of the human being? Are we by nature evil? Selfish? Good? Hungry for knowledge? What? Borrowing from Charles K. Warriner's (1970) argument, whatever we are, whatever "human nature" is, is highly dependent on society. This statement refers to two human characteristics in a sense. One is that we become violent, selfish, peaceful, or loving, owing in large part to the society. But also we are in our very nature, social beings, dependent on society for all our most basic human qualities, such as conscience, language, and the ability to reason. However, Warriner also emphasizes that the nature of human society is highly dependent on the nature of the individual, both in the sense that individuals shape society, and in the sense that individuals—highly complex, intelligent, creative, and flexible—are necessary for society to exist.

It is the nature of the *symbol* that makes this interdependence most clear. Each individual depends on society for symbols; without other people each individual would be without a symbolic life and all the things that symbols make possible. But the relationship is also reversed: Complex human society demands and depends on human symbolic life—symbolic communication.

There are two important terms for us to consider carefully before we examine the symbol. These are *reality* and *social objects*.

THE NATURE OF REALITY

To begin with, we must consider further the nature of "reality" for human beings. Because, as we have pointed out, the human sees the world through perspectives, developed socially, reality is *social,* and what we see "out there" (and within ourselves) is developed in interaction with others. We interpret the world according to social definitions. It is important to emphasize, however, that social scientists (including symbolic interactionists) operate from the assumption that a physical objective reality does indeed exist independent of our social definition, that our social definitions do develop, at least in part, in relation to something "real" or physical. Although there are some who question even this assumption, most of us would indeed agree to some *objective reality* existing out there. Symbolic interactionists sometimes call this the "situation as it exists."

The important point is that we do not respond to this reality directly. Instead, we *define* the situation "as it exists" out there, and that definition is highly influenced by our social life. We are not like billiard balls responding directly to the impact of other billiard balls, nor are we like rats responding to physical stimuli. Someone may push us physically, and we must respond physically in the sense that our bodies give way to the push, but we also immediately *interpret* that act and decide on a line of action. At first our physical bodies respond to other physical bodies, but immediately we socially define that reality, putting that action into a working context (e.g., Why did he push? Did he mean to be aggressive? Is he bigger than I am? Is he dangerous?), and we define the act accordingly.

Humans therefore exist in a physical objective reality *and* a social reality. We learn in social interaction what to see in objective reality and how to define what we see. However, there is a third reality we need to recognize. Human beings also have the ability to create a reality in interaction with themselves; they each develop their own unique reality. This personal reality is not unique; it is always based on our social reality; it is built on that social reality. We learn in social interaction about the world out there, but then we go with it: We manipulate it internally, we think about it, we arrive at our own interpretation of it. Social reality begins the process of definition, but that is not all that there is for us.

Importance of a Socially Defined Reality

Howard Becker (1953), in an interesting and comprehensive study of marijuana users, done before marijuana became such a popular part of many social worlds in the United States, illustrates the central importance of a social definition of reality, even the reality that we *feel* inside our own bodies. His point: To identify the effects of marijuana as good and pleasurable is a matter of socialization; it is, in a real sense, a result of social interaction, a social reality. In conclusion, Becker writes:

> This analysis of the genesis of marihuana use shows that the individuals who come in contact with a given object may respond to it at first in a great variety of ways. If a stable form of new behavior toward the object is to emerge, a transformation of meanings must occur, in which the person develops a new conception of the nature of the object. This happens in a series of communicative acts in which others point out new aspects of his experience to him, present him with new interpretations of events, and help him achieve a new conceptual organization of his world, without which the new behavior is not possible. Persons who do not achieve the proper kind of conceptualization are unable to engage in the given behavior and turn off in the direction of some other relationships to the object or activity. (P. 242)

The importance of a socially defined reality is one of the central ideas in sociology today and it does not need to be documented extensively here. However, before we go on I would like to mention a study done by Mark Zborowski (1952). He studied people's reaction to pain, and, he points out that pain, although it is "a physiological phenomenon acquires specific social and cultural significance . . . "(p. 17). His research examined patients' definitions of their own pain in order to better understand how their group life influenced how they saw and felt it. Pain, he concludes, is defined differently, given a different meaning and reaction, at least in part because of their ethnic group membership, from which they get a perspective. There is no reason to believe that some ethnic groups actually experience more physical pain than others, yet some groups complain more than others, some groups focus on the pain itself and are thankful for immediate relief, whereas others tend to interpret pain as representing something more serious; they are not relieved just with pain killers but need assurance about their future health. It seems that for human beings something as immediate and physical as pain is defined by perspectives the individual borrows from his or her reference groups.

The importance of socially defined reality to the human is even more obvious when we look beyond our own bodies. Every day we encounter countless physical objects. To make sense out of them, the human actor must isolate, identify, and catalog them. How do we do that? To a great extent it is done by society; we come to identify and classify our world according to what we learn from others in interaction.

OBJECTS AS "SOCIAL OBJECTS"

Objects may exist in physical form, but for the human being, they are pointed out, isolated, cataloged, interpreted, and given meaning through social interaction. In the symbolic interactionist perspective, we say that objects for the human being are really *social objects*. This concept is very important in the symbolic interactionist perspective, for, as we shall see, it will become an integral part of every chapter in this book.

First, we begin with objects "as they are." Again, although objects may exist in physical form, human beings see objects not "in the raw," but only through a perspective of some kind. We learn what things are and what they are good for. Children want to know, "What's that?" The newcomer to football wants to know, "What are they doing now? What is a 'down'? What is a 'huddle'?" And a student at college for the first time wants to know, "What is a G.P.A.? What is a graduate assistant? What is sociology?" We ask. We watch. We are told. But, in the end, we learn from one another what things are in the world. This is why objects are called *social* objects by the symbolic interactionist.

Objects in nature are, of course, acted on by both human and nonhuman organisms. Bernard Meltzer (1972, 22–23) describes Mead's thesis that all organisms must single out certain things around them to use because only certain things are important to their survival. Other objects become largely irrelevant. (A tree, grass, a human, and acorns are all different things to a cow, a squirrel, a beaver, and a cat.) Objects in the physical world act as stimuli for nonhuman animals, leading to specific responses. The same object (e.g., grass) will lead to different responses depending on which species is involved. For the human being, however, all objects in nature are not fixed stimuli but *social objects* constantly changing as they are defined and redefined in interaction. "Objects consist of whatever people indicate or refer to" (Blumer, 1969, 68). Objects are given importance by us not through fixed biological patterns (as is the case in most other animals) but according to what others around us decide to give importance to. And each object changes for the human, not because *it* changes, but because people change their definition. The meaning, says Herbert Blumer, "is not intrinsic to the object" (p. 68).

But how do we define these social objects? We give them *names,* but more important, we learn what they are good for, how they are *used.* Social objects are defined according to their *use* for people involved in a situation. Meaning "arises from how the person is initially prepared to act toward it" (Blumer, 1969, 68–69). A chair becomes "something to sit in." A desk is "something to write on." A flower is "something to smell." A podium is "something to speak from." In each of these cases, however, the object changes as its use for us changes, as we change the meaning it has for us. Chairs are also something to stand on, to store things on, to draw, to put side by side in order to sleep on, and so forth. A desk is something to sit on or stand on, to collate papers on, to represent our prestige to others with, to hide something in, and so forth. A flower is also something to give to a loved one or someone in the hospital, something to send to a person in mourning, something to decorate our yard, something to draw, something to extract medicine from, something to use to attract bees. A podium is also something to represent our authority, something to store notes in, something for children to play with. Objects change for us precisely because our use for them changes. Blumer supplies some excellent examples: "A tree is not the same object to a lumberman, a botanist, or a poet; a star is a different object to a modern astronomer than it was to a sheepherder of antiquity; communism is a different object to a Soviet patriot than it is to a Wall Street broker" (p. 69). Blumer wrote this in 1969. By 1990 communism meant something different to the Soviet patriot. Most physical objects have almost an infinite number of possible uses; thus, they have almost an infinite number of social meanings, and each physical object constitutes, therefore, a multitude of social objects.

This view of objects is one that goes back to pragmatism, which was briefly discussed in Chapter 3. Between objects out there and the individual's overt action is a perspective—a definition, a meaning—socially derived.

Because we live in a world of social objects we are now able to "understand" our environment. We are able to describe it to others and to ourselves. We are able to take what we learn in one situation and apply it to a very different situation. If we understand our environment we can take that knowledge and use it to figure out new situations. No longer do we sense our environment; we represent it in our heads and are able to discuss it with ourselves and others.

Our understanding of objects has to do with our use of them. We understand that an object—say a pencil—has many uses, and when the occasion arises, we are in the position to use it appropriately. We are able to apply what we know to our actions. Understanding is not habit but is instead *applying knowledge* we have to objects. Mead, Blumer, and other symbolic interactionists maintain that we define objects according to "a line of action" we are about to take toward them. When I see a horse out there, I see something I am about to

GOSHEN COLLEGE LIBRARY
GOSHEN, INDIANA

ride, mount, pet, run from, eat, sell, buy, or use to teach my children that animals are their friends. To say we see according to a line of action we are about to take toward something is the same as saying we organize our perception of objects according to the use they have for us.

A social object, then, is *any object in a situation that an actor uses in that situation. That use has arisen socially. That use is understood and can be applied to a variety of situations.* Other objects are ignored. However, as action unfolds, the individual may change his or her use, notice new objects, ignore objects used initially, and so on. The actor *acts* toward objects, socially defined, of use to him or her in a particular situation.

Social objects include anything. Consider the following examples.

1. Physical natural objects—a tree, a flower, a rock, or dirt—can become social objects in a situation.
2. Human-made objects—a radio, a fork, a piece of paper, a computer terminal—can become social objects in a situation.
3. Animals are sometimes used as social objects by the individual.
4. Other people are social objects—both individually and in groups, we define other people as important to the situations we are in. We develop lines of action toward them, and we "use" them (not necessarily selfishly). You are someone I ask for a date one day, ask to marry, marry, live with, get angry with, share my cares with, and so on.
5. Our "past" is a social object, as is the "future." We *use* these to work through situations.
6. Our "self" is a social object (as we shall emphasize in Chapter 6).
7. Symbols are social objects. We create and use symbols to communicate and represent something to others and to ourselves.
8. Ideas and perspectives can be social objects.
9. Emotions can be social objects. Like all else, we are able to define, use, manipulate, and understand them in ourselves and in others.

Anything can become a social object for the human actor. Whatever we use is a social object to us in a given situation. Our use defines it, and almost always that use has arisen socially. "It" changes, as our use for it changes. This view alters the nature of the world humans act in. Instead of objects "turning us on," *we define them; we use them* to achieve our goals in a situation; and *we change them* according to our changing goals. We understand the world we live in and we are able to apply that understanding to situations we enter and use the objects there according to our understanding.

SYMBOLS—A CLASS OF SOCIAL OBJECTS

This is a chapter about symbols. But what are symbols? Simply, *symbols are one class of social objects.* Some social objects are symbols, some are not. Like all social objects, symbols are used and defined according to their use. *Symbols are social objects used to represent* (or "stand in for," "take the place of") whatever people agree they shall represent. A bolt of lightning stands for the wrath of God, two fingers in the air stands for victory (or peace, or loyalty to the Cub Scouts, or rebellion toward the adult world), the word "m-a-n" stands for approximately one half of the human race (or all of the human race).

Words, of course, are symbols, but so are many objects that people may make into symbols (like the cross). Indeed, most human action is symbolic: It is meant to represent something more than what is immediately perceived. I may raise a clenched fist to represent victory; I may smile to represent I like what you are saying; I may switch on my car signal to tell you I am turning. Others generally see it as representing something. Rather than responding to it, they interpret it, they determine what the action is supposed to represent.

Many social objects are not used to represent something else and are therefore not symbols. A flower is used for drugs, for smelling, for picking, for food. However, if I use it to represent my love for you, it becomes a symbol. The same physical object (e.g., a chair or lightning or a picture on the wall), therefore, can be a purely social object to some and a symbol to others. And for still others that object does not exist, because it goes unnoticed, serves no useful function in their situation.

If symbols are social objects, then we understand their use. We do not simply respond to them (as the dog may learn to "roll over"), but we are able to describe them to ourselves and to others and we are able to apply them to thousands of situations where they seem to fit. Understanding symbols means that we understand their representation. We are not simply trained to associate a symbol with what it stands for; but we can use it at will. I know what I am doing when I use a symbol; I understand what it is supposed to represent.

The distinction between symbols and social objects, however, goes beyond just representation. Symbols represent, but they are also used for communication between actors or within the actor. Symbols are therefore *social objects used by the actor for representation and communication*. We are able to tell others something about what we think, what we are, what we intend, what we feel, and we are able to communicate to ourselves (to think) about our world. A horse is just a social object until I make it into something to represent and communicate skill, prestige, wealth, or happiness to others. The word "horse" is a word symbol, used specifically to represent a certain animal as I communicate to others and to myself.

SYMBOLS ARE SOCIAL, MEANINGFUL, AND SIGNIFICANT

Symbols are *social* (recall that all social objects are social). This means that symbols are defined in interaction, not established in nature. People make them, and people agree on what they shall stand for. Some call symbols *"con-*

ventional": They represent something else only because of convention, only because of common agreement.

Symbols are *meaningful*. That is, the user *understands what they represent*. Symbols involve an understanding rather than a simple response to their presence. When we say that symbols "represent" something to the user, we are actually saying that they stand in for something else, and that the user understands that relationship. A symbol is "any object, mode of conduct, or word toward which [people] act *as if it were something else*. Whatever the symbol stands for constitutes its *meaning*" (Shibutani, 1961, 121). For instance, Shibutani gives us the example of a colored piece of cloth, what we call a "flag":

> A flag is a symbol for a nation. The piece of colored cloth often evokes patriotic sentiments and plays an important part in the mobilization of millions of men for war. Seeing someone treat the flag with disrespect can arouse the most violent emotional reactions, for men often regard the piece of cloth as if it were the nation with which they identify themselves. . . . Soldiers risk their lives on battlefields to save a flag from falling into the hands of the enemy; the cloth in itself is of little value, but what it stands for is of great importance. (Pp. 120–21)

Symbols are *significant*. By this Mead means that symbols are meaningful not only for the actor who receives them but also to the user. The user of symbols uses symbols *intentionally*, not by mistake. "What is essential to communication is that the symbol should arouse in one's self what it arouses in the other individual" (Mead, 1934, 149). The person who uses symbols does so *for the purpose of giving off meaning* that he or she believes will make sense to the other. A crying infant does not at first use symbols to communicate to parents, although the parents do see the act of crying as important, interpret it, and act. Crying becomes symbolic only when its meaning is understood by the one who produces it, the infant. Then, as the infant intentionally communicates through crying, there is a request for an act by the other, and we can begin to speak of symbolic behavior between child and parents. Symbols, then, because they are meaningful to the actor, are used *purposively* to give off meaning to others. Sheldon Stryker (1959) describes the process by which a small child comes to share meaning:

> The early activity of the child will include random vocalization. Eventually, too, he will imitate sounds others make. Others respond to the initially random vocalization by selecting out particular sounds and responding to these. They respond to the imitated sounds as well by acts which contain the adult meanings of these sounds. For the child, the correspondence between sound and meaning will be initially vague, but in the process of interaction over time the correspondence will become more pronounced. So, for example, the child may use the sound "ba" to refer to any approximately round object and, having played this game with daddy, may be led to roll any such object—ball, orange, egg—around the floor. The response of parent to the rolling of an egg—especially an uncooked one—will soon make clear that an egg is not a "ba" and thus is not to be rolled on the floor. In the course of time, child and parent will come to agree on what is and is not a ball, and thus a significant symbol will have come into existence. A

sound, initially meaningless to the child, comes to mean for the child what it already means for the adult. (P. 116)

It is important to realize that symbolic communication can actually take two forms: In one, an actor can use symbols to talk to self (think); in another, an actor can use symbols to communicate to others. However, to be symbolic in the second sense (in communicating with others), the actor simultaneously talks to self (the actor understands the meaning of his or her act).

A symbol, then, is a *social object* used for *communication to self* or *for communication to others and to self.* It is an object used *to represent* something else. It is *intentionally* used. The actor's aim is to use it. Without intention, the actor may be communicating, but we do not call it symbolic.

Meltzer (1972, 12–13), borrowing from Mead, contrasts significant symbols with the clucking of a hen or the barking of a dog. He argues: Communication is "nonsignificant" as with the crying infant, or "nonmeaningful" in the sense that the actors do not understand the meaning of the other's act or of their own. A hen clucks and chicks respond. "This does not imply, however, that the hen clucks *in order* to guide the chicks, i.e., with the *intention* of guiding them." A dog barks; the bark serves as a cue for a response by a second dog. There seems to be little evidence that each thinks, "What does he mean by that?" or, "How should I respond to that?" or, "If I run away now, he'll think I'm chicken, so I'd better fight." Meltzer points out: "Human beings on the other hand, respond to one another on the basis of the intentions or meanings of gestures. This renders the gesture *symbolic*, i.e., the gesture is a symbol to be interpreted. . . ." David L. Miller (1973) contrasts significant symbols with the dance of the bees:

> First of all, the dance is not learned; it is committed impulsively. Second there is no evidence that the dancer intends to evoke responses by other bees. Should there be no others present, it will perform the dance anyway; and if others are present but do not "obey the request," the dancer does not perform the dance again, as if to say, "I have told you once, why aren't you on your way?" There is no evidence, in short, that the dancer intends anything by its gesture or that it is in the least aware of the behavioral consequences of its behavior. (Pp. 86–87)

Finally, symbols are *arbitrarily* associated with what they represent. That is, there is nothing inherent in the association. It is not the same as a black sky "representing" a coming storm, or a fever "representing" illness. The meaning of symbols is not found in nature, but only through arbitrary designation by people. People create symbols, and they, not nature, designate that something shall stand for something else. The fact that two fingers in the air means peace is arbitrary—it could just as well be a thumb in the air, a hand closed over our head, a black mark on our forehead.

Examples of symbols are everywhere. The more we examine our world, the more it is transformed from a purely physical world to a fully symbolic world. Let me emphasize:

1. Words are symbols—they stand for something; they are meaningful; they are used by actors to represent physical objects, feelings, ideas, values. They are used for communication. Their meaning is social.
2. Our acts are often symbols. Whatever we do is often meant to give off some meaning, to communicate with others. We tell one another in what we do, what we think, feel, see; what our intentions are; what is coming next. Acts are not symbolic if they are not intentional, or if they are not meant for anyone else. Let me give you some examples of acts as symbolic:

    Writing an outline of my lecture on the blackboard (symbolic of "This is important" or "I care that you understand")
    Looking into someone's eyes as he or she talks
    Walking out in the middle of a lecture
    Gunning a car engine at the corner
    Winking
    Kissing
    Looking at a watch as someone talks to you

    Each one of these is not simply an "act"; it is symbolic. Each person is telling the other something; each is meant for communication of meaning. Acts, for most of us most of the time, are meant to be symbolic; they are more than physical movement—they represent something.
3. Many *objects* can take on a symbolic quality. We can agree that a red star shall represent a certain political philosophy; a Cadillac, status; a diamond, luxury; a man's long hair, rebellion.

It is easiest to understand what is and is not a symbol from the standpoint of the one who gives it off. Simply put: It is a symbol if an individual uses it intentionally to communicate and represent.

What is or is not a symbol becomes more complicated when we look at it from the standpoint of the observer in the situation. He or she may *interpret* the actions of the other even when the other did not mean to communicate. You yawn and I think you are bored with me. The yawn is not a symbol to you, but it communicates and represents something to me. Your unintended body language is not a symbol to you, but it is an important clue to me as to what you are thinking. Your unintended facial expressions are not symbols to you, but they are important for my understanding of you in the situation.

All of your acts that I interpret are actually *social objects* to me. I use them to understand you. They are not, however, symbols to me, because I am not using them for communication and representation. To be a symbol, it is critical that something have meaning to the actor who gives it off. As he or she communicates to others, he or she understands the action. Whatever is given off—symbols or unintentional forms of communication—is noticed and used by others (and is therefore a social object) or goes unnoticed and unused. It is this remarkable ability to manipulate representations intentionally, for the purpose of communication, that gets at the nature of the human being.

There is obviously a lot of room for misunderstanding in human communication. My body language tells you something, but it is not something I may really want you to know. You may notice a twinkle in my eye, a nervous twitch, a frown, and you understand something about me. Or I may think you are using a certain act as a symbolic act, but I am incorrect. For example, when you do not take an exam with the rest of the class, I might interpret that as rebellion, when in fact it is simply because you really did miss the bus. Whatever you intentionally give off may have one meaning to me and another to you. In fact, nothing ever has the same meaning to different people. The ambiguity of symbols does not take away from their importance. Indeed, as Hugh Duncan (1968) writes, "perhaps it is the ambiguity of symbols which makes them so useful in human society" (p. 7).

LANGUAGE

Language is a special kind of symbol. More than any other symbol, it can be produced at will, and it can represent a reality that other symbols cannot. Before we look at language, let us summarize what has been said about social objects and symbols:

1. Social objects result from interaction, and they are defined according to their *use.*
2. Many social objects are not symbols, for their use by the actor is not in representation and communication.
3. Some social objects are symbols. They are *used* for representation and for communication among people and within the individual actor.
4. Symbols can be physical objects, human acts, or words.
5. Symbols are significant, meaningful, conventional, and arbitrary.

Language is a set of words used for communication and representation. Words—symbols that are spoken or written—are the basis for all other symbols. Acts and objects have meaning to us only because they can be described through using words. Meaning involves understanding what symbols stand for—that association is made not through simple training, but through a description that involves words. Words, then, are not simply one kind of symbol but are in fact the most important kind, and make possible all others:

> *The key and basic symbolism of man is language.* All the other symbol systems can be *interpreted* only by means of language. It is the instrument by means of which every designation, every interpretation, every conceptualization, and almost every communication of experience is ultimately accomplished. What is not expressed in language is not experienced and has no meaning; it is "beyond" the people. . . . Fundamentally, the spoken *word,* or its equivalent or functioning counterpart in the languages that do not have "words," is the only all-inclusive and basic medium of communication. There are, of course, other forms of conveying messages interpersonally, which express ideas, emotions, intents, or direc-

tives: laughter, . . . gestures, facial expressions and postures; . . . especially, writing. But these *other* signs, signals, expressions, and marks, and all other symbolic systems relate to words, imply words, are translations, substitutes, adjuncts, or supplements of words. . . . Bereft of their relation to, and interpretation in terms of, language they would be meaningless. Thus, for example, among us the raucous guffaw means "You're a fool!!"; the wave of an arm by an acquaintance means "Hello"; the green light at the intersection means "Go!"; the nod and wink means "Come on"; the beckoning gesture means "Come!"; the Civil Defense siren means "Be on the alert!"

When a people have reached the stage of literacy in their language development, they have *writing* or written language. . . . These, in various combinations, make possible the recording and perpetuation of meanings and their transmission across space and time. But speech always precedes writing. In societies like our own, communication by language is further facilitated and extended by mechanical means of transmitting either speech or writing, such as postal service, printing in its multiple uses, telegraph, telephone and teletype, radio, photography, motion pictures, and television. These are sometimes referred to as secondary symbolic systems. (Hertzler, 1965, 29–31)

Joyce O. Hertzler defines language as "a culturally constructed and socially established system . . . of standardized and conventionalized . . . symbols, which have a specific and arbitrarily determined meaning and common usage for purpose of socially meaningful expression, and for communication in the given society" (p. 30). Language is made up of *words,* each one having meaning alone and also having meaning when combined with others in a standardized way, according to certain established rules. Roger Brown (1965) refers to the "miracle of language":

Fewer than one hundred sounds which are individually meaningless are compounded, not in all possible ways, to produce some hundreds of thousands of meaningful morphemes, which have meanings that are arbitrarily assigned, and these morphemes are combined by rule to yield an infinite set of sentences, having meanings that can be derived. (P. 248)

It is a *symbolic system,* defined in interaction, and used to describe to others and to ourselves what we observe, think, and imagine. Language describes all other social objects, all that people point out to one another in interaction. Language is used to *refer to* or *represent* a part of reality.

Words as Categories

Words are really categories, used to *refer* to a class of objects that are distinguishable to the human being. To say that words refer to something else is to say that they *represent,* "they take the place of," their referent. And to say they refer to a "class of objects" means that they rarely refer to a single object. Brown uses the example of the word "larger," a symbol that stands for a difference in size. Not only can it describe the difference between two specific objects (a single cat and a single rat), but it can be applied to all cats and rats, and indeed to all objects. The word can be applied to a host of things once its meaning is grasped by the person. If words did not refer to some general category, humans would need a huge increase in the number of their words, and the real value would be lost. Each concrete object would need a name, and its similarity to and differences from other concrete objects would be lost to us. That specific object named Charles Mole is a "man," a "teacher," an "American," a "father," a "moral person." Each of these words is a category that tells us what Charles has in common with other objects and what some of his differences are. Without words Charles Mole would be Charles Mole to us and nothing more (and he would be a physical object, not "Charles Mole"). Our ability to categorize and transfer past experiences to new situations depends on this generalizing capacity—this contrasts with the nonsymbolic world of most other organisms, where they must learn specific responses to specific stimuli in order to "know" what to do.

SYMBOLS, PERSPECTIVES, AND INTERACTION

It is now easier to understand what *perspectives* are. Perspectives are a *set of symbols*. We approach reality with the symbol; we see according to our *symbolic framework*. Recall that perspectives (i.e., symbols) arise in interaction with others and in our social worlds (or reference groups). Our symbols are therefore our guides to what we see, what we notice, how we interpret—as well as what we miss—in any situation.

Figure 4–1 illustrates the point that human interaction gives rise to such things as social objects, symbols, language, and perspectives, which in turn lead to an interpretation of a situation and, ultimately, action in it.

FIGURE 4–1

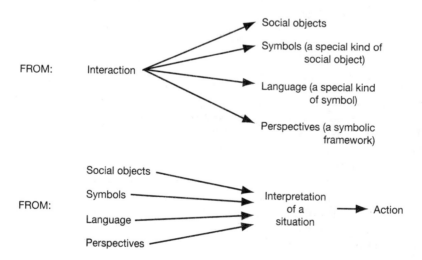

We are really saying more, however. Interaction is a dynamic process: As it progresses over time our definitions may also change, and our interpretation and action will be affected. Social objects, symbols, language, and perspectives are also dynamic and not static "things"; they arise in and are transformed through interaction.

HUMANS AND "INFRAHUMANS"

"Infrahumans" (the term Mead uses to label presymbolic infants and nonhuman animals) are not symbolic, do not define social objects in interaction, do not use symbols or language as we defined it above, and do not use perspectives to define the reality they respond to. Infrahumans—at least the vast majority of them—seem to have a passive relationship with their environment. Behavior is usually instinctive (biologically programmed) or learned through imitation and experience. There is communication among many infrahumans, but it is what might be called a conversation of *nonmeaningful gestures,* where the act of one organism becomes a cue for the response of the other. "There the beginning of the act of one is a stimulus to the other to respond in a certain way, while the beginning of this response becomes again a stimulus to the first to adjust his action to the oncoming response" (Mead, 1934, 144–45). Meltzer (1972) borrows a good illustration from Mead:

> Two hostile dogs, in the pre-fight stage, may go through an elaborate conversation of gestures (snarling, growling, baring fangs, walking stiff-leggedly around one another, etc.). The dogs are adjusting themselves to one another by responding to one another's gestures. (A gesture is that portion of an act which represents the entire act; it is the initial, overt phase of the act, which epitomizes it, e.g., shaking one's fist at someone.) Now, in the case of the dogs the response to a gesture is dictated by pre-established tendencies to respond in certain ways. Each gesture leads to a direct, immediate, automatic, and unreflecting response by the recipient of the gesture (the other dog). Neither dog responds to the *intention* of the gestures. Further, each dog does not make his gestures with the intent of eliciting certain responses in the other dog. Thus, animal interaction is devoid of conscious, deliberate meaning. (Pp. 12–13)

Infrahumans may have highly complex instinctive behavior, their learning through imitation or experience may be extensive, and their communication may be very important, but as far as we know, symbols, social objects, perspectives, and language (as we have defined these things) are not part of their worlds.

It is true that humans have taught chimpanzees symbols—even written words (languages)—and most recently, even how to combine the words. So far as we know, however, although chimps may have *potential* for language, they do not produce it through interaction with one another in nature in the sense that humans do. Most symbolic interactionists would probably agree with John Hewitt's (1984) position:

A symbolic capacity, however simple or complex, is one thing; language is quite another. The apes embarked on an evolutionary course different from ours. Our biological nature, unlike theirs, evolved in tandem with our elaboration of a symbolic capacity into a full-blown language. Our speech came to be controlled by the cerebral cortex, while the vocal call systems of other primates remained under the control of the more ancient limbic system. We developed a refined, biologically-based capacity to produce, hear, and reproduce sounds, whereas they did not. Our brains grew larger than theirs. And while we became progressively more dependent on learning and language use in a complex social environment, their development left them still dependent on a call system and with simpler modes of social organization. (P. 49)

Evidence is still being sought to determine if symbol use exists in non-human animals. The symbolic interactionist, by and large, sees the human as unique in nature, and unique precisely because of symbol use. If, however, it is established that other animals use symbols too, then this fact will in no way detract from the perspective; indeed, our understanding of both the human and other symbol-using animals will be greatly increased. However, if some other animals do indeed use symbols in the sense defined here, it must be established that (1) the symbols are developed socially, through interaction; (2) the symbols are not universally agreed on within the species but are arbitrarily established by and changed through interaction of users; and (3) a language of sounds or gestures exists that is meaningful and that includes rules allowing for combining the sounds or gestures into meaningful statements. To be symbolic means that the organism not only rotely learns responses to cues (as a dog may do from its master) but also actively creates and manipulates symbols in interaction with others and with self. Leslie White (1940) summarizes the critical differences between humans and other animals in this concise statement:

The man differs from the dog—and all other creatures—in that *he can and does play an active role in determining what value the vocal stimulus is to have, and the dog cannot.* As John Locke has aptly put it, "All sounds (i.e., in language). . . have their signification from the arbitrary imposition of men." The dog does not and cannot play an active part in determining the value of the vocal stimulus. Whether he is to roll over or go fetch at a given stimulus, or whether the stimulus for roll over be one combination of sounds or another is a matter in which the dog has nothing whatever to "say." He plays a purely passive role and can do nothing else. He learns the meaning of a vocal command just as his salivary glands may learn to respond to the sound of a bell. But man plays an active role and thus becomes a creator: Let x equal three pounds of coal and it does equal three pounds of coal; let removal of the hat in a house of worship indicate respect and it becomes so. This creative faculty, that of freely, actively, and arbitrarily bestowing value upon things, is one of the most commonplace as well as *the* most important characteristic of man. Children employ it freely in their play: "Let's pretend that this rock is a wolf."

The difference between the behavior of man and other animals, then, is that the lower animals may receive new values, may acquire new meanings, but they cannot create and bestow them. Only man can do this. (Pp. 456–57)

How Animals Approach Environment

One of the best ways to understand the nature of the symbol is to contrast it with the nonsymbolic approach to environment that characterizes other animals. Such a contrast is one of the themes in a book by Ernest Becker (1962, 15–22). He makes the point that a symbolic approach to one's environment is a *qualitatively* different one from other nonsymbolic approaches. The human is unique in nature, or borrowing Warriner's term, humans are *emergent* in nature precisely because of the symbol.

Becker describes four basic approaches to environment by animals. In the first type the organism responds directly to a stimulus. The stimulus controls the action; there is total passivity on the organism's part. The second type is the conditioned response, where the organism is trained to make an association. The organism can learn to respond to a stimulus because it has learned that the stimulus is *associated* with something else of importance. The third approach to environment is the ability of some animals to make relationships in the visual field and to act. The animal is not trained but seems to make the association by itself. Becker describes this approach:

> The best example of it is the chimp who uses a stick to knock down a banana, suspended out of reach. He sees a relationship between two objects in his visual field, and swings the stick to bring down the banana. The crucial difference between this behavior and that of Pavlov's dog is that, for the chimp, the relationship between the banana and stick is something he establishes himself. It results from an alertness to a problem situation. The equation is not built into the chimp by an experimenter, in step-by-step fashion. There is some masterful autonomy here that is absent in the simple conditioned reflex. It is not easy for an animal to relate itself to two or more things in the environment. A dog, for example, seeing food through a picket fence, will detour to a gate twenty feet down the fence to get to the food on the other side. He has seen a relationship between the open gate and getting the food. But a hen, seeing the same food and the gate as well, does not establish any relationship, and runs helplessly back and forth directly in front of the food, watching it through the pickets. (Pp. 17–18)

The final type is symbolic action: response "to an arbitrary designation for an object, a designation coined by him alone, that stands for the object." Becker explains:

> The word "house," for example, has no intrinsic qualities within itself that would connect it with an object, since someone else may use "casa" or "maison" or "dom." Unlike Pavlov's dog, man *creates* the relationship between stimuli. . . . Symbolic behavior depends, of course, upon the ability to create identifiable word sounds that become object representations of infinite degrees of subtlety— from "minnow hook" to "minestrone." (Pp. 18–19)

Becker emphasizes that the differences in the four approaches are *qualitative differences,* not just a matter of degree. Each one seems to be central to the kinds of responses possible. Symbol use provides *the most flexible and active approach* precisely because the organism has a mind to deal with the environment, whereas in the other approaches to environment, organisms are tied to simple reflex, to conditioning, or to seeing relationships in the immediate environment only.

Symbols versus Signs

Symbols are often described by distinguishing them from *signs.* Ernest Becker (1962) points out that the difference is that the organism does not give meaning to signs and does not reflect on them but instead habitually responds to them. Signs may indeed be associated with something else—for example, we might argue that the flap of a beaver's tail is associated with approaching danger. The flap of the tail can also call forth an immediate response without there being any association. In either case, however, signs lead to an automatic response; they are not arbitrary or conventional, they do not arise in interaction, nor is there any meaning assigned through words. Signs are responded to because they are produced in one's physical presence, and they lead to an unthinking response. They must be *sensed,* and the receiver has *no choice* in response.

Humans do not often respond to signs. We are so highly symbolic that if we are trained to respond to a word or object without reflection, in another situation or with another group that same word or object will most likely take on a different meaning and be transformed into a symbol. To the new recruit the word "attention" may act as a sign. It is associated without reflection with an officer, with danger, with a certain act, and the response is probably made without reflection. The sign acts as a cue that leads to a response. Yet the sign "attention" is transformed when the officer leaves the room and the soldiers may play at "attention," making fun of the whole matter. We are so thoroughly symbolic that our most habitual behavior is transformed as we move from situation to situation, from group to group, from context to context. We act in our worlds according to interpretations of objects in a context, rather than through specific responses to specific stimuli, cues, or signs.

Even "signs" in nature become profoundly complex and symbolic and do not exist for us at all in any pure sense. Most other animals, it seems, respond only to signs, cues, and stimuli.

This symbolic nature of ours is profoundly significant to what humans are capable of. It is basic to almost everything we are. Even if other animals do use symbols as described here, none will be found to depend on them as humans do, and probably none will be found whose central qualities are traceable to symbol use. The contrast with the rest of the animal kingdom, be it comfortable for you or uncomfortable, should not be disregarded as unimportant. Kenneth Burke (1966) illustrates this contrast through the interesting example of a wren. He reports how the mother wren was able to get all the baby wrens out of the nest except for one. Nothing seemed to work. "Then came the moment of genius. One of the parent wrens came to the nest with a morsel of food. But instead of simply giving it to the noisy youngster, the parent bird held it at a distance" (pp. 4–5). Slowly the baby was teased out of the nest. The parent pushed, and by obtaining the needed leverage on the baby, whose balance was shaky, was able to push it out. Pure genius, Burke announces. But, on the other hand, the wren is not now able to write a dissertation on "The Uses of Leverage," nor can this be shared throughout the wren kingdom so that others too can try it. Three important points to note, according to Burke, are

1. The ability to describe this method in words would make it possible for all other birds to take over the same "act" of genius, although they themselves might never have hit upon it.
2. The likelihood is that even this one wren never uses this method again, for the ability to conceptualize implies a kind of *attention* without which this innovation could probably not advance beyond the condition of a mere accident to the condition of an invention.
3. On the happier side, there is the thought that at least, through lack of such ability, birds are spared our many susceptibilities to the ways of demagogic spellbinders. They cannot be filled with fantastic hatreds for alien populations they know about mainly by mere hearsay or with all sorts of unsettling new expectations, most of which could not possibly turn out as promised. (Pp. 4–5)

SUMMARY

Human beings learn about and come to understand their environment through interaction with others. Thus, reality is largely social for them. This does not deny the existence of a reality "out there," nor does it ignore the fact that human beings also come to unique understandings through interaction with themselves.

Human beings exist in a world of social objects: This means that they understand and use their environment, that they come to understand their environment through interaction with others and self, and that the environment is always changing for them as their goals change.

One class of social objects is symbols, which are social objects used intentionally to communicate and represent something. They are understood by the actor who communicates and they are normally interpreted by the others. Symbols include words and many objects, and almost all acts around others contain a symbolic element. Words are the most important symbols, making human thinking possible. Although other animals communicate, they do not seem to use symbols, and their whole approach to their environment differs greatly from the human being's because of this.

Symbols are the basis for almost everything which characterizes the human being in nature. In order to appreciate this fact, we will examine their importance in Chapter 5.

REFERENCES

BECKER, ERNEST
1962   *The Birth and Death of Meaning.* New York: Free Press.
BECKER, HOWARD S.
1953   "Becoming a Marihuana User." *American Journal of Sociology* 59:235–42.
BLUMER, HERBERT
1969   *Symbolic Interactionism: Perspective and Method.* Englewood Cliffs, N.J.: Prentice Hall. Copyright © 1969. Reprinted by permission of Prentice Hall, Inc.
BROWN, ROGER
1965   *Social Psychology.* New York: Free Press.
BURKE, KENNETH
1966   *Language as Symbolic Action.* Berkeley: University of California Press.
DUNCAN, HUGH DALZIEL
1968   *Symbols in Society.* New York: Oxford University Press.
HERTZLER, JOYCE O.
1965   *A Sociology of Language.* New York: McGraw Hill, Inc.
HEWITT, JOHN P.
1984   *Self and Society,* 3d ed. Boston: Allyn & Bacon.
KELLER, HELEN
1954   *The Story of My Life.* Garden City, N.Y.: Doubleday. Copyright © 1902, 1903, 1905 by Helen Keller.
MEAD, GEORGE HERBERT
1934   *Mind, Self and Society.* Chicago: University of Chicago Press. Reprinted by permission of The University of Chicago Press. Copyright © 1934 by The University of Chicago. All rights reserved.
MELTZER, BERNARD N.
1972   *The Social Psychology of George Herbert Mead.* Kalamazoo: Center for Sociological Research, Western Michigan University.
MILLER, DAVID L.
1973   *George Herbert Mead: Self, Language and the World.* Chicago: University of Chicago Press.
SHIBUTANI, TAMOTSU
1961   *Society and Personality: An Interactionist Approach to Social Psychology.* Englewood Cliffs, N.J.: Prentice Hall. Copyright © 1961. Reprinted by permission of Prentice Hall.
STRYKER, SHELDON
1959   "Symbolic Interaction as an Approach to Family Research." *Marriage and Family Living* 21:111–19.
WARRINER, CHARLES K.
1970   *The Emergence of Society.* Homewood, Ill.: Dorsey Press.
WHITE, LESLIE A.
1940   "The Symbol: The Origin and Basis of Human Behavior." *Philosophy of Science* 7:451–63.
ZBOROWSKI, MARK
1952   "Cultural Components in Responses to Pain." *Journal of Social Issues* 8:16–30.

5

The Importance of the Symbol

Imagine a world without symbols, without language, or without social objects. Our actions would be fixed; we would *respond* to stimuli, not to meaning. We would not problem solve, reflect, imagine, recall the past at all, or teach others anything other than simple responses learned through imitation. We would not be able to depend on culture for our action but would have to rely instead on instinct and/or simple learning. Understanding would cease, worlds outside our immediate physical space would not exist for us, and so much that is abstract—goodness, love, God, freedom, life, and death—would not be examined at all and would not exist as a reality for us. Certainly communication with one another would not contain anything like concepts but would be confined to simple "nonmeaningful" gestures.

It is difficult to imagine a world without symbols because the human world is so overwhelmingly symbolic at its very core. Very few cases of non-symbol-using humans appear in history, and the few that do are incomplete studies, making generalizations difficult. Symbol use by the human begins at a very early age, first through understanding others' symbols, then through intentional symbolic expression.

The symbolic interactionist emphasizes that all that humans are can be traced to their symbolic nature. Our world is a symbolic one: We see, we think, we hear, we share, we act symbolically. Symbols are critical for the human precisely because (1) they *are our reality*, (2) they *make our complex group life possible*, and (3) they *make the human being possible*. The purpose of this chapter will be to explore each of these points in detail in order to show more fully the implications that symbol use has for the human.

SYMBOLS AND SOCIAL REALITY

The human acts within a world of social objects. That is, we act not toward a world out there but rather toward a world defined by others through symbolic communication. We share with others a definition of the world and its objects. Objects are transformed from physical stimuli responded to automatically into objects socially constructed. Each time we interact with others we come to share a somewhat different view of what we are seeing. We see what is out there in a new light. As we interact we develop a perspective as to what is real and how we are able to act toward that reality.

> *This interaction that gives rise to our reality is symbolic—it is through symbolic interaction with one another that we give the world meaning and develop the reality toward which we act.*

Symbols are important simply because they replace physical reality for us. they become our reality. Herbert Blumer (1969) expresses this simple principle in this way: "Meaning . . . arises out of social interaction that one has with one's fellows" (p. 2), and this meaning involves an understanding with symbols.

The first important function of symbols then is that they transform our relationship with our environment. Objects in our environment do not reveal to us what they are. Meaning does not come from them. Instead, we label these objects with symbols, we discuss these objects with one another, we come to develop ideas about what they are and how they are to be used, and we carry these ideas in our heads from situation to situation. The environment is no longer a physical stimulus for us; instead it is interpreted through symbols that we apply to it. The reality that we act in becomes truly a symbolic reality.

> Man operates within an *ideational framework*—that is, a body of ideas of interpretations and analyses, which he has developed, and by means of which his observations of the universe and all that it contains, as well as his reactions to it, become meaningful. He can be said to live in a world of ideas. But it is within and by means of the *linguistic framework* that the ideationally established world exists and operates. Language is the means and mode of man's whole mental existence. (Hertzler, 1965, 42)

Kenneth Burke (1966, 5) writes that our reality in the world at this split moment is nothing other than what we have learned from a "cluster of symbols about the past combined with whatever things we know mainly through maps, magazines, newspapers, and the like about the present" (p. 5). Whatever we experience *now* is seen through the symbols we use to see, and our ability to tie the present to a bigger picture depends on symbols. Burke concludes:

> To meditate on this fact until one sees its full implications is much like peering over the edge of things into an ultimate abyss. And doubtless that's one reason why, though man is typically the symbol-using animal, he clings to a kind of naive verbal realism that refuses to realize the full extent of the role played by symbolicity in his notions of reality. (p. 5)

"A person learns a new language, and as we say, gets a new soul. . . . He becomes in that sense a different individual" (Mead, 1934, 283).

SYMBOLS AND HUMAN SOCIAL LIFE

Human beings are social, as are many other animals. However, throughout our lives we learn to be social, to interact, and understand one another, and we learn the roles, rules, values, and ideas that others want us to learn. We are socialized into a particular society. None of this occurs from instinct. We become social beings because we have to in order to survive and we learn this right from the start as we interact with others. The way we live our lives around others in society is not something we are born with, nor something we simply learn through imitation. Instead,

> *human society is based on symbols. The second contribution that symbols make to what human beings are is that symbols create and maintain the societies within which we exist. They are used to socialize us, they make our culture possible, they are the basis for ongoing communication and cooperation, and they make possible our ability to pass down knowledge from one generation to the next.*

Let us examine each of these aspects of human society in turn.

First of all, *it is through symbols that individuals are socialized*—coming to share the rules, ideas, and values of the group as well as coming to learn their roles in relation to everyone else. We do not know how to act in society through instinct; we do not learn how to act in relation to others simply through imitation or experience. Each individual learns how to act in society through symbols and thus becomes part of society through symbols:

> This does not happen by instruction, at least not in the pre-school years; nobody teaches him the principles on which social groups are organized, or their systems of beliefs, nor would he understand it if they tried. It happens indirectly, through the accumulated experience of numerous small events, insignificant in themselves, in which his behaviour is guided and controlled, and in the course of which he contracts and develops personal relationships of all kinds. All this takes place through the medium of language. And it is not from the language of the classroom, still less that of courts of law, of moral tracts or of textbooks of sociology, that the child learns about the culture he was born into. The striking fact is that it is the most ordinary everyday uses of language, with parents, brothers and sisters, neighborhood children, in the home, in the street and the park, in the shops and the trains and the buses, that serve to transmit, to the child, the essential qualities of society and the nature of social being. (Halliday, 1978, 9)

Symbols are also central to society because society's culture is dependent on them. Recall Tamotsu Shibutani's (1955) "Reference Groups as Perspectives" (Chapter 3): It is, he writes, through symbolic communication that we come to share culture, and it is through this communication and resulting culture that social worlds (groups, societies) are able to continue. Culture, a central quality of every human society, is learned through symbols, and it is itself symbolic. We share ideas, rules, goals, values (all symbolic), and these allow us to continue to interact cooperatively with others.

We seem to grasp almost intuitively the central importance of symbols for our group life. We set up rules (symbolic) to be taught (usually through written or spoken *words*) to newcomers entering an already established group. We assure that the ideas we have developed are somehow shared and that what takes place is fully understood (has the right meaning) to the newcomer. That is true for college-orientation week, where students learn new rules, abbreviations, course names, teacher names, buildings, and requirements for graduation. It is true of the poker club, which must, during breaks in the action, teach the rules, the meanings, the taboos, the appropriate language, the proper betting to the newcomer. Both the college and the poker club know that without some shared reality their very existence may be at stake. And if we look at the group situation from the standpoint of the newcomer, he or she wants to understand the *meanings* attached to all the various acts—to learn immediately the shared reality in order to operate within the group.

Human society depends on ongoing symbolic communication. Communication means sharing, and sharing is one very important way that society is held together. Very complex forms of cooperation occur because human beings are able to discuss with one another how to resolve the problems that they face. Indeed, as Ralph Ross (1962) emphasizes, the words "community" and "communication" show an immediate similarity:

> They emphasize commonness, togetherness. People gather or live together for certain purposes, and they *share* meanings and attitudes; the first presupposes the second, for without communication there is no community. Community depends on shared experience and emotion, the communication enters into and clarifies the sharing. Forms of communication like art and religion and language are themselves shared by a community, and each of them contains and conveys ideas, attitudes, perspectives, and evaluations which are deeply rooted in the history of the community. (Pp. 156–57)

But there is much more. Groups have histories, and a long history means a very large corpus of knowledge. *It is by means of symbols that the past is recorded—knowledge and wisdom are not lost but are accumulated.* We can reflect and build on them—each interaction need not start from scratch. What one generation learns does not die when it dies. Joyce O. Hertzler (1965) states that language is "the major vehicle whereby we transmit—that is, impart or send and receive—our factualized experience . . . to others across space and time . . . from one individual, one area, one generation, one era, one cultural group to another" (pp. 50–51). Complex ongoing societies depend heavily on this function of symbols.

Symbols, therefore, are important to the human being because they are the basis for both social reality and society. Social reality is created in symbolic interaction and we come to see reality through symbols we take on. Society depends on symbols for socialization, culture, communication, and the cumulation of knowledge (Figure 5–1).

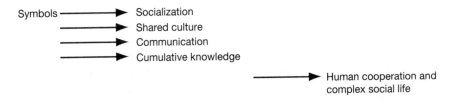

FIGURE 5–1

SYMBOLS AND THE INDIVIDUAL

What exactly is the human being? What is our essence? Mead emphasizes that our real essence is traced to our use of symbols. This goes beyond the reality we see and the society within which we live. It goes to the heart of our qualities as individual human beings. Whatever else we may be born with, it is only when we take on symbols that we are able to act like other human beings.

> *This third reason symbols are important to the human being is that there are many qualities that the individual possesses that arise only because of our use of symbols. We are transformed from a being who is weak, helpless, unintelligent, and simple, to one whose complexity, flexibility, and intelligence bring about a uniqueness in nature.*

There are at least nine ways that symbols transform the individual human being, and we will briefly examine these in turn at this time.

Naming, Memory, Categorizing

Through calling something a name we have identified it, "marked it out," "distinguished" it, and we are able to "store" it for later application. We can recognize similar objects and call them by that name. Naming an object allows us to apply it to another situation without its immediate physical presence. We can identify individual objects that we have never seen before because we have learned their names, that is, what they "are." The name can be stored in memory and can be purposely recalled in a multitude of situations. It might be possible that memory can exist without language (e.g., other animals may be able to recall pictures), but language allows for a much more complex, efficient memory system, one that can be more easily activated, whose parts can be more easily interpreted, transferred, and isolated. As Hertzler (1965) puts it: "The words of language, functioning as categories of experienced reality, not only facilitate more precise analysis, but also aid in the comparison of one portion of experiential data with other portions" (p. 41).

Related to the naming function, of course, is categorizing. Language is the tool the individual uses to make order out of experience. Language is used to discriminate, to generalize, to make ever so subtle distinctions in one's environment. The world is literally divided up by means of the language we use:

> Language has to interpret the whole of our experience, reducing the indefinitely varied phenomena of the world around us, and also of the world inside us, the processes of our own consciousness, to a manageable number of classes of phenomena: types of processes, events and actions, classes of objects, people and institutions, and the like. (Halliday, 1978, 21)

Perception

Language guides us through what our senses experience. It constitutes the individual's *perspectives,* and thus it serves the function of alerting the individual to some parts of the environment and not to others. "A language, once formed, has a self-contained organization somewhat like mathematics, and it previsages possible experience in accordance with accepted formal limitations . . . perception is limited by each language; men put what they perceive into preexisting linguistic categories" (Shibutani, 1961, 122). Symbols are the individual's eyes to the world.

Thinking

Hertzler calls language "our means of thinking." Thinking can be conceptualized as symbolic interaction with one's self. Thinking is talking to oneself; it is an activity, a constant, ongoing process. Almost every moment, the individual is thinking in this sense—according to Blumer, constantly modifying reality through an "interpretive process." When we act alone we are usually engaged in self-communication; when we are with others we engage in symbolic interaction—we communicate with, we give off meaning to others, but because symbols by their nature are understood by their user, there must be a simultaneous communication with ourselves in all social encounters. To get others to understand us, we must understand ourselves, which demands that we symbolically interact with ourselves as we communicate with others. We are thus constantly engaged in active thinking, often without realizing that we are doing it. Thinking is so central to all we do that it, like language itself, is taken for granted unless pointed out to us.

Deliberation and Problem Solving

Deliberation is a type of thinking, but it is more "deliberate" and conscious self-communication than the constant, ongoing thinking just described. It occurs most often when a problem is presented, when the situation requires analysis before action. It involves an attempt to consciously manipulate one's situation. The individual views self as an object in the situation, holds back action, analyzes, engages in lengthy discussion with self as action unfolds. In a sense, there is no difference between deliberation and the thinking described in the preceding paragraph, for the difference is really a matter of the degree of consciousness and the degree that one holds back overt action until the situation is fully understood. In fact, it is useful to understand almost all human behavior—but especially social behavior—as involving some deliberation.

Life can be thought of as a multitude of problems confronting the individual, each one calling for handling and solving, and each one demanding at least some deliberation. Each time we interact with someone else, "problems" are presented to us: how to understand the other, how to make ourselves understood, how to influence the other, how to avoid or get to know the other, how to work together or successfully dominate or successfully resist domination. Every time we enter a situation, working through that situation is a problem that demands decisions on our part. Deliberation means we analyze situations (sometimes very rapidly), interpret the ongoing action (our own and others'), consider alternative plans of action, rehearse our acts before we commit ourselves to overt action, and recall past situations that may be applicable. Problem solving in any situation is an evolving process, so that what we do at any one point can be analyzed at a later point, possibly leading to a new strategy or a new line of action. Deliberation as described here, as well as the ongoing thinking described above, is an integral part of human action and depends fully on the manipulation of *symbols*.

Transcendence of Space and Time

Problem solving and reflection involve transcending the immediate. Hertzler (1965) states that language

> enables men to overcome the limited time-and-space perceptions of the sub-human creatures. It is, in fact, man's means of mentally breaking through the space-time barrier . . . he is also able to inhabit simultaneously the past (through legend, traditions, and formal records), the present and the future (by means of declared ideals, projections, anticipations, plans and programs). (Pp. 53–54)

Language allows individuals to understand worlds they have never seen; it allows them to see the future before it occurs and to integrate past, present, and future. For example: I "know" ancient Greece without having been there, and I have a strong notion of what the United States will become in twenty years. I also believe that the United States' unjust treatment of minorities *today* is a result of a painful *history* of racism, and I also see today's policies as having some impact on a more just society *tomorrow*. The individual is guided in social situations by recalling the past, and by looking to the future, immediate and distant. When an individual acts, others outside the immediate situation may be the most important influences, the struggles of societies the individual has never had any contact with may be his or her most important inspiration, and what is going on "in the next room" outside the immediate field of vision and hearing may be perceived to be most influential on the individual's future. Language allows the individual to break out of the present and immediate stimulus environment and adds immeasurably to the factors that influence action.

Transcendence of One's Own Person

Not only do symbols allow individuals to leave the immediate space-and-time environment, but also symbols allow them to leave their own bodies, to get outside of their selves and imagine the world from the perspectives of others. This very important human quality, which symbolic interactionists refer to as "taking the role of the other," allows us to understand others, to manipulate them, to sympathize with them, to love them. It allows for human beings' understanding of one another's ideas, because the more we are able to see things from the perspective of the people with whom we communicate, the more we are able to truly "see" what other people are saying. It is through language that we come to understand other people, their perspectives, their perceptions, their feelings, and their behavior. This ability to take the role of the other, itself dependent on our symbolic nature, is so central to human social life that its nature and its importance are the subject of Chapter 8.

Abstract Reality

Language also allows the human being to imagine and perceive a reality beyond the concrete. Only through language can we establish objects like God, love, freedom, truth, good and evil, afterlife, and a host of other abstract objects that are so much an integral part of our existence. A reality beyond physical reality is open only through words and the manipulation of words into ideas. The concrete world of our senses is transformed by language into a reality not possible to nonsymbol users. Hertzler (1965) puts it nicely:

> By means of conceptualization, [the human] is able to develop and live in the abstract world of intellectual experience—the world of ethical, aesthetic, evaluational, teleological, spiritual, and supernatural considerations . . . "goodness" as an ethical aspect, or "beauty" as an aesthetic characteristic, are not inherent in the event or the object, they are nonexistent, except in so far as we "perceive" and "conceive" them in terms of words. With language, we can wrestle with such perplexing questions as "truth" and "error," "right" and "wrong," "existential" and "transcendental." Words can stand for such abstractions as electricity, force, justice, time, space, future, deity—ideas which cannot possibly be represented by any visual picture. (P. 55)

Because human beings are symbol users and are able to create an abstract world, human beings can thus imagine goals, ideals, values, and morals that themselves become important motivating factors in human behavior. To die for "my country," to work for "freedom," to try to end "poverty" show a kind of motivation impossible to any except symbol users. This means that the human potential is limited only by human imagination. As long as we believe, for example, that "love" and "goodness" and "equality" are worth working for, we can constantly try to guide our behavior toward those ends. And if we believe that "materialism" or "destruction of others" or "power over others" is important, it becomes a guide to behavior. But symbols by their very nature open up a wide range of behavior possibilities. In a sense, no action is "unnatural" to us, because symbols allow for virtually any possibility.

Creativity

The symbolic interactionist emphasizes the central importance of language in creating the active rather than passive person. It is through thinking with symbols that each individual is able to create his or her own world beyond the physical, develop highly individual interpretations of reality, and act uniquely toward that reality. Language arises from society, yet it is the tool that the human can use to think about and challenge that society. The key is not so much the symbol as it is the *symboling,* the *manipulation of symbols* by active persons, defining and redefining their social situations. Give the child an understanding of certain *words,* and it is impossible to control fully how these words will be combined and recombined. This is the magic of language. To teach "love your country" and to teach "hate other countries," is to create the possibility of students deciding to hate their country and love other countries. To teach a child what "little" means, what "big" means, and what "in a little while" means is to invite from him or her: "No, I'll go to bed *in a big while.*" Every sentence is, in a sense, a creative act. To manipulate the words we learn from interaction is to become an individual—creative, active, and shaping, not passive and conforming. Although not all creativity depends on symbols, much of it does: We learn what is known, we understand it, and we go further than what we have been taught. We create our own reality. And some of us produce great creations in literature, science, music, and art through playing with the understandings we have learned through symbols.

Self-Direction

Language allows the human being to exercise self-direction. Our communication with ourselves is a form of giving orders: Cooperate! Rebel! Listen! Get away! Run! Walk! Turn right! Work harder! Sleep! Think! Any control that we have over ourselves (and the symbolic interactionists claim it is considerable) comes through symbolic interaction with ourselves, through telling ourselves what is going on, what alternatives there are, and what line of action to take. The decision to conform and cooperate as well as the decision to rebel are a matter of the individual's deciding through symbolic interaction with self what to do.

THE IMPORTANCE OF SYMBOLS: A SUMMARY

The importance of the symbol for the individual can best be summarized by combining all of these contributions to the individual into a single central point: The human being, because of the symbol, does not respond passively to a reality that imposes itself but actively creates and re-creates the world acted in. Humans name, remember, categorize, perceive, think, deliberate, problem solve, transcend space and time, transcend themselves, create abstractions, create new ideas, and direct themselves—all through the symbol.

Ernst Cassirer (1944) describes the human as discovering

> a new method of adapting himself to his environment. Between the receptor system and the effector system, which are to be found in all animal species, we find in man a third link which we may describe as the *symbolic system*. This new acquisition transforms the whole of human life. As compared with the other animals man lives not merely in a broader reality; he lives, so to speak, in a new *dimension* of reality. There is an unmistakable difference between organic reactions and human responses. In the first case a direct and immediate answer is given to an outward stimulus, in the second case the answer is delayed. It is interrupted and retarded by a slow and complicated process of thought. (Pp. 24–25)

There is probably no better summary of the central importance that symbolic interactionists give to symbols than that of S. Morris Eames (1977):

> Pragmatic naturalists conceive of humans as a part of nature. Although they share many organic processes with other animals in their life in nature, humans emerge above the animals in certain forms and functions. For instance, humans can construct symbols and languages, they can speak and write, and by these means they can preserve their past experiences, construct new meanings, and entertain goals and ideals. Humans can make plans and by proper selection of the means to the ends carry them through. They can write poetry and novels, compose music and painting, and otherwise engage in aesthetic experiences. They can construct explanatory hypotheses about the world and all that is in it, of electrons, protons, and neutrons, and solar systems far away. They can dream dreams, concoct fantasies, erect heavens above the earth which entice their activities to far-off destinies, and they can imagine hells which stimulate fears of everlasting torture. The emergent functions of symbolic behavior make it possible for humans to transcend parts of their immediate undergoing and experiencing and to know that death and all that it entails is a part of organic life. (Pp. 40–41)

Symbols make three contributions to the human being: They are our reality, they form the basis for our social life, and they are central to what it means to be human (see Figure 5–2).

FIGURE 5–2

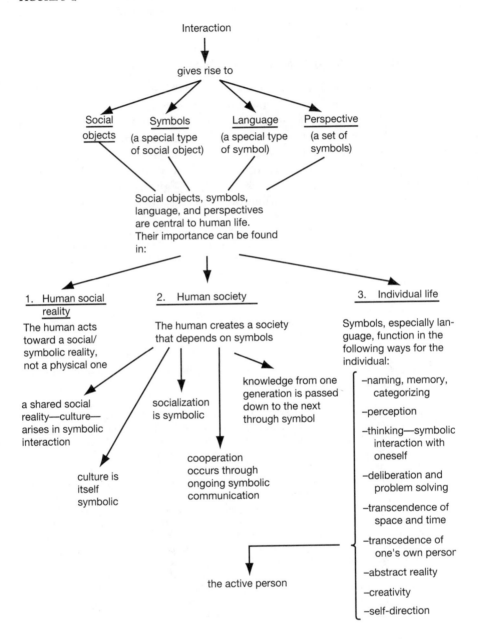

REFERENCES

BLUMER, HERBERT
   1969 *Symbolic Interactionism: Perspective and Method.* Englewood, Cliffs, N.J.: Prentice Hall. Copyright © 1969. Reprinted by permission of Prentice Hall.

BURKE, KENNETH
   1966 *Language as Symbolic Action.* Berkeley: University of California Press.

CASSIRER, ERNST
   1944 *An Essay on Man.* New Haven: Yale University Press.

EAMES, S. MORRIS
   1977 *Pragmatic Naturalism.* Carbondale: Southern Illinois University Press.

HALLIDAY, M. A. K.
   1978 *Language as Social Semiotic.* Baltimore, Md.: University Park Press.

HERTZLER, JOYCE O.
   1965 *A Sociology of Language.* New York: McGraw Hill, Inc.

MEAD, GEORGE HERBERT
   1934 *Mind, Self and Society.* Chicago: University of Chicago Press. Reprinted by permission of The University of Chicago Press. Copyright © 1934 by The University of Chicago. All rights reserved.

ROSS, RALPH
   1962 *Symbols and Civilization.* San Diego, Calif.: Harcourt Brace Jovanovich.

SHIBUTANI, TAMOTSU
   1955 "Reference Groups as Perspectives." *American Journal of Sociology* 60:562–69.

   1961 *Society and Personality: An Interactionist Approach to Social Psychology.* Englewood Cliffs, N.J.: Prentice Hall. Copyright © 1961. Reprinted by permission of Prentice Hall.

6

The Nature of the Self

Thus far, our emphasis has been human beings coming to understand their world through interaction. We indicate objects to one another, we share meanings, we create symbols as we interact with each other. Bernard Meltzer (1972, 11) points out that everything ultimately comes back to society, to interaction. In fact, Meltzer feels that George Herbert Mead's (1934) book *Mind, Self and Society* should really be entitled *Society, Self and Mind* because individuals are always born into a society, and that is what gives them such human characteristics as self and mind. Of course, this was also the point in Chapter 5: Our symbols, which are so central to what we are, arise from interaction. The human is so thoroughly social that society provides our most basic elements: symbols, self, and mind.

SELF AS A SOCIAL OBJECT

There are many views of self in philosophy and social science, and few are either clear or consistent. The term "self" is used in so many different ways in our everyday speech that it is often hard to pin down what we mean by it.

In the symbolic interactionist perspective, "self" has a very specific meaning, not perfect but very usable. As Morris Rosenberg (1979, 6–8) points out, this meaning is different from so many other meanings that are popular today. For example, it does not have the same meaning as Freud's "ego." It does not mean the "real" person nor the "productive person" nor "the total person."

For the symbolic interactionist, the self is an object of the actor's own action. The individual acts toward others; the individual also acts toward himself or herself. It is not the self that acts; it is the actor that acts, and the actor is able to act back on self as well as the environment that exists outside. The self is best defined as a social object, one of the objects in the situation that the actor finds useful in achieving his or her goals. Every one of us is then an actor (*one who acts*), and we are the *objects of our own actions*—that is, we have a self. It is probably easier to understand this if you consider your self as part of the environment toward which the actor acts. It is our internal environment.

When we say that the self is a social object, we mean, first of all, that *it is an object* and that *it, like our symbols, arises in our social interaction*. This means that the individual comes to see himself or herself as an object in the environment through interaction with others—other people point out to the actor that he or she exists as an object. Others label and define the self to the actor, and they help the actor understand himself or herself in the environment. "You are Andrew," "You are a boy," "You are a big boy," "You are Mom's favorite person." "You exist in the world just like other objects you see around you; you are like other people, chairs, telephones, mice, doorknobs." "Others see you as an object too; they will act toward you." "You were born, you live, and someday you too will cease to exist as an object in the natural universe." Each actor becomes an object to himself or herself because of the actions of others toward him or her. "In the beginning [the actor] is quite unable to make a distinction between [himself or herself] and the rest of the world" (McCall and Simmons, 1966, 207). Eventually this is learned in social interaction. Thus, our social life not only makes possible our symbolic abilities, but it also makes possible the development of self and all that goes with our ability to act toward ourselves in every situation we enter.

Mead (1934) emphasizes the social origin of the self in *Mind, Self and Society*. He asks:

> How can an individual get outside of himself experientially in such a way as to become an object to himself? . . . [It is through] the process of social conduct or activity in which the given person or individual is implicated. . . . The individual experiences himself as such, not directly, but only indirectly, from the particular standpoints of other individual members of the same social group . . . [he] becomes an object to himself just as other individuals are objects to him or in his experience . . . it is impossible to conceive of a self arising outside of social experience. (Pp. 138–40)*

Because the self is a social object, it is constantly changing for the actor because it continues to be defined and redefined in social interaction. Its social nature means that it is process rather than a stable entity. How I view myself, how I define myself, how I act toward myself throughout life is highly dependent on the social definitions I encounter every day of my life. Peter Berger (1963) calls this view of the self radical in the sense that the self "is no longer a solid, given entity that moves from one situation to another. It is rather a process, continuously created and recreated in every social situation that one enters . . . . man is not *also* a social being, but he is social in every respect of his being that is open to empirical investigation" (p. 106). The self is therefore not what the psychologist means by "personality," nor is it a true transcendental authentic person. It is simply a continuously changing object, one that we see and use in one situation one way and another in quite another, and these actions toward ourselves are influenced by the social interaction

*Reprinted from *Mind, Self and Society* by George Herbert Mead by permission of the University of Chicago Press. Copyright © 1934 by the University of Chicago. All rights reserved.

that takes place on a continuing basis with other people. Sheldon Stryker (1959) makes this point nicely:

> . . . the human organism as an object takes on meaning through the behavior of those who respond to that organism. We come to know what we are through others' responses to us. Others supply us with a name, and they provide the meaning attached to that symbol. They categorize us in particular ways—as an infant, as a boy, et cetera. On the basis of such categorization, they expect particular behaviors from us; on the basis of these expectations, they act toward us. The manner in which they act toward us defines our "self," we come to categorize ourselves as they categorize us, and we act in ways appropriate to their expectations . . . as the child moves into the social world he comes into contact with a variety of persons in a variety of self-relevant situations. He comes, or may come, into contact with differing expectations concerning his behavior and differing identities on which these expectations are based. Thus he has . . . a variety of perspectives from which to view and evaluate his own behavior, and he can act with reference to self as well as with reference to others. In short, the socialization process as described makes possible the appearance of objectivity. (P. 116)

Stryker concludes his description of the self with the word "objectivity." Socialization makes possible the fact that the individual is able to get outside of himself or herself and look back at the self objectively, as an object like all the objects defined in interaction. Mead makes a very big point of this ability to get outside of oneself, to take the perspective of the other, and as we shall see in the description of the development of the self in children, it is through "taking the role of the other" that the self emerges.

SELF AS SOCIAL: FOUR SOCIAL STAGES FOR SELF-DEVELOPMENT

At first the individual does not have a self. However, the individual is born into a world that acts on him or her, and most of those actions are the acts of other people, and those acts almost always make use of symbols. At first, we do not understand symbols and simply imitate the acts of others, but very quickly we understand who we are through the use of symbols, and, over time, the individuals who are important in our self-understanding—significant others—become a group or society—what Mead calls our generalized other. As we become adults, there is first a consistency in how we see ourselves because of this generalized other, but over time, we come to interact with many different others, and the one generalized other becomes a number of reference groups, each one having a different impact in how we see and act toward ourselves.

This description emphasizes the central role of our interaction with others in the development of our self, and it emphasizes the self as process. The first three stages are drawn from the work of Mead, and the last is suggested by Tamotsu Shibutani in the article discussed in Chapter 3 called "Reference Groups as Perspectives."

The Prepatory Stage

The earliest stage of the self is referred to as the *preparatory stage,* with an almost primitive self emerging, a presymbolic stage of self. Mead probably did not explicitly name this stage, but he implied it in various writings (Meltzer, 1972, 15). The child acts as the adult does. The child imitates the others' acts toward other objects and toward himself or herself as object. The parent may push the chair and so may the child. The parent may point to the child as object, the child may also point to self. The parent may say, "Dad," and the child may imitate "da." But the interaction, so long as it is only imitation, lacks meaning, lacks a symbolic understanding. The person as object can really emerge only when objects take on some meaning, that is, when objects are defined with words. When Andrew realizes that he is Andrew, separate and distinct from others, someone represented with a name and described with word qualities, then a symbolic self emerges. That is why Mead refers to this first stage as preparatory; it is purely imitation, and social objects, including the self, are not yet defined and understood with words that have meaning to the child.

The Play Stage

The second stage, referred to by Mead as the *play stage,* comes early in the individual's development, during the acquisition of language. For most children language comes very early and meaning arises early, really making the preparatory stage insignificant in terms of length of time. The child, learning language, is now able to label and define objects with words that have shared meaning, so objects originally acted toward because of imitation now are acted toward according to the meaning shared in interaction with others. The self is pointed out and labeled by the significant others. "Hi, Andrew!" (Hey, Andrew stands for this object: *me, myself.*) "Good boy!" (Hey, *I* am good.) "Are you sleeping?" (Am *I* sleeping?) "Go play!" (She is telling *me* to play.) As others point us out to ourselves, we see ourselves. We become social objects to ourselves. Others point us out; they give us names. The "creation of self as social object is an identification of that object. . . . Identification involves naming. Once an object is named and identified a line of action can be taken toward it" (Denzin, 1972, 306). Our names, as well as various pronouns and adjectives, are used to identify "me" in relation to others. *Susan, girl, baby, good, you, she, smart, pretty, slow, funny, bad, wise, American, New Yorker:* That's *me!*

During this play stage, the child assumes the perspective of certain *individuals,* whom Mead refers to as "significant others," those people who take on importance to the individual, those whom the individual desires to impress; they might be those he or she respects, those he or she wants acceptance from, those he or she fears, or those with whom he or she identifies. Significant others are usually role models, who "provide the patterns of behavior and conduct on which he patterns himself. It is through interaction with these role models that the child develops the ability to regulate his own behavior" (Elkin and Handel, 1972, 50). For the child, role models are most likely parents but can also be other relatives, television heroes, or friends. As the child grows older, the significant other possibilities increase greatly and can be a whole number of individuals, including Socrates, Jesus, mom, wife, son, the boss, the president of the United States, Madonna, and Bart Simpson. Whoever our significant others are at any point in our lives, they are important precisely because their views of social objects are important to us, including, and especially, our view of ourselves as social objects. The concept of significant others recognizes that "not all the persons with whom one interacts have identical or even compatible perspectives, and that, therefore, in order for action to proceed, the individual must give greater weight or priority to the perspective of certain others . . . others occupy high rank on an 'importance' continuum for a given individual" (Stryker, 1959, 115). To the small child significant others are responsible for the emergence of the self; the child comes to view self as an object because of significant others. In a sense, I fail to see myself without my awareness that these significant others see me.

The reason Mead calls this second stage the *play* stage is that the child assumes the perspective of only one significant other at a time. In this stage individuals are incapable of seeing themselves from the perspective of many persons simultaneously. The child segregates the significant others, and the view of self is a segmented one. The self is a multitude of social objects, each one defined in interaction with a single other. Play refers to the fact that *group* rules are unnecessary, that the child and a single other are necessary for controls at any single point in time. The child needs to guide self, needs to see self, needs to judge self from the view of only one individual at a time in order to be successful at play. Play is an individual affair, subject to the rules of single individuals. Mead's play stage is a time when the child takes the roles of significant others—father, Superman, mother, teacher—and acts in the world as if he or she were these individuals. In taking the roles of these others the child acts toward objects in the world as they act, and that includes acting toward self as they do. This stage is the real beginning of the self as social object.

The Game Stage

The third stage is the *game stage*. The "game" represents organization and the necessity of assuming the perspectives of several others simultaneously. Cooperation and group life demand knowing one's position in relation to a complex set of others, not just single others. They demand taking on a group culture or perspective. This stage is, to Mead, the adult self, a self that incorporates all one's significant others into one "generalized other." The self becomes more a unitary nonsegmented self, changing in interaction but not radically changing each time another significant other is encountered. The child puts together the significant others in his or her world into a whole, a "generalized other," "them," "society." The self matures as our understanding of *society* matures: It is the other side of the coin. Interaction with others brings us face to face with *their* rules, *their* perspectives, and it also brings us *their* perspective of self, and the self becomes an object defined not only by the individual (play stage) but also by *them* (game stage):

> The play antedates the game. For in a game there is a regulated procedure, and rules. The child must not only take the role of the other, as he does in the play, but he must assume the various roles of all the participants in the game, and govern his action accordingly. If he plays first base, it is as the one to whom the ball will be thrown from the field or from the catcher. Their organized reactions to him he has embedded in his own playing of the different positions, and this organized reaction becomes what I have called the "generalized other" that accompanies and controls his conduct. And it is this generalized other in his experience which provides him with a self. (Mead, 1925, 269)

The development of a generalized other by the individual is really the internalization of society as the individual has come to know it, society's rules and perspectives become the child's, and society's definition of self becomes the individual's. "In one sense socialization can be summed up by saying that what was once outside the individual comes to be inside him" (Elkin and Handel, 1972, 53). Meltzer (1972) emphasizes the central significance of internalizing a generalized other:

> Having achieved this generalized standpoint, the individual can conduct himself in an organized, consistent manner. He can view himself from a consistent standpoint. This means, then, that the individual can transcend the local and present expectations and definitions with which he comes in contact. An illustration of this point would be the Englishman who "dresses for dinner" in the wilds of Africa. Thus, through having a generalized other, the individual becomes emancipated from the pressures of the peculiarities of the immediate situation. He can act with a certain amount of consistency in a variety of situations because he acts in accordance with a generalized set of expectations and definitions that he has internalized. (Pp. 16–17)

The Reference Group Stage

Mead does not always make it clear if the individual has just one generalized other or several. It seems that what begins as one increasingly becomes several. Tamotsu Shibutani (1955) makes this explicit, emphasizing what amounts to a fourth stage of self, the *reference group stage*, a stage that seems especially characteristic in an industrial urban "mass society."

The individual interacts with many different groups and thus comes to have several reference groups (social worlds or societies), and he or she shares a perspective, including a perspective used to define *self*, with each of them. If he or she is to continue to interact successfully with a reference group, then that perspective must, at least temporarily, become the individual's generalized other, used to see and direct the self in that group.

This notion is highly consistent with the definition of social objects discussed in Chapter 4: Social objects are defined in interaction and change in the process of interaction and as the people with whom we interact change. The self as a social object has these identical qualities. In interaction with students I define myself one way, with my family another, with sociologists another, and with male friends another. Think of your life: Your self changes as you interact with friends, family, salespeople, strangers at a party. In each case, our view of self is somewhat different, and it is always undergoing change. William James (1915) points this out nicely:

> Properly speaking, *a man has as many social selves as there are individuals who recognize* him and carry an image of him in their mind. To wound any one of these images is to wound him. But as the individuals who carry the images fall naturally into classes, we may practically say that he has as many different social selves as there are distinct *groups* of persons about whose opinion he cares. He generally shows a different side of himself to each of these different groups. Many a youth who is demure enough before his parents and teachers, swears and swaggers like a pirate among his "tough" young friends. We do not show ourselves to our children as to our club-companions, to our customers as to the laborers we employ, to our own masters and employers as to our intimate friends. From this there results what practically is a division of the man into several selves; and this may be a discordant splitting, as where one is afraid to let one set of his acquaintances know him as he is elsewhere; or it may be a perfectly harmonious division of labor, as where one tender to his children is stern to the soldiers or prisoners under his command. (Pp. 179–80)

SELVES AS EVER-CHANGING SOCIAL OBJECTS

Let us try to bring some central ideas together here. The small child, before the language-play stage, has the beginnings of self. Then the child with language begins to assume the perspectives of significant others, then of a generalized other, and finally of several reference groups, in each case entering into a new stage of the self. The self rests on other people, both individuals and reference groups. To some extent we have several distinct selves, but because our interaction overlaps, because our significant others and reference groups probably form a relatively consistent whole, our self is not as segmented as might have been implied in this discussion.

Let us look at some examples of the social nature of the self as well as its complexity. A president of the United States may use various individuals, groups, and categories of people in defining self, including, for example, "the Republican party," "the American people," "the corporate rich," "the 1776 revolutionaries," a small group of loyal advisers, Thomas Jefferson, his or her spouse, their children, the United Nations, the World Bank, or those who died in the Vietnam War. Whoever's perspective is assumed in the definition of the president's self will be critical to how the president acts. If Ivan matters and Ivan defines the president as one who cares about human beings, then in the presence of Ivan (or even away from Ivan) the president will define his or her self as "one who cares" and will behave accordingly. It is much more complex, but we will better understand self-definition and its consequences later in this chapter. Or take the example of Felix the freshman: mom, dad, girlfriend, Ernest Hemingway, the Rolling Bones, the alienated generation, the Catholic Church, the business world, Johnny Cash, the Harwood football team—each will influence how Felix defines himself and how he acts. If it is the alienated generation that constitutes his reference group, then he will act in relation to the college authorities as a noncooperative and distant role player.

It should be emphasized that the individual may or may not use people in his or her presence as significant others or reference groups. If people in the present situation are not important, then their perspective is not important and their definition of self is also not important. They are not significant others or reference groups. Thus, the poor teacher is often the one whose reference group does not include the students, and the "moral" person may be the one who rejects the standards of those who are *immediately* around him or her doing things people (significant others, reference groups) elsewhere consider immoral.

THE SELF AS OBJECT

We have stated that the self is an object, a social object. It is a thing, like other things pointed out and shared in interaction. As Herbert Blumer (1962, 181) emphasizes, the importance of the self as object cannot be understated: It means that the individual can *act* toward himself or herself as he or she acts toward all other people. In a sense the individual has an additional person to act toward in the situation. Because we sometimes judge other people, so we can also judge our self. Because we can talk to others, so we can also talk to our self. Because we can point things out to our self about other people, so we can actually point things out to our self about self. We can direct others, so we can direct our self. When we say that selfhood means that the person is object we mean that the actor can act toward his or her self. "The individual achieves selfhood at that point at which he first begins to act toward *himself* in more or less the same fashion in which he acts toward other people. . . . It is still he who is doing [the acting]" (McCall and Simmons, 1966, 54). Blumer (1962) emphasizes the central importance of the self as object:

> The key feature in Mead's analysis is that the human being has a self. This idea should not be cast aside as esoteric or glossed over as something that is obvious and hence not worthy of attention. In declaring that the human being has a self, Mead has in mind chiefly that the human being can be the object of his own actions. He can act toward himself as he might act toward others. Each of us is familiar with actions of this sort in which the human being gets angry with himself, rebuffs himself, takes pride in himself, argues with himself, tries to bolster his own courage, tells himself that he should "do this" or not "do that," sets goals for himself, makes compromises with himself, and plans what he is going to do. That the human being acts toward himself in these and countless other ways is a

matter of easy empirical observation. To recognize that the human being can act toward himself is no mystical conjuration. (P. 181)

One way to appreciate the meaning of self as object is to consider emotions. Many other animals emotionally respond to their environment. Adrenalin flows, clenched teeth are bared, a growl is expressed. What then distinguishes human emotion from that of other animals? It all has to do with self. It is the fact that we can look back on what we do. We can see, recognize, and understand what is taking place within us: I am angry. I am sad. I am jealous. I am in love. I am afraid. This is what is meant when we say the human actor is able to see himself or herself as object. We see what we are and what we do—we even are able to look back on how we feel.

To better appreciate the importance of the self we need to examine more closely the various actions that the individual takes toward it, or the way we use it in situations. There are three general categories of action that we need to consider:

1. *Self-communication.* We talk to ourselves. Our self is an object we talk to.
2. *Self-perception.* We see ourselves in situations. Our self is an object we notice. Because we can recognize and understand our relationship with other objects in the situation, we are able to develop a self-concept, including self-judgment and identity.
3. *Self-control.* We tell ourselves what to do in situations. Our self is an object we use in order to control our own actions. To claim that humans direct or control their own actions means that humans have an ability to act back on and direct themselves in situations.

ACTION TOWARD SELF: SELF-COMMUNICATION

The human being is an actor who is able to communicate to himself or herself. In short, the actor talks to himself or herself. The individual is both a subject (a communicator) and an object of that action (has a self to whom he or she communicates). Talking to self with symbols is what the symbolic interactionist means by thinking. Self therefore makes possible thinking, the ability to point things out to ourselves, to interpret a situation, to communicate with ourselves in all of the diverse ways we are able to communicate with all other humans. "The possession of a self," Blumer (1966) concludes, "provides the human being with a mechanism of self-interaction with which to meet the world—a mechanism that is used in forming and guiding his conduct" (p. 535). Mead (1934) points out that "the essence of the self . . . is cognitive: it lies in the internalized conversation of gestures which constitutes thinking, or in terms of which thought or reflection proceeds" (p. 173). To think is to speak to one's self, to continuously point things out, to sometimes reflect, to carry on conversation toward that social object called self in identically the same manner as one speaks to others, except that, in most cases, conversation with one's self is silent.

Without self-communication, the human would not be able to communicate symbolically with others, for it is only because the human can simultaneously give off meaning to other people and understand (through communication with self) what he or she communicates, that effective symbolic communication with others can take place. "From Mead's point of view . . . only humans can self-consciously and purposively represent to themselves that which they wish to represent to others: this, for Mead, is what it means to have a self and what it means to be human" (Elkin and Handel, 1972, 50). "What is essential to [symbolic] communication," Mead (1934) states, "is that the symbol should arouse in one's self what it arouses in the other individual" (p. 149).

All other action we take toward the self depends on this first action. Self-communication makes it possible for us to see ourselves and direct ourselves, for the latter two mean the ability to *talk to ourselves about our self,* and the ability to *talk to ourselves about what we are to do in situations.* The use of the symbol to talk to our self becomes the most important action we engage in toward our self. The self, remember, is not the source of that communication, but the object. It is the actor who talks to self.

ACTION TOWARD SELF: SELF-PERCEPTION

When we communicate back toward the self, what are we able to say? We are able to communicate about all the objects in the situation that are useful for us: other people, tools, and the clock, for example. We are also able to indicate to the self information about the self in the situation. *The fact is that selfhood means that the actor is able to see himself or herself in the situation and is able to consider that object as he or she acts.* We see ourselves in relation to the situation; we think about ourselves; we judge ourselves; we identify ourselves.

Self-perception is no small matter. The self allows the human to look at his or her own action in the situation. The actor can understand the others in the situation and the influence they are trying to have on him or her. The actor can appraise his or her own actions as they unfold in the situation. We understand our situations in relation to ourselves. C. Addison Hickman and Manford H. Kuhn (1956) point out that the self "anchors" us in each situation, because unlike other objects, the self is present in all situations. The self serves as the basis from which a person "makes judgments and subsequent plans of action toward the many other objects that appear in each situation" (p. 43). We imaginatively see ourselves in relation to others, and we determine appropriate actions. For example, when I engage in conversation with others, I engage in a self-interaction that attempts to assess the other's understanding of me and what I must continue to say in order to get my thoughts understood. As I hold my loved one close to me, I try to assess not only her activity but also my own activity—for example, if my action in relation to her is appropriate, tender, manipulative, or immoral. How I assess myself in these acts and all others will be important guides for my ongoing action. It goes without saying that this activity is ongoing and gives the human actor a social intelligence that is not open to animals without selves. It allows the actor to understand his or her own action, overcoming the simple responses other animals seem to give off in situations.

Self-Perception: The Development of Self-Concept

Self-perception over time develops some stability. We develop knowledge about who we are and what we do. We come to understand ourselves as objects in contrast to the other objects around, and we come to expect certain things from our action since there is a familiarity we develop toward ourselves.

The term "self-concept" is sometimes used to describe the fairly stable picture we have of ourselves. Rosenberg (1979) describes the self-concept as the "totality of the individual's thoughts and feelings with reference to himself [or herself] as an object" (p. ix). It is *what we see* when we look back on ourselves. It is our "picture" of ourselves. Of course, this picture will change over time in every situation: It is a process, not a fixed entity. Yet, to some extent the picture is stable over time and across situations. It is sometimes useful to call this consistency "self-concept" and describe it as somewhat different from the particular "self-image" we have in a certain situation. Our self-concept is enduring and built up over time: When others surprise us or act toward us in ways that are unusual to us, the self-concept continues without a great deal of change because of its stability. On the other hand, a serious confrontation with someone may have much more of an effect on us than that stable self-concept, and if that confrontation continues to be important in our life, may have a significant influence on our self concept.

It is also important to regard this picture of our self as a changing process. It is a "shifting, adjustive process" that influences what we do in every situation. Although we may carry an "average tone of self-feeling" (self-concept), the individual still "has as many different social selves as there are distinct groups of persons about whose opinion he [or she] cares" (James, 1915, 294). Think beyond "the groups of persons" James refers to; think instead of the continuous social interaction we enter into all day long.

Self-Perception: Self-Judgment as Part of Self-Concept

Our view of ourselves involves judgments about ourselves. We give ourselves credit; we blame ourselves; we like what we do and are; we reject what we do and are. Here is the issue we sometimes call "self-esteem." We not only see ourselves as objects in situations but we also appraise ourselves. The self is something we judge, evaluate, like or reject, love or hate. We may feel good as we look at ourselves; we may feel bad. Good boy! Stupid! Insensitive! Klutz! Beautiful! Wow! Ugh! We judge ourselves and those judgments involve feelings we have toward ourselves. Charles Cooley (1970) emphasizes this aspect of the self in his description of "looking-glass" self: He states:

> As we see our face, figure, and dress in the glass, and are interested in them because they are ours, and pleased or otherwise with them according as they do or do not answer to what we should like them to be; so in imagination we perceive in another's mind some thought of our appearance, manners, aims, deeds, character, friends, and so on, and are variously affected by it.
>
> A self-idea of this sort seems to have three principal elements: the imagination of our appearance to the other person; the imagination of his judgment of that appearance; and some sort of self-feeling, such as pride or mortification. (P. 184)

"He sees that I am talking a lot. He likes that about me. I like me too." "She sees me walking toward her slowly and deliberately. She thinks I'm cool. Yes, I'm cool!" "I must appear to them to be skillful at this game. They hate me for it, for I threaten them. Maybe I shouldn't be so showy. I don't like this aspect of me!" What we think of ourselves and what we feel about ourselves, like all else about the self, result from social interaction: What I end up liking or not liking about myself is, to a great extent, the result of the acts of others toward me, and my acts toward them. Shibutani (1961) describes the interrelationship of self-judgment and social interaction in this manner:

> Like other meanings, sentiments toward one-self are formed and reinforced in the regularized responses of other people. Through role-taking a proud man is able to visualize himself as an object toward which others have feelings of respect, admiration, or even awe. If others consistently address him with deference, he comes to take it for granted that he deserves such treatment. On the other hand, if someone is consistently mistreated or ridiculed, he cannot help but conclude that others despise him. If a person is always ignored, especially in situations in which others like himself are given attention, he may become convinced that he is a comparatively worthless object. Once such estimates have crystallized, they become more independent of the responses of other people. (Pp. 434–35)

And it is important to reiterate that it is not all people we interact with whose perspective we assume in judgment of self, but our significant others and reference groups:

> Since men are socialized creatures whose perspectives develop through communication, the criteria by which they evaluate themselves are cultural. Standards differ from one reference group to another. In the social worlds that make up American society there are an amazing variety of attributes of which people are proud or ashamed: their speaking voices, the straightness of their teeth, their ancestry, their muscular strength, their ability to fight, the number of books they have read, the number of prominent people they know, their honesty, their ability to manipulate other people, the accessories on their automobiles, or their acquaintance with exotic foods. Each person sees himself from the standpoint of

the groups in which he participates, and whatever he believes will impress his audience becomes a source of pride. (Shibutani, 1961, 436)

Of all the propositions derived from symbolic interactionism, this one—the relation between the judgment of others and self-judgment—has been the most empirically supported and has been the subject of the most studies. In a sense it is the easiest to study precisely because within the symbolic interactionist perspective it comes closest to a simple causal relationship in the traditional scientific sense.

Yet this causal relationship is not a simple one. On the one hand, it is not the judgments of others per se that affect our self-judgment; rather it is our perception of other people's judgments that is important. They may actually like us, but we define their acts as negative toward us. They may think of us as stupid, yet we may think they are kidding. On the other hand, even if others consistently see us in a certain way, and even if we correctly interpret that perception, we still do not necessarily accept it, because we also interact with ourselves, and whatever others say or do we can define in any way that is useful to us. We can, for example, reject the judgments of others as unfair, inaccurate, or close-minded ("They really do not know me"). Or others might continuously tell me that I am thin, intelligent, smart, ambitious, but because I do not like what I am I find it useful to label them polite, kind, and easily taken in. There are several studies that show that self-judgment and the appraisals of others do not match perfectly (Gecas, 1982, 6). We select from whatever others may think of us; we interpret, ignore, exaggerate, alter whatever fits what we think about ourselves. We may even select our significant others in order to enhance or reaffirm our self-judgment, thus making self-judgment a factor in influencing what others think of us (Rosenberg, 1979).

The importance of self-judgment, of course, is in the consequences it has for the individual's behavior. Kinch (1963, 482–83) relates the following story about the importance of self-judgment for action. It also underlines the central importance of interaction and its relationship to self:

A group of graduate students in a seminar in social psychology became interested in the notions implied in the interactionist approach. One evening after the seminar five of the male members of the group were discussing some of the implications of the theory and came to the realization that it might be possible to invent a situation where the "others" systematically manipulated their responses to another person, thereby changing that person's self-concept and in turn his behavior. They thought of an experiment to test the notions they were dealing with. They chose as their subject (victim) the one girl in the seminar. The subject can be described as, at best, a very plain girl who seemed to fit the stereotype (usually erroneous) that many have of graduate student females. The boys' plan was to begin in concert to respond to the girl as if she were the best-looking girl on campus. They agreed to work into it naturally so that she would not be aware of what they were up to. They drew lots to see who would be the first to date her. The loser, under the pressure of the others, asked her to go out. Although he found the situation quite unpleasant, he was a good actor and by continually saying to himself "she's beautiful, she's beautiful . . ." he got through the evening. According to the agreement it was now the second man's turn and so it went. The dates were reinforced by the similar responses in all contacts the men had with the girl. In a matter of a few short weeks the results began to show. At first it was simply a matter of more care in her appearance; her hair was combed more often and her dresses were more neatly pressed, but before long she had been to the beauty parlor to have her hair styled, and was spending her hard-earned money on the latest fashions in women's campus wear. By the time the fourth man was taking his turn dating the young lady, the job that had once been undesirable was now quite a pleasant task. And when the last man in the conspiracy asked her out, he was informed that she was pretty well booked up for some time in the future. It seems there were more desirable males around than those "plain" graduate students. (Pp. 482–83)

This story makes clear that judgment of self is a complicated interacting process, one where other individuals influence self but also where the individual, in interaction with self, actively defines and judges self. Thus, although this woman may have at first been highly dependent on others for self-judgment, she was able to break away and become increasingly independent in relation to self. The story also highlights the role of power in human relationships, and it reveals some of the selfish and harmful effects that may result from people in unison "picking on," "scapegoating," and "stereotyping."

Erving Goffman (1959, 14–60) describes the situation where the individual's judgment of self is almost completely in the hands of other people who have very great control over the physical and social environment the individual is in. He calls these instances total institutions, institutions that are apart from the wider society, isolated, where for a length of time the individual's life is in an enclosed, regimented space. Prisons, mental hospitals, the army, and some religious orders are examples. Goffman describes the process by which the total institutions systematically (but not always intentionally) manipulate the individual's world so that the individual comes to redefine self—to reject or question the conceptions of self brought in from the outside, which resulted from interactions in various social worlds. One is, in a real sense, redefined at first through "a series of abasements, degradations, humiliations, and profanations of self." Isolation itself, as well as the dispossession of property and loss of one's name, contributes to the pattern. Individuals may be stripped of privacy and also of the ability to present themselves to others in the way they choose. For example, clothes, cosmetics, haircuts are all restricted. A host of other acts that the individual is forced to perform, such as the constant use of "sir," asking permission, and figuratively bowing to those in authority, all operate to bring about a "mortification of self." New self-judgments slowly replace the old ones. Gradually, any positive self-judgments depend on the authorities and on the actions they wish to support. To obey passively becomes action rewarded with praise and approval, so a positive self-judgment, as it becomes more and more dependent on authorities, is tied to obedience. This whole process depends on (1) isolation from significant others and reference groups outside the institution, (2) total control of the individual's environment by a few powerful individuals, and (3) constant interaction within a social world whose perspective is assumed, including perspective on self.

This model, although extreme and unusual for most of our lives, still serves to sensitize us to a multitude of situations where people do have power and do indeed manipulate self-judgments. Parents, teachers, and peers may do this to the child. Sometimes the judgments of these others are highly consistent and lead the individual to reject self totally or love self fully. More often, significant others and reference groups are inconsistent and the judgment of self is to some extent a continuously changing process. Many religious cults resemble the total institution, and some societies do on occasion: isolation of the individual, control over the environment, limited interaction with outsiders, rejection of self-judgments developed elsewhere, and assumption of the group's perspective. Most of us, however, are not controlled by anything resembling a total institution. Instead, we live in a highly complex world, where many significant others and reference groups make possible self-judgments that are not easily manipulated but where the individual actively forms them.

One more point. Self-judgment makes possible moral choice. Individuals are able to assess and monitor themselves. They can praise themselves for good behavior and censure themselves when they are bad. Self-control involves threatening and punishing self as well as congratulating and rewarding self:

> Unlike the animals in the researcher's laboratory, people exert considerable control over the rewarding and punishing resources available to them. They congratulate themselves for their own characteristics and actions; they praise or abuse their own achievements; and they self-administer social and material rewards and punishments from the enormous array freely available to them (Mischel and Mischel, 1977, 34).

Self-Perception: Identity as Part of Self-Concept

The self then is an object toward which we direct symbolic communication. It is also an object we see in situations, and, because of self, we are able to understand ourselves in relation to situations, and we are able to picture our self in situations. We develop a fairly consistent self-concept over time, yet our image of ourselves changes in every situation to some extent. We also judge ourselves, and this constant evaluation is a part of what our self-concept is. The other part of self-concept we call *identity*.

Identity is the name we call ourselves, and usually it is the name we announce to others that we are as we act in situations. All social objects have names for us; this allows us to identify and classify our world. So too do we give names to people, and ultimately we give names to ourselves. This allows us to understand our environment, and it allows us to understand ourselves in the environment. Gregory Stone (1962, 93) describes identity as the perceived social location of the individual: Where one is "situated" in relation to others, who one tells the self one is, and in his or her actions, the name one tries to communicate to others.

Identities then are part of what we mean by self. Self is the object we act toward. Identity is the naming of that self, the name we call ourselves. As with all objects, identities are "socially bestowed, socially maintained, and socially transformed." (Berger, 1963, 98) Thus, defining who the self is, like all other actions the actor takes toward his or her self, is carried out in interaction with others. As others label me, so I come to label myself. The names given us become our names, our social addresses, our definitions of who we are in relation to those with whom we interact. The identities are labels used, not by all others, but by the reference groups and significant others of the individual. And these identities become central to us over time as our interaction reconfirms them them over and over.

"Identities are meanings a person attributes to the self," wrote Peter Burke (1980). They are relational, social, placed in a context of interaction, and they "are a source of motivation" (p. 18). "I am a man! That is important to me! Like many other men I must develop male friendships that mean having fun without sexual involvement, and like other men I must date, court, and have sexual contact with women!" Needless to say, such a male identity will matter in an individual's interaction and relationships. Indeed, as Harold Garfinkel (1967, 116) notes, sexual classification is especially important to all societies for dividing people and placing them into "natural" categories of male and female. The individual sense of "the real me" begins with sex identity—it is central to who we think we are. Spencer E. Cahill (1980) concisely describes how children take on this identity:

> From the very first day of life the child is responded to by caregivers in terms of his or her sex. Caregivers' sexually differential responsiveness is associated with their use of sex designating terms. By the second year of life the child has incorporated these complexities of responses to his or her self and their association with sex-specific verbal labels into his or her self-conception. The child then attempts to actively confirm his or her gender identity and is influenced in these attempts by the responses of others. Through initiation, playing at gender specific roles, selection of dress and objects of play, and increased interactional experience the child becomes increasingly competent in the subtleties of gender expression. During this same period the child learns the importance of anatomical features to the confirmation of gender identity. Of course, the content of this process is dependent on cultural definitions and common sense understanding of sex and gender. (P. 133)

The central importance of identity to the individual is the subject of a great deal of theoretical and empirical work at the State University of Iowa. Much of this work has been done or inspired by Kuhn, who developed the Twenty Statements Test (TST), which simply asks the individual to answer the question *Who Am I?* with twenty statements. The answers to the question tell the researcher the central identities or self-definitions of the person (boy, Christian, Smith, student, and so forth). As one would expect, as the person identifies his or her self, there is almost always a simultaneous identification of reference group. The instructions for the TST are as follows:

> There are twenty numbered blanks on the page below. Please write twenty answers to the simple question "Who am I?" in the blanks. Just give twenty different answers to this question. Answer as if you were giving the answers to yourself, not to somebody else. Write the answers in the order that they occur to you. Don't worry about logic or "importance." Go along fairly fast, for time is limited. (Kuhn and McPartland, 1954, 70)

Hickman and Kuhn (1956) describe their view of self that is operationalized by the TST:

> There is nothing mystical about this self. It consists of the individual's attitudes (plans of action) toward his own mind and body, viewed as an object. We may think of it as consisting of all the answers the individual might make to the question "Who am I?" (Pp. 43–44)

Probably "identity" would be more correct than "self" because the answers to the questions are core names with which the individual labels self. As Stone (1962, 93) emphasizes, identities are *social locations,* and individuals will usually answer a question like "Who am I?" by identifying themselves in groups or in social categories. "I am a woman" is a valid social category in that it refers to the fact that women constitute an important reference group, that in the individual's relations with others she sees this as an important identity, and she *believes* others also regard it as such. Several hypotheses can be made on the basis of the order in which subjects list their identities, the degree to which the order changes over time, or the relationship between identities and such things as age, sex, social class, and marital status.

There are different types of identities. Some are central to the individual; others are not very important and are easily changed. It is important to make this distinction. Stone, for example, distinguished three types: basic (such as age and sex), general (such as priest or father), and independent (such as part-time employee). These go from the very basic, central, difficult-to-change identities to the nonpervasive, easy to change. A more recent attempt to do the same thing is by Stryker (1980, 60–62), who distinguishes between identities according to "identity salience" and according to "identity commitment." Salience refers to the level of importance a given identity has to many situations. Some identities are important only occasionally; others are important to the individual all the time. We must recognize that all individuals have a hierarchy of salience, with some identities being at the top and others at the bottom. My identities as sociologist, teacher, father, and husband are very salient; homeowner, golfer, union member, and author are less so. Stryker also describes "commitment," the degree to which a certain identity matters to the individual in relation to certain other people. When I am around family, my identity as a family member is very important to me; when I am around students, I have strong commitment to the identity of professor. Some identities—sociologist, for example—have high salience to me, and among many people with whom I interact I give these identities high commitment. Other identities—tennis player, for example—have low salience but high commitment when I am with my friends on the tennis court. There are yet other identities—full professor, for example—that are not salient and that I do not give much commitment to.

Ralph Turner (1968) makes the same type of distinction. However, he refers to core identities as "role-person merger" or "real selves." By real self Turner means that the individual believes that a given identity reflects who he or she really is: The person and the role are seen to be one and the same. Who am I? I am a man, I am a moral being, I am a Confucianist, I am a breadwinner. This is who I *really* am! Of course, Turner points out, this is not who people really are, but who they think they are.

Identity is an important part of self-concept. It is who the individual thinks he or she is and who is announced to the world in word and action. It arises in interaction, it is reaffirmed in interaction, and it is changed in interaction. It is important to what we do. Not all identities matter. However, some may matter almost all the time.

ACTION TOWARD SELF: SELF-DIRECTION

We act toward ourselves through our symbols: We talk to ourselves. As we talk to ourselves, we also see ourselves as objects in situations, and over time we develop a self-concept, including both self-judgment and identity.

As we talk to our self, we are also able to direct what we do. *The self is an object that we are able to direct, influence, control.* By acting back on ourselves, action toward our environment is in the hands of the actor to some extent. Objects that exist out there are manipulated by us, internally, and the same goes for our self: Because we have a self we can manipulate what we do with it. I am able to direct Martha, I can tell Daniel what to do, and I can try to influence Friska the freshman, but I can also do such actions with *myself.* That the individual has a self is important precisely because the individual has this ability to order self, control self, direct self. That is what we mean by "self-control," or "self-direction." The actor is in control; the actor does not passively respond to commands but is able to hold back action, consider options, hesitate, act aggressively or quietly, guide action according to a set of morals learned in other times and in other places, change lines of action, and so on. To direct oneself is to point at oneself and give orders to oneself. It is difficult here to describe exactly goes on in this action, except to state that it is important to recognize that it is the *actor* who is doing the action, not the self. To say we are in control of our selves and direct our selves, means that in the actions we take toward our selves we are able to exercise some control over the actions we take toward our environment.

Self-control and self-direction allow us to cooperate and to exercise freedom. Because we act toward self we are able to align our action with others and therefore to do our part in any cooperative venture. We see what others are doing, and we determine our line of action in relation to them. A basketball team is a number of actors who exercise self-control throughout the game, and, if successful, each forms his or her action as they go along and take one another's actions into account.

Also, at any time, self-direction and self-control mean we are able to say, "I must determine what the truth is for myself," or "Stop! Don't you do that with those guys! You know better, Me!" Individuality, freedom, and nonconformity as well as cooperation depend on this ability to exercise control over our selves. Action is organized by the human being for a purpose: It is "elicited and directed without the presence of immediate rewards, external agents of control, or controlling conditions" (Wells and Marwell, 1976, 43). Without a self that we are able to act back on, there is only direction and control by outside forces.

Our self-direction and self-control, like all else, depend on other people. Our self is pointed out by others, and our self-control is in large part guided by others. We direct/control our action according to those whose perspectives we assume in the situation we encounter, those who are in the situation, and/or those outside of it. We are thus not "free" to direct and control self in any complete sense, but we are guided by the perspectives of others. The guides to our behavior, the guides we use to determine "right" action, appropriate action, rational action, depend on the perspectives of significant others and reference groups. When Mead points out that the self and society are two sides of the same coin, he is referring to society's perspective becoming the individual's, the rules of society becoming the standards by which the individual controls his or her own action. According to Mead "the principal outcome of socialization that makes self-regulation possible is the development of the *self* (Elkin and Handel, 1972, 50). Human conscience in this sense is the assumption of a social world's perspective, and use of conscience is acceptance of this perspective as a guide for one's actions. The individual uses perspectives not to "determine response" but to converse with self, guide self, control self, and direct self. Each situation we enter is different, and each, to some extent, demands active participation by the individual in relation to self.

Self-direction is neither completely social nor is it completely determined by the actor. Like all else human, it is interaction with others and with self that matters. Although the acts of others play an important role in how we direct ourselves, because we are able to act back on ourselves, part of what we do is independent of the acts of others. We plan our own actions, we figure out what to do in situations, we work in relation to our goals or values or morals we believe in. Although the self must be understood as socially created and socially anchored, it is equally important to recognize that once the self is developed, the actor has the ability to act on his or her own to a great extent.

The power "out there" is tempered by the fact that the actor comes to exercise self-control. To possess a self means that the actor is able to direct self in situations, and if freedom means anything, this is what it seems to mean. We may be free or we may not, but without self, freedom is unthinkable. As Tom Goff (1980) describes it:

> The human being's] relationship to nature is a *self*-conscious, reflexive relationship. . . . Other animals react to stimuli: [Human beings] can, in addition, react to themselves as stimuli. . . . [This fact] is understood as the basis of the ability to inhibit overt and immediate reaction to stimuli, to think or act implicitly, or in mind, before responding overtly and intentionally to the environment. [Human beings] thereby acquire a control over their own activity and their environment which is denied to other species. (Pp. 56–57)

And Blumer (1966) emphasizes exactly the same point:

> With the mechanism of self-interaction the human being ceases to be a responding organism whose behavior is a product of what plays upon him from the outside, the inside, or both. Instead, he acts toward his world, interpreting what confronts him and organizing his action on the basis of the interpretation. (P. 536)*

It seems truly paradoxical that the origin of the free actor—selfhood—should be a *social* creation.

CENTRAL IDEAS ABOUT THE SELF

The self is highly complex and very important. Let us review some of the key ideas discussed so far.

1. The self is social. It arises in interaction, and it changes or remains stable due to interaction.
2. The self arises in childhood through symbolic interaction with significant others (play stage). The child develops a mature self with the development of a generalized other (game stage). With adulthood come reference groups, each influencing a different view of the self and making the self somewhat different in each situation.
3. The meaning of the self is that the individual becomes an object to his or her own action. The actor is able to look back on self in situations and is able to imagine himself or herself in the situation. This process involves social interaction with others, and it depends to a large extent on seeing and acting toward self according to our definition of the acts of others toward us.

*Reprinted from "Sociological Implications of the Thought of George Herbert Mead" by Herbert Blumer in *The American Journal of Sociology*, by permission of the University of Chicago Press. Copyright © 1966 by The Univesity of Chicago.

4. Much of our action with other people is symbolic communication; all of our action toward the self is symbolic communication. The basis for all selfhood is that we are able to talk to ourselves. This is what is meant here by thinking.
5. As we communicate toward self we are able to see ourselves in the situation, to recognize who we are in relation to others and vice versa, as well as to evaluate our own action in the situation. We are able to judge ourselves and to establish an identity.
6. The self is one object that exists in and is used by the individual in all situations. Actions toward self are central to our understanding of all situations.
7. Self means that the individual is able to be active in relation to the world, for self makes possible self-control and self-direction. The ability of the individual to influence the direction of his or her own action makes possible both individuality and cooperative action. It allows the individual to agree to cooperate or to refuse to conform.

THE SELF AND THE SYMBOLIC INTERACTIONIST PERSPECTIVE

Throughout this chapter the self has been shown to be tied, like everything else we discussed earlier, to interaction as diagrammed in Figure 6–1.

FIGURE 6–1

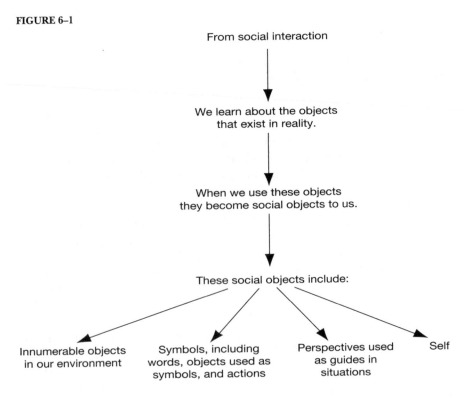

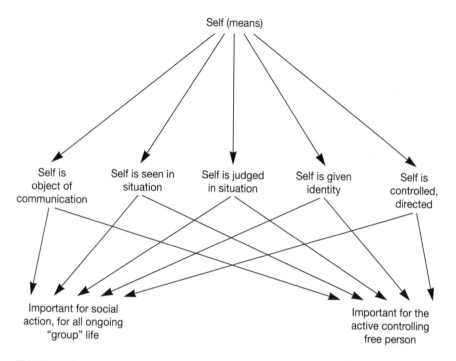

FIGURE 6–2

The self is social because it arises from social interaction and because our actions toward self are continuously tied to social interaction.

Yet, this socially anchored self, once developed, allows the individual to break away from the influence of others to some extent and to control his or her own action.

The point so far is that the social self—the me—is an *object* created in social interaction and an *object* the actor is able to act back on. It, like the symbol, is central to both complex social life and the life of the individual. (Figure 6–2)

THE "I" AND THE "ME"

Wouldn't you know it? There is a lot of confusion when it comes to self, partly because of something I have thus far ignored in this chapter.

Mead described the self as consisting of the "I" and the "me." Herbert Blumer, one of his students, focused our attention entirely on the me, the social self, the self as object, and self as described in this chapter. My interpretation of symbolic interactionism is like Blumer's: It is the self as social object that is to be emphasized. I believe this is also Mead's emphasis. However, Mead also describes something in addition to this—the "I"—and this has led to problems I would like to address at this time.

The "I" has been interpreted to mean a lot of things, and as I read and listen to symbolic interactionists, I can readily see that each tries to fit it into his or her own theory of the actor. Even Mead is not consistent in his use of the term, so this allows others to plug it in where they want.

There are several ways I have noticed this term is used. In introductory sociology textbooks it is introduced as a very neat point, although I personally do not understand this meaning. The "I" is described in these texts as one of two sides to the self. Each human actor has an I and a me. All action arises from the conversation between the I and the me, the I being the actor as subject and the me being the actor as object. Somehow our action is the result of this interaction. If you think about it, this does not fit very well with the discussion in this book. Here, I have argued that it is the actor who acts, and the actor acts toward self as object. I do not even introduce this other "part of self."

Some make the distinction even more complex—and interesting. The "I" is the beginning of the act and the "me" is the end. We start with the actor being propelled, but soon the actor is able to converse with self and act according to a socially developed set of rules.

A related distinction is that the "I" is the free actor and the "me" is the socially shaped and controlled actor. Somehow, interpreters ignore the meaning of freedom to Mead: Freedom is the control by the actor of his or her own action; it is a result of self and symbol—both socially created—not the result of a biological response that has nothing to do with society.

In his writing, Mead does not clearly describe the "I," probably because the "me" is such a central part of his view of self. However, there are places that the "I" described by him fits well with the discussion in this chapter. It is a recognition by Mead that there is part of all human beings that goes untouched by other humans. To say that part of our self is an "I" means to Mead—and to me—that part of what we do is nonsocial and noncontrolled. It is action that does not arise from thought; it is action that even surprises the actor—"Did I really do that?" It is action that we might call impulsive, unlearned, unpredictable, unplanned. This is not freedom to Mead, however—it may lead to more freedom if it opens up choices to us as we act. It is really action that we do not control when it occurs and therefore is closer to an internal response. It is how Mead tells us that humans do more than engage in action toward the self—part of what we do occurs because this action does not take place and we act without consideration of the situation.

There is no assumption here that this is good or bad. Impulsive action often gets people into trouble. Creativity and spontaneity breaks us out of controls by others around us. The "I" can lead to destructive or creative action, but its essence is that it is neither learned nor controlled. Mead is reminding us that no matter how much we learn to control what we do in situations, we all are to some extent impulsive, spontaneous, and creative in the situations we act in.

The "I" sometimes plays an important part in what we all do, but by far it is the "me" that really characterizes our ongoing action in the world. Some of us do lack control over ourselves, and sometimes this means action that gets us into trouble with other people and at other times it allows us to go in directions we never imagined. However, the "me" is so much more important to symbolic interactionists that I will use the term "self" in this book to mean the "me," the self as object.

SUMMARY

The self, like symbols, is a social object the actor uses in situations to achieve goals. The actor acts toward objects in the outside environment; the actor is also able to act toward himself or herself as an object. By doing this, the actor is transformed; the actions we take toward self—communication, perception, and direction—change what we are in nature. We take some control away from our outside environment, and we are able to choose what we do in the world. We do not simply respond to stimuli but act back on ourselves: discussing, evaluating, holding back, and commanding action.

The self is socially created. What better evidence is there that human beings are social beings? The "I," discussed briefly in this chapter, is sometimes considered a part of the self, but for purposes of understanding the nature of the human being, it is far more important to recognize that it is the "me"—the actor as the object of his or her own actions—that plays far more of a role in human action.

The "mind" is also a part of this mixture. In fact, to Mead (1934), the mind is the "twin emergent of the self." The *object* we have here called "self," and the *activity* toward the self we call "mind" arise in social interaction. In fact, they are really triple emergents: mind, self, and symbols, all qualities that are central to the human being, and they arise together and are hopelessly interlinked. The mind is, in a sense, easier to understand now that we have discussed symbols and self. Whereas self and symbols are social objects, mind is a a certain type of *action: all the symbolic action the actor takes toward the self.* This will be the subject of Chapter 7.

REFERENCES

BERGER, PETER
    1963   *Invitation to Sociology.* Garden City, N.Y.: Doubleday. Copyright © 1963 by Peter L. Berger. Reprinted by permission of Doubleday & Company, Inc., New York, and Penguin Press, Harmondsworth, Middlesex, England.

BLUMER, HERBERT
    1962   "Society as Symbolic Interaction." In Arnold Rose, ed., *Human Behavior and Social Processes*, pp. 179–92. Boston: Houghton Mifflin.
    1966   "Sociological Implications of the Thought of George Herbert Mead." *American Journal of Sociology* 71:535–44. By permission of The University of Chicago Press. Copyright ©1966 by The University of Chicago.

BROOKS, RICHARD
    1969   "The Self and Political Role: A Symbolic Interactionist Approach to Political Ideology." *Sociological Quarterly* 10:22–31.

BURKE, PAUL J.
    1980   "The Self: Measurement Requirements from an Interactionist Perspective." *Social Psychology Quarterly* 43:18–29.

CAHILL, SPENCER E.
   1980   "Directions for an Interactionist Study of Gender Development." *Symbolic Interaction* 3:123–38.
COOLEY, CHARLES HORTON
   1970   *Human Nature and the Social Order.* New York: Schocken Books.
DENZIN, NORMAN K.
   1972   "The Genesis of Self in Early Childhood." *Sociological Quarterly* 13:291–314.
ELKIN, FREDERICK, AND GERALD HANDEL
   1972   *The Child and Society.* New York: Random House.
GARFINKEL, HAROLD
   1967   *Studies in Ethnomethodology.* Englewood Cliffs, N.J.: Prentice Hall.
GECAS, VIKTOR
   1982   "The Self Concept." *Annual Review of Sociology* 8:1–33.
GOFF, TOM W.
   1980   *Marx and Mead.* London: Routledge & Kegan Paul.
GOFFMAN, ERVING
   1959   *Asylums.* Chicago: Aldine.
HICKMAN, C. ADDISON, AND MANFORD H. KUHN
   1956   *Individuals, Groups, and Economic Behavior.* New York: Dryden Press.
JAMES, WILLIAM
   1915   *Psychology.* New York: Holt, Rinehart & Winston.
KINCH, JOHN W.
   1963   "A Formalized Theory of the Self-Concept." *American Journal of Sociology* 68:481–86.
KUHN, MANFORD H., AND THOMAS S. MCPARTLAND
   1954   "An Empirical Investigation of Self Attitudes." *American Sociological Review* 19:68–76.
MCCALL, GEORGE J., AND J. L. SIMMONS
   1966   *Identities and Interactions.* New York: Free Press. Reprinted with permission of The Free Press, an imprint of Simon & Schuster. Copyright © 1966 by The Free Press.
MEAD, GEORGE HERBERT
   1925   "The Genesis of the Self and Social Control." *International Journal of Ethics* 35:251–77.
   1934   *Mind, Self and Society.* Chicago: University of Chicago Press. Reprinted by permission of The University of Chicago Press. Copyright © 1934 by The University of Chicago. All rights reserved.
MELTZER, BERNARD N.
   1972   *The Social Psychology of George Herbert Mead.* Kalamazoo: Center for Sociological Research, Western Michigan University.
MISCHEL, WALTER, AND HARRIET N. MISCHEL
   1977   "Self-Control and the Self." In Theodore Mischel, ed., *The Self,* pp. 31–64. Oxford: Basil Blackwell.
ROSENBERG, MORRIS
   1979   *Conceiving the Self.* New York: Basic Books.
   1981   "The Self-Concept: Social Product and Social Force." In Morris Rosenberg and Ralph Turner, eds., *Social Psychology,* pp. 593–624. New York: Basic Books.

SHIBUTANI, TAMOTSU

  1955 "Reference Groups as Perspectives." *American Journal of Sociology* 60:562–69.

  1961 *Society and Personality: An Interactionist Approach to Social Psychology.* Englewood Cliffs, N.J.: Prentice Hall. Copyright © 1961. Reprinted by permission of Prentice Hall, Inc.

STONE, GREGORY P.

  1962 "Appearance and the Self." In Arnold Rose, ed., *Human Behavior and Social Processes*, pp. 86–118. Boston: Houghton Mifflin.

STRYKER, SHELDON

  1959 "Symbolic Interaction as an Approach to Family Research." *Marriage and Family Living* 21:111–19.

  1980 *Symbolic Interactionism: A Social Structural Version.* Menlo Park, Calif.: Benjamin/Cummings.

TROYER, WILLIAM LEWIS

  1946 "Mead's Social and Functional Theory of Mind." *American Sociological Review* 11:198–202.

TURNER, RALPH H.

  1968 "The Self-Conception in Social Interaction." In Chad Gordon and Kenneth J. Gergen, eds., *The Self in Social Interaction*, pp. 93–106. New York: Wiley.

WELLS, L. EDWARD, AND GERALD MARWELL

  1976 *Self Esteem.* Beverly Hills, Calif.: Sage Publications.

7

The Human Mind

When social scientists emphasize that people are conditioned, caused, shaped, moved, controlled, and driven by such forces as their past, social structures, roles, culture, social institutions, and other people, they are supporting the notion that people lack the tools necessary to act back on their world, to determine their own action, to direct themselves through some decision making on their part, some free choice in what to do. Charles Warriner (1970) calls this the "stable-man" view of the human being and contrasts this view with what he call the "emergent-man" view, a view that emphasizes an actor in control of his or her own action in the present, defining, thinking, controlling his or her own choices. The symbolic interactionist, as we emphasized in the previous four chapters, rejects the "stable-man" view as exaggerated and incomplete and focuses instead on the "emergent-man" view primarily because humans depend on the symbol and on self in situations. As soon as these concepts are introduced, the human becomes much less passive, moved much less by deterministic forces. We can begin to identify ways that human beings take control from their environment. We can begin to see that human beings act in relation to their environment because they define that environment and tell themselves what to do. As Mead emphasized, humans are able to turn back on their environment and not simply respond to it once we give them symbols and self.

THE MEANING OF MIND: SYMBOLIC INTERACTION TOWARD SELF

However, the picture is more easily understood if we add a third element. This third element is *mind*, and it is important to consider this if we are to understand human beings and the active relationship they have with their environment.

Mead (1934) discusses mind extensively in his book *Mind, Self and Society*. There are important links between these concepts. Humans with *minds* and *selves* create a certain type of *society*; human *society* creates a unique being that possesses *mind* and *self*. Also, mind and self are linked, and everything, in turn, is linked to *symbols*.

Mind is an active concept: It is a certain kind of *action* the actor engages in. It is what we call *thinking*, or covert action (action not open to observation by others), talking to oneself, engaging in conversation with oneself about the environment and one's action in that environment. Mead (1982) writes that mind is "activity, and the different phases of consciousness are parts of this activity." Mind is not an object like the self or symbols; it is *action* that the individual takes, all action the individual takes toward himself or herself.

The distinctions here are far from perfect, but still important to make. Recall that the *actor* is the one who acts. Actors act toward their outside environment. They "do things." They do things with their bodies toward that environment. They manipulate objects in their environment to achieve their goals. The action that others take toward the outside environment we call *overt action* (action that is "open"). However, actors also act toward themselves; this we might call action that is *covert* (action that is "covered" because it occurs inside each actor; it is internal). *All this covert action is called "mind." Mind is all the action that the actor takes toward himself or herself. It is all thinking, all active manipulation of symbols by the actor in conversation within his head and toward self.*

Then what is the *self*? Remember the self is the *object* that the actor talks to when he or she engages in covert action. The actor acts; the actor acts toward the outside environment; when the actor acts toward the self he or she is engaging in mind action. In almost every situation the actor is simultaneously engaged in both overt and covert (or mind) action. Our overt action is caused by our covert action; our own covert action is considered by us when we engage in covert action back toward the self.

The mind is probably best defined as symbolic action toward the self, the symbolic activity the actor directs toward his or her own self. It is active communication toward the self through the manipulation of symbols. Mead (1936) describes it as that which arises and is interdependent with the self, "an inner flow of speech . . . that calls out intelligent response . . ."(p. 381). Active symbolic interaction means that the human *manipulates symbols* covertly: We *think*, we engage in minded behavior, we literally hold conversations with ourselves—yes, we constantly talk to ourselves, and we often answer to ourselves. Stop and reflect a moment; Herbert Blumer's (1962) insight that we engage in mind action all the time seems so obviously true. The mind, he states, is "anything the individual indicates to himself, . . . and the individual . . . from the time that he awakens until he falls asleep, is a continual flow of self indications—notations of the things with which he deals and takes into account" (pp. 181–82). We do not, then, *sometimes* think; we are constantly thinking in every situation we encounter. As we hold conversation with others, we hold conversation with ourselves: That is mind activity. As we walk into situations, we determine what is important for us in those situations; we define the situations: That is mind activity. The manipulation of symbols is not the same as simple recall of pictures. We may be stimulated in a situation and recall a picture, and the picture may lead to a response by us, but the internal active manipulation of things demands symbols that are capable of being purposely combined and recombined in a number of different ways. A picture cannot be manipulated alone; words can be. "A mind cannot be located in the brain or nervous system or anywhere inside the body. Mind is not a thing, and certainly not a thing to be located. It is *conduct*. . . . Mind then, will subside and disappear when communication is not going on, and come back when communication is resumed" (Ames, 1973, 50–51). It is important to regard mind as *activity*.

Mind, then, should not be confused with brain. The two are not the same. All animals may have brains, but that is not to say that they have minds. Brains with the capacity to store and manipulate large numbers of symbols are necessary for minds, but "brains, *per se*, do not make mind" (Troyer, 1946, 200). It is the manipulation of symbols, made possible through the learning of those symbols and the development of self, that makes mind. And these tools, you will recall, are developed in interaction with others. William Troyer puts the case clearly and to the point: "It is society—social interaction—using brains, which makes mind" (p. 200). Give the human the self and the words to communicate with the self, and the active person emerges, manipulating words, thinking, and creating.

MIND ACTION: MAKING INDICATIONS TOWARD SELF

Mind is action made possible by the fact that humans have both symbols and self. It is ongoing conversation. It is, as Mead (1938) emphasizes, actors "making indications" toward themselves: "He [or she] talks to himself [or herself]. This talking is significant. [He or she] is indicating what is of importance in the situation. . . indicating those elements that call out the necessary [action]" (p. 384).

Simply put, mind action means that actor is able to pull things out of the environment that he or she has words for, and use them as he or she considers what to do in the situation. We isolate, label, and develop plans of action toward objects around us. We do not simply respond to these objects but define and discuss these objects internally. We notice certain objects and ignore others, and those we notice we perceive and define according to our specific goals in that specific situation. Mind means we are actively telling ourselves what exists around us, and, because we understand these things, we are able to determine how we are going to use them.

Initially, we may notice certain objects, but then leave these aside and move on to other objects. Our goals may change or other actors in the situation may inform us of something, and we indicate to ourselves different objects or new definitions of objects already indicated to ourselves. I may walk down the street and note the cold weather. I notice the wind on my thighs and realize I have not worn my long underwear today. I note a subtle change in the weather and wonder if there is a storm approaching. I walk toward a snow-covered car I pray will start. If I am religious, my prayer may not simply be a hope, but I will even take note of a God I think may be listening to me. On another occasion I may walk down this same street noticing the tickets on the cars and worrying about my car, which may have a ticket on it. Or I may take note of the different styles of clothing people are wearing this year. Or I might be walking down the same street noting the faces of everyone because I am looking for someone in particular: my friend in need of help or the no-good guy who stole my wallet, or the person who looks like a good experimental subject, someone who would make a good model or the one who might protect me from a gang, or the one who might make a good date. The point is that people point things out to themselves as they walk down the street, or run or talk or play. Things that are out there are noticed and defined in our heads through minded activity. The world is transformed into a world of definitions because of mind. Blumer (1966) emphasizes this throughout his work. We pull things out of our world, define them, and give them meaning according to the use they have for us at the time, and we act. We act, therefore, as we manipulate these things in our heads:

> To indicate something is to stand over against it and to put oneself in the position of acting toward it instead of automatically responding to it. In the face of something which one indicates, one can withhold action toward it, inspect it, judge it, ascertain its meaning, determine its possibilities, and direct one's action with regard to it. With the mechanism of self-interaction the human being ceases to be a responding organism whose behavior is a product of what plays upon him from the outside, the inside, or both. Instead, he acts toward his world, interpreting what confronts him and organizing his action on the basis of the interpretation. (P. 536)*

Blumer (1969) argues that "by virtue of engaging in self-interaction the human being stands in a markedly different relation to his environment than is presupposed by the widespread conventional view" (pp. 14–15).

MIND ACTION: THE ABILITY TO CONTROL OVERT ACTION

Mind stands in marked contrast to simple response to a stimulus. If we respond to something, we mean that "we can't help it." Mind, on the other hand, means we take some control away from the stimulus. This is what Blumer means in the previous paragraph when he writes that we have a "markedly different relation" to our environment.

Because of mind, we tell ourselves how to act toward the environment around us. We are able to apply what we know to the situation, to make plans of what to do, and to alter our plans and definitions as we and others act in the situation.

---

*Reprinted from "Sociological Implications of the Thought of George Herbert Mead" by Herbert Blumer in *The American Journal of Sociology* by permission of The University of Chicago Press. Copyright © 1966 by The University of Chicago. All rights reserved.

To point things out to ourselves means our own acts make sense to us. We understand what we are doing, the failure or success of what we are doing, the reactions to what we are doing by others. Through all of this we are changed from responders to planners, from beings "who can't help what we do" to beings who understand what they are doing, understand what they did, and understand what they are going to do before they do it. We are able to rehearse our actions before we actually act out in the environment. We are able to predict the actions of others to what we do before we do it. Mead calls mind the ability to approach objects in our environment according to what we plan to do with them in the future. There is, he writes, an organization of parts of our own "nervous system that are going to be responsible for acts, an organization which represents not only that which is immediately taking place, but also the later states that are to take place." Mead gives the example of the hammer. "If one is approaching a hammer, he is muscularly all ready to seize the handle of the hammer. The late stages of the act are present in the early stages." The actor is in control of the ongoing act. The actor controls the process. How we will use an object in the near future influences "the steps in our early manipulation of it" (1934, 11).

This control over action that mind allows means that at any point we can speed up action or delay it. Mind means we are able to hold back, to put off acting in the immediate so we can achieve goals that can be achieved only by planning. Trial and error gives way to problem solving; the immediate sensed present gives way to pointing out to ourselves events from our past and future; stimulus response gives way to understanding and holding back what we are able to do. Just as symbols and self make the active human being—maybe even some free choice—possible, so does this ability to engage in mind action. It is Blumer (1981) who highlights the significance of this ability:

> The organism is not just there—in a relation of merely responding to the thing—it points it out to itself and consequently, it can do something. By indicating the thing to itself, the organism can stop and figure out what it will do before it acts toward the thing. To indicate something to oneself is to put oneself in the position of being able to talk to oneself about the thing. This cannot be done by the organism which doesn't have the means of pointing out the thing to itself. (Pp.115–16)

Maurice Natanson (1973) also makes this same case nicely: "The human animal has the unique capacity of isolating his responses to environmental stimuli and controlling those responses in the very act of these both to himself and to [others]" (p. 7). Troyer (1946) reminds us that mind is what Mead means by "choice and conscious control" (p. 199). "Mind makes it possible," according to Meltzer (1972), "to control and organize" action, and thus to do considerably more than respond to the environment" (p. 20).

The ability to direct oneself, to hold back what one does, to rehearse action is all mind activity, and this activity is one that changes our relationship to the environment into an active manipulating one.

MIND ACTION: THE ABILITY TO PROBLEM SOLVE

The ability to represent the environment that exists outside of us with words we can manipulate internally means that we are able to figure out how to act in our situations. We can plan, rehearse, and try to overcome whatever stands in the way of our achieving the goals we have in a particular situation. To create goals and then define a situation in relation to those goals means what we do is constantly being evaluated by us and altered in relation to our successes and failures. We change what we do because it no longer works for us.

Mead emphasizes (1938) that mind action is most likely to arise where problems arise for us:

> Consciousness is involved where there is a problem, where one is deliberately adjusting one's self to the world, trying to get out of difficulty or pain. One is aware of experience and is trying to readjust the situation so that conduct can go ahead. There is, therefore, no consciousness in a world that is just there. (P. 657)

Mead is telling us something very important about mind. It is focused on goals, and when something stands in the way of our achieving those goals smoothly, we must stop and carefully discuss the situation and what we are doing there. Although he does not clearly say so, Mead at least implies that to some extent each situation poses a problem that must be resolved if goals are to be achieved. We need to think about it to some extent. It is, in the end, a matter of degree: The more our action is interrupted because something stands in the way of our achieving our goals, the more important our mind action becomes, the more deliberate and conscious it becomes, the more planning, rehearsal of action, and making deliberate choices must be made. However, pure overt action without any mind activity is unusual simply because each situation is unique, poses at least a minor problem to be resolved, and therefore demands some covert action.

The story of Robinson Crusoe as described by Van Meter Ames highlights the role of mind in the affairs of the human being. Robinson Crusoe sailed on many voyages before his ill-fated one. Without question every one of those voyages involved mind action on his part. As he worked from day to day, his stream of mind action accompanied what he did on his ship. Usually he did tasks he had faced before, and so little deliberate mind action was needed. Undoubtedly, serious problems arose every day that involved deliberation, and occasionally a brand new situation arose that involved much. Even hearing commands from officers and conversing with other sailors involved mind action. But one day he found himself thrust into a very dangerous and life-threatening situation, one that involved him in having to take stock of the situation quickly but carefully and having to assess himself in relation to a brand new future. Everything changed for him as he discussed the situation with himself. Here Van Meter Ames (1973) describes Defoe's story in a symbolic interactionist context.

Robinson Crusoe was in the act of sailing for Guinea when this act was interrupted by shipwreck. Other voyages and adventures of his had preceded, but the
story associated with his name begins with his being wrecked off an unknown
island. There the ongoing act of the voyage was halted when he was plunged into
the sea. Now it was no longer a question of going to Guinea but of reaching a
rock he could hold on to until a huge wave subsided. Then he made a dash for
shore and clambered up a cliff. On the next page, as Defoe relates:

> After I had solaced my mind with the comfortable part of my condition, I began
> to look around me to see what kind of place I was in, and what was next to be
> done. . . . I was wet, had no clothes to shift me, nor anything either to eat or
> drink. . . . I had nothing about me but a knife, a tobacco-pipe, and a little tobacco
> in a box. . . . All the remedy that offered to my thoughts at that time was, to get
> up into a thick bushy tree. . . .

Things appear, with their limitation and promise, as he looks about. Taking in
the surroundings, with himself as an organism in their midst, an object among
objects, he sees things loom up on account of the antecedent act which had
been thwarted. What Defoe tells is pure Mead. Mead is generalizing and analyzing what Defoe or any storyteller knows: that the appearance of things of interest must follow upon the blocking of activity. . . . Only then does the individual
appear to himself as an object caught in the midst of things, scanning them for
hints of how to get going again. Robinson Crusoe was previously too immersed
in a smooth ongoing [act] to confront himself as something separate. He
appears to himself, along with other objects, when he has to sort them out in
search of cues for getting under way again. The situation takes on a structure
momentarily lifted out of passage, by the fact that alternative options of different courses appear in the guise of different objects, before any one or one set of
them is chosen for pursuit. Surveying land and sea, Robinson Crusoe brings distant points into his own breathing moment, suppressing the time it would take
to get to them and touch them. The hills and trees, the rocks in the sea and the
wreck beyond, are all magically present in his present, as if the completion and
consummation of arriving at each of them were all achieved simultaneously.
(Pp. 46–47)

We all enter brand new situations that call for a careful examination of
objects in the situation. Someone insults us or surprises us and suddenly we
need to figure out what to do next. We lose our keys or the car won't start, we
cannot find our purse, or we realize we forgot an appointment. What happens? We carefully consider what to do next, objects around us take on new
meaning, a new plan of action is hatched and followed.

When our identity is threatened—"You are a stupid person," "You are a
child," "You are boring"—our situations become problematic and thus must
be thought out and acted on appropriately. If we desire money or honor or
love or sex and we are unable to get it in a situation, we will perceive that situation as a problem with which we must deal. When we see that someone is taking advantage of us, or when we are late for an important appointment, or
when we have little time to study for an important test, or when we want someone to think well of us, or when we want to tell our roommate to cut out the
chatter so we can get some sleep, we are faced with problems to be solved in
order to continue our flow of action without hassle. We may carefully and
deliberately look around for useful objects to help us in the problem situation.

Problem solving is the key point in Mead's approach to mind. Bernard Meltzer (1972) reminds us that mind action inhibits action, holds action back in order to first appraise the future consequences of what we are about to do.

> It consists of presenting to oneself, tentatively and in advance of overt behavior, the different possibilities or alternatives of future action with reference to a given situation. The future is, thus, present in terms of images of prospective lines of action from which the individual can make a selection. The mental process is, then, one of delaying, organizing, and selecting a response to the stimuli of the environment. This implies that the individual *constructs* his act, rather than responding in predetermined ways. . . . When the act of an animal is checked, it may engage in overt trial and error or random activity. In the case of blocked human acts. . . consequences can be imaginatively "tried out" in advance. . . . What this involves is the ability to indicate elements of the field or situation, abstract them from the situation, and recombine them so that procedures can be considered in advance of their execution. (P. 20)

The human pursues interests, values, goals, and in these pursuits problems arise that must be resolved. Here lies the essence of minded activity to Mead (1936): "It is this process of talking over a problematic situation with one's self, just as one might talk with another, that is exactly what we term 'mental.' And it goes on within the organism" (p. 385).

MIND ACTION IS PART OF ALL SOCIAL INTERACTION

When humans act in a social situation, other people become objects for them that they point out to self. To interact with others involves taking account of others, to make indications about them to ourselves, to define and redefine what they are doing in relation to us, and to evaluate what we our doing in relation to them. All of this activity is mind, and thus it is important to recognize that human interaction is not stimulus response or fixed and automatic, or simply overt and physical. Like everything else in our action, it is accompanied by ongoing conversation with ourselves.

We engage in mind action when we are alone and when we are around others who somehow make a difference to us at the time. When others act in our presence, we need to interpret and understand those actions if we are to know what to do. In their actions (including their speech, their simple symbolic gestures, and their unintentional body language) we try to understand their thoughts, their intentions, their past actions, their plans, their age, their belief system, their perspectives, their abilities, and, by indicating these to our self, we consider such things as we act in the situation. Sometimes we are concerned about what they think of us, or perhaps what we think of each other. We may wonder what they had for breakfast or how they look naked or on the toilet, or we may consider what their marriage is like or what their childhood consisted of. We may also consider how to escape the social situation, how to control it, how to appear to conform to others at least until we can get away, or how to disrupt the situation. We might escape the situation in our minds by thinking about last night's party, tonight's book that we're definitely going to get to, tomorrow's Super Bowl, or next year's job. But whenever we are with others, just as whenever we are alone with our own self, we are engaging in a constant conversation with self—not always a conversation that we are fully aware of, but a conversation nevertheless.

It is important to consider not only what others are saying to us but also what we are saying to others. To give off symbols to others is to give them off to ourselves simultaneously. Our communication is an attempt to share something with others. What we share therefore has meaning to us. We are able to "know" the meaning that our words will have to others, only because the words have meaning to us. Van Meter Ames (1973) points out that

> Mead's tremendous discovery is that the mind begins to appear at the point when certain gestures tend to call out in the individual making them the response which they simultaneously arouse in another form. Mead noted that the vocal gesture is especially apt to have this double effect, because it can be heard by the form which makes it in practically the same way and at the same moment as by another form. This is the main basis of communication among men: that the same utterance or other gesture should affect the organism initiating it as it does another. (P. 50)

Minded activity, therefore, includes the conversation with the self that necessarily must accompany the conversation with others.

Mind is involved in all social situations because other people are objects that must be defined like everything else. People pose greater problems for us, however, than other objects because we must understand what they are doing, we must make ourselves understood by them, and we must actively interpret their acts in situations in order to revise our own acts. We develop lines of action toward other people, but these lines of action are constantly being revised in the situation because each actor is also acting back and we must adjust accordingly. Rehearsing our acts before we act overtly is especially important in social situations because what we do overtly is seen and defined by others.

Games provide especially good examples of individuals engaging in mind action, rehearsing overt action, redefining the other person, and altering overt action. In a sense, games are slow-motion human action. In chess, for example, a move by Ivan may be preceded by something like: "I think that the capturing of his queen will be accomplished in three moves if I now move my castle to this position. The American might interpret this as meaning I am after his knight, and if he does, I have him. If he figures out my move, then I will have to alter my plans." Then as he moves, Ivan reexamines the situation, looking especially at John, his opposition. Noting that John moves the pawn, Ivan realizes that John has not fallen for the trap, and Ivan must now revise his line of action. Self-communication, making indications, rehearsing acts, developing and altering lines of action, understanding the meaning of the other—

all these activities characterize both Ivan and John playing chess, but they also characterize all of us in every social situation we encounter. Or consider the game of football: "I think the action should be right through the center of the line, because they won't be expecting it. Their backs are expecting a pass, and the center is weak. However, if they line up as if they are expecting a run, I will change the play by calling number 88." After the play is run: "We did that well, but they were somewhat ready for us. I wonder now if the time is right to try the same thing again." That is the quarterback, but all the actors on the field, including tackles and guards, the opposition, the referees, the coaches, and the fans, are making indications to self, rehearsing acts, and doing all the other activities called mind.

These formal games are replayed throughout our lives in all social situations: the classroom, the party, the bull session, the meeting, through traffic, while shopping at the store, and while getting ready to meet someone for dinner. But mind is like all else—we become most conscious of it when it is pointed out to us by others and when we, in turn, point it out to ourselves. In a sense, what the perspective of symbolic interactionism does is to make us more aware of the mind activity that characterizes much of our lives.

SUMMARY

Mind then is not the same as self or symbols, but mind depends on both self and symbols. Mind is defined as the ongoing symbolic action the actor takes toward the self. It is the constant process of making indications to ourselves about objects in our environment and especially their use for aiding us in achieving our goals.

Mind action allows us to control our own overt action, and in that way we are able to take an active role in relation to our environment. Mind action allows us to problem solve in situations, going beyond trial and error and habitual response. Mind action accompanies all human social interaction, since social interaction demands constant understanding, interpretation, and definition of the others in the situation.

There are two emphases concerning mind introduced in this chapter. At first, we emphasized that mind action is a continuous process of the individual making indications to self all day long. This is Blumer's point. The actor moves from situation to situation, defining goals and social objects, thinking, rehearsing, evaluating. Then we emphasized that mind action takes place around problems in situations: Where our goals are not immediately met, we need to figure out what to do. Where action is blocked, we have a problem and we must engage in mind action. This is Mead's emphasis.

Although different, both views are very important for understanding mind action. Mind action becomes most deliberate and conscious when we must stop and figure out how to solve a problem facing us in a situation. Yet Blumer is also correct in suggesting that mind action—often less deliberate and conscious—is necessary throughout our day, in every situation. Each situation is new for us, at least to some extent, and that means some problem solving is necessary. Each has objects we make into social objects around the goals we seek; each involves perceiving self in situation. Every situation we enter demands some adjustment on our part, presents itself as a "problem" to be resolved. Every situation takes some covert action, some self-indication, some rehearsal of various lines of action. When we speak to others, it may be a minimal problem to be understood, but it is still a problem, and we must pay some attention to organizing our presentation. To understand others is usually a minor problem, but it is a problem nevertheless, and we must pay some attention to meaning. Mind activity becomes more deliberate, and we become more conscious of it, when a major problem confronts us, and we must sit down and carefully analyze the situation, considering the consequences of what we are about to do. Mind covert activity should be conceptualized as present in all our situations, as a constant flow of activity, and this activity is organized around situations we encounter, where some definition and adjustment on our part must be accomplished. Sometimes it is rapid and we are barely aware of it; sometimes it is obvious and deliberate, but almost always it accompanies overt action since each situation is unique and demands some definition.

We are, then, symbol users, we possess a self, and we engage in mind activity throughout everything we do. Is this the end of what we are? These qualities are interdependent with one other quality, one that is central to everything else, and one we have not even touched on up to now. This quality is called *taking the role of the other*, and it is important enough to spend all of Chapter 8 on.

REFERENCES

AMES, VAN METER
    1973   "No Separate Self." In Walter Robert Corti, ed., *The Philosophy of George Herbert Mead*, pp. 43–58. Winterthur, Switzerland: Amriswiler Bucherei.

BLUMER, HERBERT
    1962   "Society as Symbolic Interaction." In Arnold Rose, ed., *Human Behavior and Social Processes*, pp. 179–92. Boston: Houghton Mifflin.

    1966   "Sociological Implications of the Thought of George Herbert Mead." *American Journal of Sociology* 71:535–44. By permission of the University of Chicago Press. Copyright © 1966 by The University of Chicago.

    1969   *Symbolic Interactionism: Perspective and Method.* Englewood Cliffs, N.J.: Prentice Hall. Copyright © 1969. Reprinted by permission of Prentice Hall, Inc.

    1981   "Conversation with Thomas J. Morrioni and Harvey A. Farberman." *Symbolic Interaction* 4:9–22.

DEWEY, JOHN
    1922   *Human Nature and Conduct.* New York: Modern Library.

McCALL, GEORGE J., AND J. L. SIMMONS
  1966 *Identities and Interactions.* New York: Free Press. Reprinted with permission of The Free Press, an imprint of Simon & Schuster. Copyright © 1966 by The Free Press.

MEAD, GEORGE HERBERT
  1934 *Mind, Self and Society.* Chicago: University of Chicago Press.
  1936 *Movements of Thought in the 19th Century.* Ed. Merritt H. Moore. Chicago: University of Chicago Press.
  1938 *The Philosophy of the Act.* Ed. Merritt H. Moore. Chicago: University of Chicago Press.
  1982 "1914 Class Lectures in Social Psychology." In David L. Miller, ed., *The Individual and the Social Self,* pp. 27–105. Chicago: University of Chicago Press.

MELTZER, BERNARD N.
  1972 *The Social Psychology of George Herbert Mead.* Kalamazoo: Center for Sociological Research, Western Michigan University.

NATANSON, MAURICE
  1973 *Social Dynamics of George Herbert Mead.* The Hague: Martinus Nijoff.

TROYER, WILLIAM LEWIS
  1946 "Mead's Social and Functional Theory of Mind." *American Sociological Review* 11:198–202.

WARRINER, CHARLES K.
  1970 *The Emergence of Society.* Homewood, Ill.: Dorsey Press.

8

Taking the Role of the Other

It has been very difficult up to now to refrain from introducing one of the central concepts in the symbolic interactionist perspective: taking the role of the other. This concept is intimately connected to every other concept discussed so far in this book. Taking the role of the other is central to the development of selfhood, it is probably the most important mind activity, and it is necessary for both the acquisition and the use of symbols.

DESCRIPTION OF THE CONCEPT

Taking the role of the other is the activity that people do in every social situation. It is how children play when they try to think and act like mom or dad, a firefighter or a teacher, a rock star or a cartoon character. It is what people do on a date when they try to figure out what the other is thinking, and it is what parents do when they try to help their children. It is also what salespeople, political leaders, and television preachers do when they try to imagine how best to appeal to those whom they are trying to influence. Role taking is *imagining the world from the perspective of another.* As we imagine, so we act; we use what we imagine to deal with the situation we confront.

When George Herbert Mead discusses the importance of significant others and the generalized other in the development of self, he emphasizes that these others who are so important to the child constitute those whose roles the child takes in viewing self. It is this ability to get outside himself or herself, and to see the world imaginatively in the roles of others, that allows the child to see himself or herself as an object, from out there.

When Mead analyzes the nature of society, he also emphasizes the importance of taking the role of the other; this time it is the role of the whole, the society. Here, he points out, it is critical for the individual to understand the point of view of the society and take it, internalize it, and then control himself or herself accordingly. Taking the role of the other for Mead is essential for human conscience and cooperation.

In a real sense, taking the role of the other (or "role taking") is best understood as *taking the perspective of the other*, seeing the world from the perspective of other individuals or groups, and directing one's own actions accordingly.

The emergence of self is clearly dependent on this process. The four stages in the development of self, discussed in Chapter 6, depend on this role-taking process:

1. *The preparatory stage:* The child *imitates the acts of significant others*; the act of symbolically imagining self from the perspective of others is not yet possible. Role taking here is a matter of imitating other individuals' acts rather than understanding their perspective. We come to imitate their acts toward *self,* and thus begin to become aware of self as an object.

2. *The play stage:* The child *takes the role of significant others,* seeing self, directing self, controlling self, judging self, identifying self, and analyzing self from the perspectives of important individuals. No organized perspective on the self has yet formed. The child takes the role of one significant other at a time.

3. *The game stage:* The child's selfhood has matured into an organized whole. Here the child *takes "their role,"* the perspective of the generalized other, assuming the role of "the Community, the Law, the rules of the game, and so on. Such role taking involves generalizing the attitudes of constituent members of the whole and reacting to one's self from the standpoint of those generalized attitudes" (Natanson, 1973, 14).

4. *The reference group stage:* The individual's self is not a single whole so much as it is divided between various social worlds. Here the self to which we communicate changes depending in part on which group's perspective is being assumed in a given situation. We are here able to assume the perspective (take the role of) *one of several groups,* depending on the situation.

This ability to take the role of the other is a central quality of the human being which does not seem to be shared with other animals. As Robin Vallacher (1980) reminds us: It is difficult for all organisms—even the human being—to overcome the "egocentric viewpoint and understand things from different points of view . . ."

> The perspective-taking inherent in self-reflection requires abstraction, the ability to manipulate symbols—words, for example—as though they were concrete objects. You do not literally "see" yourself from others' point of view; rather, you infer their conception of you in terms of abstract qualities like "sincere," "flamboyant," and "perky." (P. 7)

Taking the role of the other *is an important mind activity.* We imagine the other's perspective; we communicate that perspective to self on the basis of what we see and hear the other do. We take the other's role though inferring perspectives from the other's action. It is through mind (symbolic interaction toward the self) that individuals tell themselves how others see things and how other people's perspectives operate, and it is through mind that individuals understand the meaning that other people's words and acts have. As others act, we put ourselves into their perspectives, and we begin to understand the meaning their acts have for them. That is the essence of taking the role of the other, and it is obviously dependent on the development of mind in the individual. It is, however, so central to human activity that we are treating it as a *special mind activity* rather than including it in the chapter on the mind.

ROLE TAKING'S RELATIONSHIP TO MIND, SYMBOLS, AND SELF

Taking the role of the other is usually mind activity, but in the very initial stage, it seems to precede mind, symbols, and self in the child's development. Mead argues that role taking is first, that we come to know the *other* first, before we come to distinguish self, that the child first imitates the acts of others, and in an early presymbolic stage, assumes the action, but not yet the perspective, of the other. From this simple beginning in imitation, we might argue, come the earliest glimmerings of that object we call self, as the child directs imitative acts toward his or her self, then with self, develops mind and symbols, followed by more complex symbolic role taking, or taking the *perspective* of the other (see Figure 8–1).

The importance of the *order* of these human qualities should *not* be over emphasized because, in the long run, it makes little difference. A good case might be made for a different order, but doing so can be like splitting hairs or counting the number of angels dancing on the tip of a needle. It matters little. The important point is that the four qualities are linked together and are interdependent in their development. It is most accurate, perhaps, to see self, symbols, mind, and role taking *emerging together* as we interact with others. Something such as the diagram in Figure 8–2 would be in order.

Another way of showing the interdependence is to indicate how each of these qualities arise only because of the other three. Self arises from symbols, mind, and role taking; mind arises from self, symbols, and role taking; symbols

FIGURE 8–1

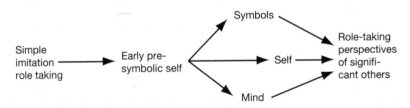

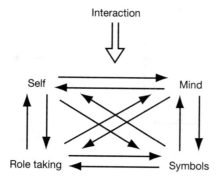

FIGURE 8–2

arise from self, mind, and role taking; and role taking arises from self, mind, and symbols. Briefly, let us turn our attention to these in turn.

Self

The self arises only because the actor possesses symbols, uses mind, and takes the role of the other (Figure 8–3).

The emergence of self arises from symbolic action by others toward the actor. Others use symbols to talk to, encourage, restrain, identify, and describe the actor. The actor takes these same symbols to act back on himself or herself. The human being comes to understand who he or she is through using symbols, and throughout life continuously uses symbols in all actions taken toward self.

Mind is also necessary for self. It is only through the action—with symbols—the actor performs internally, that he or she becomes aware of self, takes note of self, perceives self, judges self, and develops identities.

Role taking is how we originally see ourselves. It is through the perspectives of others that we become aware of self and act toward self.

FIGURE 8–3

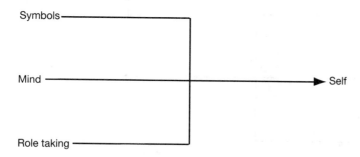

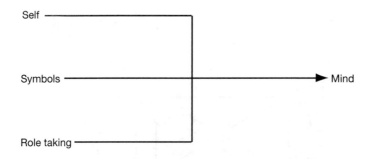

FIGURE 8–4

Mind

Mind exists only because the actor has self, symbols, and the ability to take the role of the other (Figure 8–4).

Self is a necessary ingredient for mind. Mind is all covert action the actor takes toward self. Thus, self is assumed for there to be mind.

Symbols constitute the other ingredient for mind. All action toward the self is symbolic. We point things out to self through labeling and describing these with symbols. We manipulate things through symbolic action.

Taking the role of the other makes mind possible through creating both self and symbols.

Symbols

Symbols arise because the actor possesses mind, the ability to role take, and self (Figure 8–5).

Mind makes symbols possible. A symbol is a representation that the actor understands; that is, it is meaningful to the actor in that the actor communicates to self at the same time he or she communicates to others.

Role taking is also necessary for symbols. As we act symbolically toward others, Mead emphasizes, we imagine the reaction of those to whom we communicate.

FIGURE 8–5

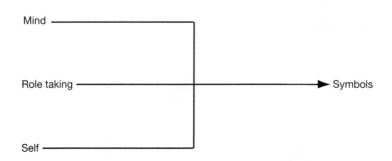

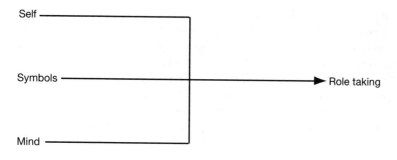

FIGURE 8–6

Self makes symbols possible. To be a symbol, an act of communication must be communicated back toward the self. When we think with symbols, we act toward the self; when we communicate to others with symbols, we know what we are doing—we must talk back toward our self.

Role Taking

Role taking is dependent on self, symbols, and mind (Figure 8–6).

Self is necessary for role taking. It is the object toward which we communicate as we take the perspective of others.

Symbols are the tools which allow us to escape our own bodies and imagine the world from the outside. Imagination is representing the environment symbolically; imagining other people's perspectives is symbolically communicating their perspectives to ourselves.

Mind makes role taking possible. Indeed, role taking is one type of mind action. Role taking is made possible because we are able to tell ourselves what is going on in our environment, including how others perceive the situation in which we are acting.

The point of this description is to show the *interconnectedness* of these concepts. In a real sense, they make one another possible and they arise together. The difficulties we face in trying to separate them in a clear manner should be obvious. We are really talking about specific qualities whose real significance is grasped only when we put them together.

THE IMPORTANCE OF ROLE TAKING

Its Central Place in All Social Interaction

Obviously, taking the role of the other is much more than the child playing at the roles of others. Play is a good example of role taking, but role taking is done by both children and adults in more serious moments, indeed, in all interaction with others. The child takes some cookies, then looks at the parent's stern face and searches that face in order to determine the meaning that the face is giving off, the action that is symbolized. The child tries to see himself or herself at that moment from the parent's perspective in order to know if it is best to laugh or cry or run away or look sorry. Understanding the meaning of others demands that we role take, so that we understand from the other's perspective. So role taking is more important than play and more important than simply figuring out mom's view of our cookie stealing: It becomes an integral part of all interaction, *necessary for understanding the other and being understood by the other.*

If we pause a second and analyze our everyday interaction, it will become more and more obvious how important role taking is. The child figures out what adults are thinking in order to please them, to manipulate them, to get the most from them, to escape bad consequences, and sometimes just to be left alone. The child takes the role of other children and figures out how to stay away from fights, how to win in a game, how to make and keep friends. The conscientious parent takes the role of the child in order to know what the child needs at any moment. The teacher figures out what students need through taking their role, and the students figure out what the teacher wants through taking his or her role. A good salesperson knows what customers want by taking their roles and saying the right things. The employee who is totally dependent on the employer must know the employer through role taking and must be careful to conform or know how far he or she can go without bringing forth negative sanctions. The employer who is all-powerful need not always take the employee's role, but if this perspective is totally ignored, the employer may go too far and end up with hostile employees, low morale, and high turnover. We take the role of the other when we love or feel sorry for another, and we take the role of the other when we want to exploit or use the other.

Taking the role of the other can lead us to see things from the perspective of someone different from us, can cause us to understand that perspective and respect the person, and can make us more tolerant and loving. On the other hand, taking the role of the other can cause us to see other people's perspectives, and we can use that to manipulate them and gain our own interests without concern for them. Taking the role of the other may help us understand the problems of the poor and cause us to take action to work for the poor, or it can help us take advantage of the poor, exploit them, and become rich at their expense.

Nine Ways Role Taking Is Central to All Human Life

Taking the role of the other, or taking the perspective of the other, is a basic part of all interaction. Its importance must not be missed. In the following pages we analyze systematically its contribution to all interaction, to the individual, and to all group life.

1. *Taking the role of the other is important to the emergence of the self.* Mead (1934) makes this point clearly:

> The individual experiences himself as such, not directly, but only indirectly, from the particular standpoints of other individual members of the same social group, or from the generalized standpoint of the social group as a whole to which he belongs. For he enters his own experience as a self or individual, not directly or immediately, not by becoming a subject to himself, but only in so far as he first becomes an object to himself just as other individuals are objects to him or in his experience; and he becomes an object to himself only by taking the attitudes of other individuals toward himself within a social environment or context of experience and behavior in which both he and they are involved. (P. 138)*

The child takes the role of significant others, then develops a generalized other, whose perspective becomes important in the judgment of self, direction of self, and all the other self processes discussed earlier:

> So the self reaches its full development by organizing these individual attitudes of others into the organized social or group attitudes, and by thus becoming an individual reflection of the general systematic pattern of social or group behavior in which it and the others are all involved. . . . (P. 158)

2. *Taking the role of the other is important for action we take toward the self in all situations.* We take the role of the other and converse with ourselves and direct our actions accordingly. We direct ourselves, at least in part, according to what we think others will think of our acts (if not others in the situation we are in, then perhaps significant others or reference groups outside the situation). Direction of the self according to the controls of society is what we mean by social control, and this becomes possible through role taking. Each situation calls for self-communication, including self-control and self-direction, and this involves role taking in the situation. Mead (1936) describes the important link between role taking and social control:

> This of course, is what gives the principle of social control, not simply the social control that results from blind habit, but a social control that comes from the individual assuming the same attitude toward himself that the community assumes toward him . . . he will be acting toward himself as others act toward him. He will admonish himself as others would. That is, he will recognize what are his duties as well as what are his rights. He takes the attitude of the community toward himself. This gives the principal method of organization which . . . belongs to human society and distinguishes it from social organization which one finds among ants and bees and termites. (P. 377)

We exercise self-control and self-direction by understanding "the other," and that is done through the process of taking the role of the other in

*Reprinted from *Mind, Self and Society* by George Herbert Mead, by permission of The University of Chicago Press. Copyright © 1934 by The University of Chicago. All rights reserved.

each situation. We must also, in the same way, identify our selves, judge our selves, and analyze ourselves in situations; to do so demands role taking. Indeed, as was pointed out in the chapter on self, what we think of self—our self-judgment—is in large part a looking-glass image, gained through the eyes of others whose roles we take.

3. *Taking the role of the other is important for learning our perspectives on all things.* We learn how to view reality through interacting and learning the perspectives of others, not through memorizing them by rote but through understanding the others' view by taking their role. Learning the perspectives of others—from Socrates to Jesus, from the Ku Klux Klan to the Republican party, from our father to our tenth-grade world history teacher, from ancient Greece to American society in the 1970s—is to actively take the role of the other and to see from another perspective. Indeed, if this book is to be a learning experience for anyone, then reading it demands role taking: What is Charon trying to say anyway? Where's he coming from? To gain a perspective is to understand the other through taking his or her role and to come to share that perspective.

4. *Taking the role of the other is necessary for working through all social situations.* We enter a social situation and know what to do in part by taking the role of others in the situation and acting in ways expected of us, or by doing things contrary to what is expected but still within the bounds of acceptability of others in the situation, or by purposely upsetting the expectations and the situation. When we take the role of the others in the situation, according to Anselm Strauss (1959, 59), we must assess the others in terms of (1) their general intent, (2) their response toward themselves, and (3) their responses and feelings toward us. This ongoing assessment causes us to look at our own acts, which in turn leads to further action. The point is that others do indeed make a difference most of the time in what we do, and to figure out what to do in a situation we must take the role of the other. Indeed, that is crucial if we act and then want feedback from others concerning our action. We must see ourselves from the perspective of others in the situation to know what to do next.

5. *Taking the role of the other helps the individual control the interaction situation through knowing how to manipulate, direct, or control others.* The good salesperson, the good con artist, the good lover, the good politician, or the good advertising person knows the perspectives of those interacted with because he or she must "give them what they want," must persuade others to do or think a certain way: This is done through effective role taking. The effective teacher takes the role of the students, the successful student knows how to take the role of the teacher, and the good parent knows how his or her children think and may use that to influence them to go to bed. In a real sense, to know how to take the role of the other brings power in interpersonal relationships.

6. *Taking the role of the other is necessary for love.* Love implies respect for the other's ways, the other's ideas, the other's goals and values, and to have this respect demands understanding at least minimally the other from his or her perspective. Some of us may empathize with the other—see the other person's feelings, ideas, perspective, and problems and understand objectively what he or she is feeling. Some of us may come to sympathize with the other—not only understanding objectively but also *feeling* the concerns, the problems, and emotions of the other. Sympathy and empathy both demand understanding the other. Real concern for others, being able to give to others, to act in relation to their needs, demands first and foremost that we understand the other. This means understanding from the other's perspective; this means taking the role of the other.

7. *Taking the role of the other is basic to human cooperation.* To cooperate means to know where the others are at, what they are doing, and often, what they are thinking:

> By taking the attitude of the others in the group in their co-operative, highly complex activity, the individual is able to enter into their experiences. The engineer is able to direct vast groups of individuals in a highly complex process. But in every direction he gives, he takes the attitude of the person whom he is directing. It has the same meaning to him that it has to others. We enter in this way into the attitudes of others, and in that way we make our very complex societies possible. (Mead, 1936, 375)

Complex group behavior demands not only a division of labor but also an understanding of how one's own behavior fits into a whole process; knowledge of others' tasks is essential for this. To coordinate one's acts with others demands a certain amount of understanding where others are going. Cooperation at any level demands the simultaneous understanding of one's own acts and the meaning of others' acts:

> Coordination requires that each participant be able to anticipate the movements of the others, and it is for this purpose that men who are cooperating watch one another . . . anticipating what another human being is likely to do requires getting "inside" of him. (Shibutani, 1961, 141)

The football team, the marriage partners, the committee that makes the decisions for the annual dance, the General Motors Corporation—in each there must be people role taking, understanding and anticipating one another's actions, if any kind of cooperative action is to take place toward a goal. If we do not role take we are doomed to keep bumping into each other, duplicating tasks, unable to adjust our own acts to the other's acts—all of which, of course, make cooperation impossible.

8. *Taking the role of the other is the basis for human symbolic communication.* To understand the other demands taking the other's role in order to understand

where the other is "coming from," to see the meaning of the other's words and acts. Meaning is obtained through determining what a word or act represents— to the other. This suggests that the individual must "complete imaginatively the total act which a gesture stands for," and to do that "must put himself in the position of the other person, must identify with him" (Meltzer, 1972, 14). That is also true when we try to communicate with the other. We must understand where the other is at in order to get him or her to understand our words or acts:

> To indicate to another what he is to do, one has to make the indication from the standpoint of that other; to order the victim to put up his hands the robber has to see this response in terms of the victim making it. Correspondingly, the victim has to see the command from the standpoint of the robber who gives the command; he has to grasp the intention and forthcoming action of the robber. Such mutual role taking is the *sine qua non* of communication and effective symbolic interaction. (Blumer, 1969, 10)

Indeed, Mead's whole definition of the symbol, which is the basis of human communication, is dependent on role taking. Miller (1973) summarizes Mead's position: In making a significant gesture, "there is a triadic relation: 0_1 by taking the role of the other, stimulates himself in turn to respond as 0_2 will respond to 0_1's gesture" (p. 91). I am stimulated by my own words as I speak to you. That stimulation comes from my imagining the effects my words will have on you, and these effects are known by me only through taking your role in the situation. "The significant gesture involves two fundamental elements: First, the individual making the significant gesture places himself in the position of the individual to whom his gesture is addressed; second, from the point of view of the other, the individual then regards the content of his own gesture" (Natanson, 1973, 8). We do that all day long as we interact with countless others. It is impossible to be fully *aware* of our own role taking, for that would demand too much from the human being. However, continuous attempts at taking the role of others as we communicate are evident if we take the time to notice. There are times, of course, when we must very deliberately take the other's role, such as when we want to make certain that others understand us, and then we may become very aware of the other's cues as to whether or not we are being understood. A question by the other about what we are saying tells us, in a sense, if we are indeed being understood, and when we say to ourselves "What a stupid question that is!" we are usually recognizing that the other is not understanding us. A good public speaker, a good teacher, a good politician, or a good comedian makes sure that he or she is understood exactly, and that necessitates carefully taking the role of the other.

> It becomes communication when the individual indicating the object takes also the attitude of the individual to whom he is indicating it plus that of his response, while the individual to whom the object is indicated takes the attitude of him who is indicating it (Mead, 1938, 51).

Mead (1936) more clearly states this same idea in this more extensive passage:

> The common expression of this is that a man knows what he is saying when the meaning of what he is saying comes to him as readily as it goes to another. He is affected just as the other is. If the meaning of what he says affects the other, it affects himself in the same way. The result of this is that the individual who speaks, in some sense takes the attitude of the other whom he addresses. We are familiar with this in giving directions to another person to do something. We find ourselves affected by the same direction. We are ready to do the thing and perhaps become irritated by the awareness of the other and insist on doing it ourselves. We have called out in ourselves the same response we have asked for in another person. We are taking his attitude. It is through this sort of participation, this taking the attitudes of other individuals, that the peculiar character of human intelligence is constituted. (P. 379)

9. *Finally, taking the role of the other allows us to see the present both from our own past and from future perspectives.* We are able to imagine how the perspective that we held ten years ago would view what we do now. Or we may imagine how we would view what we do now ten years hence. This ability to take the role of ourselves outside the present means that whatever we do in the present can be tempered not only by other people in our past, present, and future but also by our own perspectives from our past and future. "Two years ago I would never have done such a thing." "If I marry this person now, what will I think of this decision five years from now?" "If I sign this agreement today, will I be sorry for it tomorrow?" "How can I live with myself if I do this?"

AND IF WE DON'T ROLE TAKE—SO WHAT?

In a very basic sense, the ability to take the role of the other amounts to what we might term "social intelligence." It is basic to all we do as we interact with others. If we are highly capable role takers, and if we actually make use of this ability, then we will be more able to understand others, to meet the expectations of others if we choose, to bend the rules and not get into trouble with the authorities unnecessarily, to rebel successfully in light of unjust demands, to direct others rather than to be directed, to love, to cooperate, and to communicate effectively with others.

Role-taking skills are probably not the only important skills for success in interaction situations, but they are probably the most important ones. Their importance might become even clearer if we try to understand what happens when individuals do not effectively take the role of the other while acting in situations. Here are a few examples; I am sure each reader can add another fifty.

1. The "cool" guy who is trying to talk it up with a young woman, treating her the way he treats all the women he has met before, not being sensitive to her perspective, her definition of him, her definition of herself,

her reference groups. She happens to be head of Dakota National Organization for Women. He talks. She listens. She talks. He leaves.

2. The teacher who runs the class without taking the role of the students. He is also doomed to fail. Mr. Mumble-to-himself is busy playing with words but does not attempt to see himself or what he is saying from his students' perspective. He just keeps rollin' on; then he can never really understand why those kids don't know what he is trying to teach them.

3. Then there are the many misunderstandings and conflicts that arise between parents and children. Each is intent on seeing the world from his or her own perspective. Interpretations seem right, and the other seems old-fashioned, rebellious, irrational, or crazy. Instead of compromise or negotiation, the result is confrontation or running away from one another. In fact, even manipulating the other is impossible, because manipulation demands knowing how to deal with someone effectively, and that begins with understanding the situation from his or her perspective.

Family life, possibly the most intimate interaction we participate in, is filled with role taking and problems that result from inaccurate role taking. The list seems endless. We are role taking whenever we are with others. Failure to role take or inaccurate role taking will inevitably have implications for the continuation of interaction. A friend of mine in economics, thinking that he had discovered a profound truth one day, confessed to me: "You know, Joel, there is no way that I can ever really know what's going on in your head. No matter how well we know each other, we cannot penetrate what's going on in the other person's head." Of course he is right, and we all know it. However, role taking is still something we all do: (1) We take the role of the other continuously in interaction; (2) we must do this in order to understand the other, in order to communicate effectively and to cooperate; and (3) the fact that we cannot role take perfectly makes the individual's life both exciting and highly complex, makes group life continuously tenuous, and demands that we always attempt to open up communication with those with whom we wish to interact. Most important, if we have difficulty taking the role of the other through observing action, then it is incumbent on us to ask the other, "What is going on in your head?" Otherwise, our goals, whatever they are, will not be achieved. George McCall and J. L. Simmons (1966) realistically describe the difficulty inherent in role taking:

> Our images of people will always contain some admixture of truth and error but . . . this must be a *workable* admixture. That is to say, it must contain just enough of the relevant truth about our alter to allow us to take minimally successful action toward him. Seldom are we truly *en rapport* with him, for we do not truly know him. Ordinarily, we understand him just well enough to work out a sort of fumbling, on-again accommodation in which we manage to get along with, and past, one another without serious conflict. Only rarely, and then most often in quite intimate relationships, do we truly communicate and interact in harmony. (Pp. 123–24)*

*Reprinted from *Identities and Interactions* by George J. McCall and J. L. Simmons, by permission of The Free Press, an imprint of Simon & Schuster. Copyright © 1966 by The Free Press.

Not a great deal has been done in examining the qualities necessary for accurate role taking, but McCall and Simmons (pp. 135–36) list two that they feel are important:

1. "Amount and breadth of our experiences." Our ability arises in part from a wide range of experiences with various individuals and various roles. Further, we also come to understand "from observing the counterrole performances of those who have interacted with us."
2. Our ability also depends on the nature of the other person's identity, whether or not what he or she is doing is known to us, and whether or not it is a recognized line of action.

SUMMARY

Self, mind, and taking the role of the other, which have been the topics of the last three chapters, are concerned with human *covert activity*, activity that is not directly seen by others but must be inferred. It is maintained throughout this book that this kind of activity is central to human life, that individuals and groups can be understood only by taking account of covert activity, and that covert activity is basic to all that we do overtly toward things and toward other people. Figure 8–7 summarizes the points made in the chapters on mind and role taking.

Taking the role of the other, the central topic in this chapter, is a truly wondrous ability. It makes social interaction more than the interaction of billiard balls or other physical objects, for it causes us to include the constant attempt by actors to understand the acts of others by putting themselves into the perspectives of the others. Role taking enters our lives in at least nine ways, each one contributing to understanding the covert and overt action throughout all of our lives. It is responsible for the emergence of self and it plays a big role in what we see ourselves as and what we say to ourselves in every situation. We learn our own perspectives through taking the role of the other. We know how to act by doing this, and we are able to influence others if we do this well. Taking the role of the other is necessary for love, human cooperation, and human symbolic communication. And, finally, it allows us all to imagine the present from both our past and future perspectives. It is, in truth, one of the important keys to understanding all human action.

Mind activity—including taking the role of the other—is only part of the activity that humans engage in. The other side of the coin is overt activity, which is action open to the senses of others. It is overt activity that is necessary for our dealing with our environment and achieving our goals there; it is overt activity that has consequences for what other people do; it is overt activity that gives others a clue to our covert activity; and it is the overt activity of others that allows us to understand their covert activity.

It is time, therefore, to turn our attention to overt action, and from there, move to a discussion of social action and social interaction. This is what we will do in Chapters 9 and 10.

FIGURE 8–7

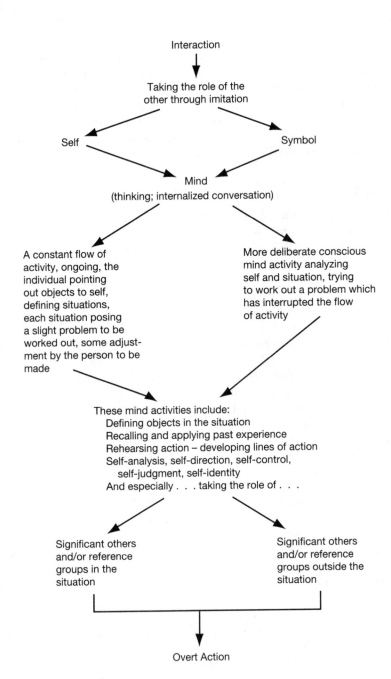

REFERENCES

BLUMER, HERBERT
1969 *Symbolic Interactionism: Perspective and Method.* Englewood Cliffs, N.J.: Prentice Hall. Copyright © 1969. Reprinted by permission of Prentice Hall.

McCALL, GEORGE J., AND J. L. SIMMONS
1966 *Identities and Interactions.* New York: Free Press. Reprinted with permission of The Free Press, an imprint of Simon & Schuster. Copyright © 1966 by The Free Press.

MEAD, GEORGE HERBERT
1934 *Mind, Self and Society.* Chicago: University of Chicago Press. Reprinted by permission of The University of Chicago Press. Copyright © 1934 by The University of Chicago. All rights reserved.

1936 *Movements of Thought in the 19th Century.* Ed. Merritt H. Moore. Chicago: University of Chicago Press.

1938 *The Philosophy of the Act.* Ed. Merritt H. Moore. Chicago: University of Chicago Press.

MELTZER, BERNARD N.
1972 *The Social Psychology of George Herbert Mead.* Kalamazoo: Center for Sociological Research, Western Michigan University.

MILLER, DAVID L.
1973 "Mead's Theory of Universals." In Walter Robert Corti, ed., *The Philosophy of George Herbert Mead*, pp. 89–106. Winterthur, Switzerland: Amriswiler Bucherei.

NATANSON, MAURICE
1973 *The Social Dynamics of George Herbert Mead.* The Hague: Martinus Nijoff.

SHIBUTANI, TAMOTSU
1961 *Society and Personality: An Interactionist Approach to Social Psychology.* Englewood Cliffs, N.J.: Prentice Hall. Copyright © 1961. Reprinted by permission of Prentice Hall.

STRAUSS, ANSELM
1959 *Mirrors and Masks.* New York: Free Press.

VALLACHER, ROBIN R.
1980 "An Introduction to Self Theory." In Daniel M. Wegner and Robin R. Vallacher, eds., *The Self in Social Psychology*, pp. 3–30. New York: Oxford University Press.

9

Human Action

In Chapter 3 we looked at the philosophical foundations of symbolic interactionism. In particular we examined pragmatism, and we emphasized that pragmatists concentrate on *action,* on what human beings *do,* rather than on what they *are* as individuals or as part of groups. To pragmatists human beings are understood as doers rather than persons, actors rather than personalities. Social scientists, according to Charles Warriner (1970), should emphasize *"action* as the ultimate referent for our ideas of man, as the source of all of our basic data about man, and as the focus of our questions about man" (pp. 6–7). Humans *act,* and from this action we can come to understand both the individual and the group. It is from a consistency in *action* over time, for example, that social scientists are able to infer "personality," and it is from a consistency in *action* between actors that a group or society is inferred. We also infer change in the individual or in the group from action. "The action orientation says that persons and societies are to be known through what they *do,* are to be postulated from continuities in action and conduct and that both [persons and societies] are equivalent inferences from these observations" (Warriner, 1970;8).

This chapter concentrates on *human action.* All the topics covered in earlier chapters come together here as we investigate the nature and causes of human action. And, after all, isn't that what thoughtful people really want to know: Why do we all act as we do?

THE "STREAM OF ACTION"

The reality of action is that it is continuous, a constant process that is never ending except when we die. It is best described as a *stream of action.* "This stream of action is complex, manifold, multiplex. It is the full reality with many aspects, characteristics, features, dimensions, and interconnections" (Warriner, 1970;15). The actor does not stop acting along this stream. One act leads to another; acts overlap; action flows with only arbitrary lines separating one "act" from another. The word "stream" describes exactly what is meant by human action.

Streams of water constantly change direction; human action also is to be understood as changing direction. We act, and our stream goes one way, then another. Our lives change direction constantly, sometimes in small ways, occasionally in very significant ways. Barriers in the water change the direction of the stream, different environments do, and changes in the weather might. So too do our directions change as we encounter new situations, as new factors enter our lives. Streams of water change because smaller brooks enter and cause a change in the direction. So too do other people—individuals and groups—enter our stream of action, and as we interact with them our directions are changed, too.

This description of human action as an ongoing stream of action is not all that obvious to a casual observer. Most of us tend to focus attention on single, isolated acts. He stole a pig; she took a bus to the store; he robbed a bank; she just completed her exam; he became a lawyer; he did the dishes tonight; she put the kids to bed. This kind of description seems sensible and accurate, but it does not describe what the actor really does, because it divides this never-ending stream into manageable segments. We watch others and we label their acts; we look at our own action and we label those acts. It is really impossible to capture this never-ending stream, even though that is in fact a more accurate portrayal.

Actually, the comparison with a stream of water is misleading in two ways. For one thing, human beings actually engage in two streams of action simulatneously. Thus far, we have focused on a stream of overt action. However, humans also engage in a continous *stream of covert action*. We are actively and continuously engaged in an ongoing conversation with ourselves about what we are encountering and doing in the situation. The novelist captures this when he or she describes the "stream of consciousness" of the main character, the internal discussion the character is having about the situation he or she is in. We see the thinking that goes into the decisions and actions, because the novelist recognizes the importance of the steam of covert action. Just as our stream of overt action is continuous and flowing in directions, so does our stream of covert action. Both are important, and both influence one another. There is absolutely no reason to believe that water "has a mind of its own," or that a continuous stream of consciousness accompanies what a stream of water does.

The second reason the water analogy is misleading is tied to the first. Because humans engage in a covert stream of action along with the overt, they are *active in their stream*, not passive as water is. Water responds to its environment. It flows because of the environmental conditions it exists in. Humans, however, make active decisions along their stream, deciding what to do as they go along, and therefore have some control over their directions. We evaluate our own action, we change our minds and establish new goals and redefine objects in new ways. When we interact with others we evaluate their acts, we role take, we interpret their actions and their acts of symbolic

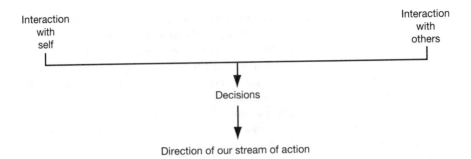

FIGURE 9–1

communication. Our relationship with the environment is therefore different from a stream of water because we determine our own directions to some extent. We are not simply pushed around by the outside environment acting on us; we are in control of our overt action. We need to see human action as illustrated in Figure 9–1.

Decision making is therefore ongoing. It has a long history, and in most cases an isolated decision must be understood within this historical context if it is to be understood. We do not simply make a decision and fix our direction in life or even end up doing a certain isolated act. We make many decisions as we go along, and this fact needs to be recognized. To decide something does not simply cause something. We do not simply make one decision to go to college—to go to college takes a number of decisions, and even if we end up going, if we are going to remain there, a large number of decisions need to be made that keep us in that particular direction. We do not simply decide to marry someone, or decide on a particular major. In every case many decisions are made to cause us to go in that direction. A series of decisions will reaffirm, slightly alter, or completely change the decisions we made earlier. And this decision making is constantly being influenced by our interaction with others and with self along the way. What others do in relation to us makes a difference to the decisions we make; in defining goals and objects along our stream we ourselves will also make a difference.

THE ACT

We all divide human action into separate acts because it is useful for us to do so. It helps us understand what is taking place; it gives us a handle on what others are doing as well as what we ourselves are doing. Like everything else, we divide up action in a way that makes sense to us at the moment. Any way we divide it is somewhat artificial, but it must be done to survive. It is important to realize that whatever way we divide action is, of course, limited and incomplete, and changes as our purposes change.

From our common-sense point of view, the human is thought to take part in a number of separate acts in a single day—we get up, wash ourselves, get dressed, make breakfast, eat breakfast, leave the house, start the car, drive the car, park it, arrive at the office, and collapse in our office chair for a morning nap. Of course, no one can capture all that an individual does in a single morning. If asked, the actor may combine all these small acts into "I went to work," or at lunch we might wonder, "Did I turn off the stove after breakfast?" We each divide up our stream of action in a number of ways, isolate individual acts that sometimes take a moment or might even take days. We give those acts names and apply them to situations at the moment. In this sense, then, *acts are social objects* the actor pulls out of the stream of action in order to decide something in the present. Each act, it should be noted, is like all other social objects: It is named, its name is social, and it changes as our use for it changes. Acts that we point out to one another and to ourselves are like the people, plants, physical objects, and symbols that we also point out. A given act, Warriner (1970) writes:

> is recognized by the members of the society as a unit act with a particular meaning. . . . The "sawing of a board" by a carpenter has primary significance for sociological purposes, not because it involves certain muscles and nerves, not because the carpenter has particular motivations, not even because the board gets sawed, but because the act is given a name, conceptually separated from the other parts or aspects of the stream of action. . . . "Thumbing one's nose," "punishing the child," "giving a speech," "going to church," "riding a bus," "going to class" . . . are all . . . acts because they are named and are identified by the conventional understandings of the members of the society. (Pp. 17–18)

Therefore, anything that humans do that is also given a name is an "act." Consistent with the chapter on mind, action includes covert action, so "thinking about a good meal," or "thinking about how to get away from an embarrassing situation," and "telling oneself not to be afraid" are all acts. "Eating a meal," "excusing oneself from a conversation," and "telling a big bully to get lost" are also acts, overt acts.

The way we divide up our stream of action and pull out segments, calling them by name, depends on the perspective we use. Some perspectives, for example, emphasize large units of action (driving a car to California), whereas others emphasize much smaller units (turning the key in the ignition). Our stream looks different from the point of view of a teenager than that of a middle-aged person, or that of an older person. An hour in our life will appear different to us if we look at it from the perspective of a wounded lover or a jealous lover or someone yearning to be free. Each segment in our stream will take on different degrees of importance—yet the actual stream of action stays the same.

One way we can understand the arbitrary nature of dividing our stream of action into separated acts in order to simplify understanding is to consider the whole notion of "decades." What is a decade? It is a ten-year period in society's ongoing stream of action, pulled out and labeled. It always begins with a year whose last digit is zero and ends with one whose last digit is nine. Think about it: Decades are really artificial arbitrary descriptions created for convenience sake:

> But being in and of itself nothing more than a chronological succession of ten numbers, a decade is soon invested by people with its own distinctive themes and motifs, thereby imparting into it a characteristic symbolic texture as well. The symbolic profile of a decade comes then to so rule collective memory that syntonic events falling somewhat outside the precise chronological boundaries of the ten-year span are assimilated to it while dystonic events actually falling within the chronological decade are either overlooked or, if occurring near either terminus of the ten-year span, are assigned conveniently to the adjacent decade with whose themes and motifs they can better resonate. (Davis, 1984;16)

Just as we divide recent history into decades and distant history into centuries, so too do we constantly divide our own lives and the lives of others into separate acts. In reality, however, there is only a constant stream of action. The reality of action is an ongoing process of decision making and doing things in relation to our environment, the environment outside and inside each of us.

ACTION, GOALS, AND SOCIAL OBJECTS

The symbolic interactionist, like everyone else, divides up the stream of action so that action is meaningful and manageable for understanding. We conveniently divide action into individual acts. Acts are sometimes even said to have a "beginning" and an "end," but such designations are usually used only for analytical purposes. Most symbolic interactionists understand full well the fact that individual acts are simply social objects pulled out from the ongoing stream of action.

Action exists in situations. Individuals define situations and act according to those definitions. We define goals, immediate or distant, and we see objects in the situation around those goals. We are planners; we use objects according to our plans. Social objects are those objects useful for achieving goals in a given situation. George McCall and J. L. Simmons (1966) describe the human being as a "thinker, a planner, a schemer," who

> continuously constructs plans of action . . . out of bits and pieces of plans left lying around by his culture, fitting them together in endless permutations of the larger patterns and motifs that the culture presents as models. The ubiquitous planning is carried on at all levels of awareness, not always verbally but always conceptually. (P. 60)[*]

---

[*]Reprinted from Identities and Interactions by George J. McCall and J. L. Simmons, by permission of The Free Press, an imprint of Simon & Schuster. Copyright © 1966 by The Free Press.

Each act begins with defined goals, and each ends with goals achieved, altered, or forgotten. Objects in the situation become tied to our goals in the situation, and they are defined according to our use for them; objects become part of our plan. Objects, of course, include other people, self, past acts, symbols, and so on. We act in a stream of action that does not stop for us during the day but focuses on first one goal and set of objects in a situation, then another goal and set of objects in another situation. My goal is to get to George's house as soon as possible. I see Marsha down the street. I decide to talk briefly to Marsha, or evade her, or kiss her and run along, or shake her hand, or treat her with cool respect, or reject her completely—and I act overtly based on that decision. Action toward the object may change during the course of action—for example, Marsha might tell me she is about to quit her job, and my goal may immediately change to trying to convince Marsha that her plan is not wise. Thus, my definition of Marsha as "someone to greet and get away from as soon as possible" is replaced by a definition of Marsha as "someone to take the time to help." I may eventually achieve my goal in getting to George's house—after helping Marsha solve her problem, giving Mark the brush, running across a beautiful lawn that is graced with a "Please Do Not Walk on the Grass" sign, and waiting for what seems like forever for a train to pass. Once at George's house my goals will change again, my social objects will be transformed, and, for example, Mark may now become someone that I had better call to explain why I was in so great a hurry. Indeed, now that I am at George's and I see who else is there, my action may be organized around getting out of George's house as soon as possible.

Each act, then, although separated for purposes of analysis, is in fact part of an ongoing stream of action. Each act has a goal or goals as well as social objects, and each involves decisions by the actor:

> In carrying out that line of action, he has to take note of things in the situation as that situation appears to him. The line of action, accordingly, may take new directions, new twists, in terms of what the individual points out to himself in that situation. Objects that the individual notes act back upon the line of action being executed. The line of action in which the individual is engaged is of great significance in determining what kinds of objects he's going to select out of what confronts him. (Blumer, 1981;114)

The human, from the moment of waking in the morning to the moment of falling asleep at night, is engaged in a continuous stream of action toward an innumerable list of social objects that are defined around a great number of goals. He or she changes lines of action, alters direction, redefines goals, and redirects action as objects in the environment act back.

The actor we make love to is someone we feel affection for, try to give happiness to, and gain happiness from. Making love is an act, and once it has been completed, our goals change immediately, objects take on new meaning, and our action changes direction. The beautiful, wonderful person whom we desired to make love to is redefined as one to speak softly to, to share a meal with, to joke with, perhaps to quietly say goodbye to until later in the day or week. As we leave that person's presence, he or she becomes someone to remember with affection, perhaps someone to talk about to parents or friends. But as we leave, we walk toward an elevator, and we act toward the button in order to get downstairs, in order to leave the building, in order to make our appointment at two o'clock. Other social objects have begun to replace our loved one ever so slowly, and our stream of action continues, centered on new goals and objects. As we prepare for bed at night, our thoughts may be directed toward the morning hours, so our action includes setting the alarm, picking out our clothes, perhaps preparing a lunch that we will take to work the next day. We might recall the isolated act of love during the previous day, making that into a social object, and feeling good. As we awaken the next day, the stream of action continues, guiding us from one social object to another. Herbert Blumer (1969) points out: "In this process, given lines of action may be started or stopped, they may be abandoned or postponed, they may be confined to mere planning or to an inner life of reverie, or if initiated, they may be transformed" (p. 16). But the action continues throughout our waking day, directions always changing, sometimes slightly, sometimes greatly.

MEAD'S FOUR STAGES OF THE ACT

If we decide to dissect the stream of action in order to understand an isolated act, we can also try to dissect the isolated act, realizing of course that beginnings and ends of individual acts or their parts are difficult to delineate clearly and that drawing lines is artificial. For purposes of understanding the nature of human action, George Herbert Mead breaks up the individual act into four stages: impulse, perception, manipulation, and consummation. Although most symbolic interactionists do not see these stages exactly as Mead did, nor do they give them the importance he did, it is widely recognized that the four stages represent a further understanding of human action.

Stage 1: Impulse

The act begins when the organism is in "a state of disequilibrium." There is "discomfort leading to behavior" and an "activation through disruption." *Impulse* is simply a "generalized disposition to act." It does not tell the organism what to do nor even what goal to achieve. It does not determine the direction of the act but only that there will be action of some sort. In every situation there is at least slight disequilibrium, discomfort, and disruption, and the organism must act out in the environment. Humans act from a state of slight or great disturbance that does not come only once in a while but characterizes their entire life (description borrowed from Shibutani, 1961;65–66).

Other symbolic interactionists do not go so far as to give a reason for the beginning of the act: We act, and that's all there is to it. John Dewey (1922) states that the human being "is an active being and that is all to be said on that score" (p. 119). Gregory Stone and Harvey Farberman (1970) announce proudly: "Man simply acts, period!" (p. 467). In essence most symbolic interactionists simply *assume* action on the part of the organism and pay little attention to why an act begins, focusing instead on understanding the direction that action takes. Mead's "impulse" is not developed extensively in the literature and is still somewhat vague, yet imbalance or disequilibrium seems as good a reason as any for the beginning of an act.

Perhaps a personal note might be introduced here. Throughout this book it has been emphasized that human beings are goal directed and problem solvers. Each situation is unique and thus is a challenge to the individual. We might simply suggest that an act begins with a problem to be solved, a goal to be reached, something to be overcome by the human being in the environment.

Stage 2: Perception

Humans perceive—or define—their situation. The acting organism seeks out objects and notices and defines aspects of the environment that can be used to attain goals in the situation. Objects are seen by us as useful to what we seek, and we act toward them accordingly. "Stimuli, therefore, do not initiate activity; they are pivots for redirection . . ." (Shibutani, 1961;68). The individual acts in a world of meaning, a world of objects, social objects, that have become defined according to their use for achieving goals and solving problems in a situation. Perception and definition are done by actors who have goals; the process is selective and ongoing. This part of the act is central to Mead's (1936) conceptualization of human action: ". . . for an intelligent human being his thinking is the most important part of what he does and the larger part of that thinking is a process of the analysis of situations, finding out just what it is that ought to be attacked, what has to be avoided" (p. 403).

Mead explains how this second stage is related to the first: Our goals in a situation are formed in order to restore our equilibrium; that is, we decide to go to lunch (goal) in order to satisfy our hunger (impulse, problem), or we decide to sing out loud (goal) in order to satisfy our uneasiness (impulse, problem) in the social situation. That is, individuals define goals, and they perceive and define objects in situations in order to reach those goals and overcome problems.

The important point that must not be lost is that human beings *define their situation*. This is the second stage of the act.

Stage 3: Manipulation

In the third stage humans manipulate their environment, act in it, handle it, and come "into contact with the relevant aspects" (Shibutani, 1961;68), using objects according to goals they have defined for themselves. Humans manipulate things and persons by physically handling them, talking to them, breaking them, writing letters to them, or caressing them. We act toward objects overtly (for all to see), after the foundations have been laid in stages 1 and 2, both covert phases.

Mead emphasizes the importance of human hands, the ability to take physical objects, dissect them, put them together with other objects, change them, use them in a creative way. We become aware of the object, we plan a use for it, we use it, we revise our plan and use it in another way. We handle objects in situations as tools, as means to an end, as objects whose purpose lies in the future. We thus manipulate objects physically in the present to achieve goals that are in our future. The house is dark; in order to change the fuse, we pick up the flashlight, find the stairs, watch out for things in the way, open doors, find the blown fuse, take it out, put in the good fuse. The lights are on; we go up the stairs, reset the clocks. . . . New goals, problems, definitions, manipulations.

Stage 4: Consummation

This stage, consummation, is the end of the act—the goal is achieved and the equilibrium is restored even though only for a moment. Acts are not always consummated, because we may start another act before ending an act, focusing our attention on something else, shifting our stream of action. After consummation, if it takes place, another sequence of impulse, perception, manipulation, and consummation takes place, and the stream of action continues.

A Brief Look at the Four Stages

The importance of Mead's description is in the fact that humans *actively* perceive, define, and manipulate their environment to achieve goals. This is the essence of action; this is the essence of each segment of action, or act. Action is both overt and covert, we act along a stream of action that involves a constant process of definition and redefinition. Dissecting the act into four stages is misleading: Perception and definition do not occur only before manipulation. It is an ongoing "stage." As we manipulate objects in the world out there we are defining and evaluating what is going on. Covert action does not simply precede overt action; it *accompanies* overt action. This is a point that should not be overlooked.

Blumer's (1966) description of action captures the essence of Mead even though it does not dissect the act into four clear phases:

Action is built up in coping with the world instead of merely being released from a pre-existing psychological structure by factors playing on that structure. By making indications to himself and by interpreting what he indicates, the human being has to forge or piece together a line of action. In order to act the individual has to identify what he wants, establish an objective or goal, map out a prospective line of behavior, note and interpret the actions of others, size up his situation, check himself at this or that point, figure out what to do at other points, and frequently spur himself on in the face of dragging dispositions or discouraging settings. The fact that the human act is self-directed or built-up means in no sense that the actor necessarily exercises excellence in its construction. Indeed, he may do a very poor job in constructing his act. . . . What he takes into account are the things that he indicates to himself. They cover such matters as his wants, his feelings, his goals, the actions of others, the expectations and demands of others, the rules of his group, his situation, his conceptions of himself, his recollections, and his images of prospective lines of conduct. (Pp. 536–37)*

Human action is not simply released in situations, nor is it caused by personality traits or the situation. It is caused by the actor making decisions actively through the stages that Mead calls impulse, perception, manipulation, and consummation but that are probably better described as goal, definition, and overt manipulation accompanied by continuous definition.

LOCATING THE "CAUSE" OF HUMAN ACTION

By dividing our stream of action into isolated acts, it is easier for us to look for the cause of an act. Why did you go to Harvard? Why did you major in history? Why did you decide not to study for your physics exam? Why did you break up with Roberta? Each of these isolated acts can be analyzed, and causes can be determined.

When people attempt to explain such isolated acts, they normally take one of three approaches:

1. *Free choice.* The individual wanted to do it; the individual chose to do it. (This tends to be a common-sense view of cause.)
2. *Personality.* The individual did it because that is the way he or she is. That is the way he or she was brought up. Those are the kinds of things he or she does because of traits that are embedded in personality. (This tends to be a psychological or common-sense view of cause.)
3. *Social environment:* The individual did it because of society, social forces, groups, or other people. (This tends to be a sociological view of cause.)

We can understand such causes. They are relatively easy to isolate, study, and comprehend. And we have something we can act on. We can punish or reward the person who purposely did it, we can try to rehabilitate the person whose action was caused by personality traits, or we can try to alter a person's environment if that is what caused it.

From a symbolic interactionist perspective, the cause of an act is seen differently. Any given act along the stream of action is caused by the individual's *decisions* at that point. A given decision in turn is caused by the individual's *definition of the situation* at that point, including goals, plans, social objects, future consequences, relevant memories recalled and applied. The definition of the situation the individual arrives at in turn is influenced by two things: *interaction*

*Reprinted from "Sociological Implications of the Thought of George Herbert Mead," by Herbert Blumer in *The American Journal of Sociology,* by permission of The University of Chicago Press. Copyright © 1966 by The University of Chicago. All rights reserved.

with self (thinking) and *interaction with others.* I took a job at Moorhead State University long ago. I took it because of several decisions I made at the time: to leave my previous job and community, to move from Minneapolis, and to stop looking for other jobs. These decisions were made on the basis of the goals I defined for myself at the time: to become a college professor, to finish my doctorate, and to settle in a community close to my family. These decisions were made because of social objects relevant to me at the time: a job offer, an attractive community, a past that I no longer wanted to continue, a job in a sociology department that looked both promising and secure, my wife's welfare, my children's welfare, the easy highway from Moorhead to Minneapolis, and a good school system for my children. I recalled situations in my past job that I wanted to escape, and I saw an opportunity for something new and exciting. Throughout it all I interacted with my wife, my adviser, my friends at the university, and people from the sociology department who had asked me to come. Many decisions had to be made, and together my stream of action was altered in the direction of university life at Moorhead State.

From the perspective of symbolic interactionism, the cause of an isolated act is the decision made at the time, caused in turn by definition and interaction. However, it is misleading to isolate an act. In fact, the cause of that act can be understood only by placing it in the larger context of a stream of action where many decisions are made. Thus, we might decide on one act and change our minds a few moments or minutes or hours later. To actually change my job and move took many decisions all made over time, and at any time the direction I ended up taking could have been changed dramatically. To decide to get married does not mean that one actually gets married; to decide to major in history does not cause us to be history majors. Instead, many decisions go into this, and all of them are influenced by interaction with self and others over time.

The cause of a single act is easier to understand than the cause of the direction of our stream of action. Streams of action are influenced by many instances of social interaction, definition, and decision making. At times our streams are steady, at other times they waver a bit, and at other times they are dramatically changed—always due to social interaction, definition, and decision making.

Let us for a moment summarize what is being said here about the cause of human action:

1. Action is caused not by our past, our personality, or social forces working on us. It is caused by the decisions we make that arise from our definition of the situation we are in.
2. The definition of a given situation results from interaction with self (thinking) and social interaction.
3. Each act is really part of a larger stream of action that flows in directions. The direction of our stream of action is due to many decisions we make over time along that stream.

Two final points should be made. When we say that interaction influences our definition of the situation, we mean that as actors act toward each other, the action of each becomes part of the situation that each actor is defining, and thus each actor becomes a social object to the other. The acts of each are influenced, and the stream of action of each is influenced. It is interesting to note that social interaction really is the intersection of different actors' streams of action, each altering his or her own stream according, in part, to what others do. And, as we shall see later, over time such interaction leads to a shared view of reality—a perspective—and this too enters into definition, decision making, and the direction of action.

Finally, there is also the question of freedom as an important reason for our action in situations. Because the actor is continuously defining the situation in conversation with self, part of the reason for a given act is the free choice that is made in the decision making. We are conceived here as active participants in what we do in a given situation; our action in part springs from decisions made by us through manipulating the situation in our heads and making choices. It is hard to prove that this is in fact an act of freedom; however, if there is any freedom for the actor, this is what must be done. The perspective of symbolic interactionism explains more than most other perspectives the possibility for this free choice in this description of cause.

Figure 9–2 summarizes the cause of human action from the perspective of symbolic interactionism.

FIGURE 9–2

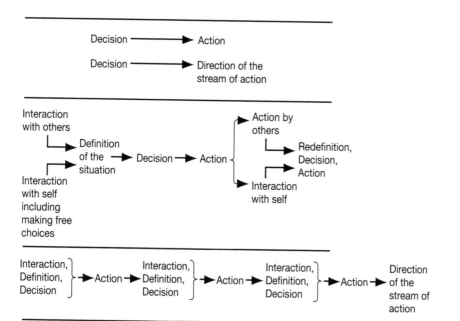

THE DEFINITION OF THE SITUATION

To better understand cause we will now turn our attention to the concept "definition of the situation," which we have identified up to now as the process that leads to the decisions the actor makes along the stream of action.

William and Dorothy Thomas (1928) wrote: "If men define situations as real, they are real in their consequences" (p. 572). Their point is simple: Humans act in a world they define, and although there may actually be a reality out there, their definition is far more important for what they *do*. In the end, it does not matter if you are a scoundrel or not; what matters is that I see you as a scoundrel and I act toward you as if you were one. And you in turn may not be a scoundrel, but you may accept my definition of you as one and then proceed to act that way. If I see a situation as threatening, then I will act accordingly, even if people in that situation did not mean to appear threatening. If I define school as hard or good or silly, then I will act toward school in that manner, no matter if others feel as I do and no matter if it is in reality harder, better, sillier than other schools. Our realities are our definitions of situations. Definitions of the situation may be influenced by others but in the end, each individual must define the situation (including those others) by engaging in mind activity. We each act in a world that we create through interaction with self influenced in part by interaction with others.

Donald Ball (1972) defined the definition of the situation as the "sum total of all recognized information, from the point-of-view of the actor, which is relevant to his locating himself and others, so that he can engage in self-determined lines of action and interaction" (p. 63). It is, as we have described throughout this book, the definition of social objects the actor regards as relevant for action. It is a "social construction of reality," and it is reality the actor creates within himself or herself that has consequences for overt action in the situation.

Although it is difficult to summarize all the different activities that are included in defining a situation, recall the following:

1. Establishing goals in the situation
2. Applying a perspective from a significant other or a reference group to the situation
3. Pointing out to self the relevant objects in the situation—this may include other people, natural and human-made objects, ideas, words, and so on
4. Taking the role of the other—both of individuals and of the group as a whole
5. Defining self in the situation, including
   assessing what one is doing in relation to the situation
   assessing what is happening in the situation in relation to the self
   judging self in the situation
   giving self an identity in the situation
   interpreting what one is experiencing emotionally

6. Defining the future, distant and near, and imagining the effects of one's acts before one performs them
7. Applying knowledge and memories from the past to the present situation

It is therefore imperative to understand human action from the definition of the actor. How he or she defines the situation is central to how he or she acts in it. The cause of action is always definition, and the definition is not easily understood: Goals, perspective, significant others, reference groups, objects, other people, view of future and past, and assessment of what is taking place in the situation all are matters that must be considered if action is to be understood. And to make cause even more difficult to isolate, recall that the situation always changes; the actor engages in an ongoing stream of action, defining the situation one way at one point, another way later on.

HABITUAL ACTION

Of course, our definition of the situation is not usually a matter of careful deliberation, but rather quick assessment. It is when we are confronted by interruptions in our stream of action, when we are faced with problems, that we become more aware and deliberate. However, every situation is at least somewhat new for us, goals and objects must be worked out, others are taken account of, and therefore some definition is almost always involved.

Habitual action does not involve definition, but simply response to a certain type of situation that we have developed over time. It does not involve covert activity. Habitual action takes us through some situations; we may be able to respond based entirely on past learning, but usually such action is short in duration. Habitual action is sometimes functional, allowing the individual to act without hesitating; it is good where immediate response is demanded. On the other hand, action that is purely habitual is dysfunctional for most situations because each situation is unique, each involves other people acting, and therefore each demands some adjustment on the part of the actor. Walking to work in the morning may become highly habitual, but often we must tell ourselves to speed up or slow down or watch out for a car at this intersection, or we must adjust to an increase in traffic, perhaps by taking a slightly different route. Driving a car may also be a highly habitual act much of the time, but that too is loaded with covert action—giving ourselves direction, acting in response to traffic signals, other cars, pedestrians, and detours.

Indeed, the more habitual our actions, the less prepared we become for alterations in situations that demand some adjustment on our part. Perhaps we can afford habitual action for small, simple acts such as putting the key in the ignition, but when acts are larger than simple motor movements, such as driving a car to California, we must rely less on habitual response and more and more on covert definition and interpretation of the ongoing situation. Purely habitual action would be especially inappropriate to activities where other people are involved because the individual must constantly make adjustments to an ever-changing interactive situation. Definition and analysis of self and others are absolutely essential to working out social situations.

Purely habitual action is extremely rare. In most cases ongoing definition while we act overtly in situations is the rule. In some cases careful deliberation is necessary.

THE ROLE OF THE PAST IN HUMAN ACTION

Needless to say, action always takes place in the present. We act *now,* and when we are through our act becomes part of our past. Past is massive; the present is a split second.

Throughout this discussion, we have emphasized that our action in the present is not determined by what went before, but by the definition of the situation in the present. This is in sharp contrast to most of what psychologists emphasize. My past does not cause my acts in the present; my definition in the present does, and that definition is also not caused by my past but by interaction with self and others *in the present.*

Does the past play any role in what we do? Of course it does, but not because it has shaped our personality, but because *we use it in our definition of the present.* What we know and remember from our past is applied to situations we encounter. Significant others, reference groups, perspectives, beliefs, information from our past are recalled and used as social objects to work through the present situation. When I enter Math 210 I use what I already know to make it through that class—experiences in other math classes, experiences with teachers, strategies I have developed elsewhere to get through classes like this one, knowledge of mathematics, and so on. But it is important to realize that these are items I *use* in Math 210, that I apply to the definition of that particular situation. The past, therefore, does not cause what I do in the present; instead, I use the past to define the present and to guide my action in the present. Mead (1934) describes intelligence as "essentially the ability to solve the problems of *present* behavior in terms of its possible *future* consequences as implicated on the basis of *past* experience . . . it involves both memory and foresight" (p. 100). The past is used to make sense out of the present.

The past is rich for us, and it provides us with the tools to define the present. The past changes every second because the present is always moving forward, with new experiences being added to it. Further, our past is always changing because our new experiences, the new situations we encounter, and the new perspectives we come to believe in reinterpret the past and cause us to see it as altered. As a society we are always rewriting our past: African Americans, women, and Native Americans, to name a few groups, are clearly reconstructing our past for us, causing us to see it anew, and that is affecting what we do *now.* It is also true of our personal biographies: The man who becomes a parent sees his own parents in a new light and understands their anxieties, hopes, and feelings when he was a child. He is redefining his past, as he also does when he looks back twenty years at his high school days, fully remembering some beautiful moments, conveniently forgetting the horrors of adolescence experienced at the time.

Our past is very important for another reason: *The decisions that we made in our past have brought us to the present situation.* We all have histories; our streams of action go back a long way. If our decisions had been different, the situation we are facing at the moment would also be different. Many decisions went into my marriage to Susan; had those decisions not been made in my past, then the situations I define every day that involve Susan would not confront me. Figuring out how to study for a final in a sociology class you are taking right now would not be a problem except for the fact that you made *many decisions* that have brought you to the final exam.

Finally, our past is important because *where we begin our life really matters a great deal in our direction.* We are born poor or rich or neither; we are born in Boise, Idaho, or Atlanta, Georgia, or somewhere else; we are born into a family that loves us, ignores us, or abuses us. This is the beginning of our stream of action. The situations we encounter in life depend in part on where we begin in life. Therefore, our past enters in by starting us out. Nothing is inevitable after that, but it is foolish to ignore the starting line, for the situations we end up defining are influenced by that.

To fully understand the role of the past in human action, therefore, it is important to understand three points: (1) How the individual applies the past to the present, (2) the history of decision making (including interaction with others and self) that brought the individual to the present situation, and (3) where the actor's stream of action begins. This emphasis by the symbolic interactionist is significantly different from other social science perspectives, since it does not assume that past causes action in the present, but that always it is the definition of the present that does. Where I begin my life does not cause what I do now, it is simply the origin of my stream of action. My actions in my past do not cause what I do now; instead just as they resulted from choices and decisions made at the time, so too does my action now arise from choices and decisions that I make now. My past experiences do not cause what I do now, but they become important as social objects I can pull out from memory and use to make my decisions.

THE ROLE OF THE FUTURE IN HUMAN ACTION

The future is a very important part of the individual's definition of the situation. What we do in the present depends in part on our conception of the future. Our acts have consequences, and we try to imagine these as we act. To Mead the actor sees objects according to how he or she plans to use them in the future. We develop a plan of action toward objects, the "later stages of the act are present in the early stages" (Mead, 1934;11), what we will do later is imagined in the present:

If one approaches a distant object he approaches it with reference to what he is going to do when he arrives there. If one is approaching a hammer he is muscularly all ready to seize the handle of the hammer. The later stages of the act are present in the early stages—not simply in the sense that they are all ready to go off, but in the sense that they serve to control the process itself. They determine how we are going to approach the object, and the steps in our early manipulation of it. (P. 11)*

We are planners. We consider what our present acts will lead to. We are problem solvers. We imagine the consequences of the alternatives we choose. We are social beings. We imagine the effects our acts will have on others:

The intelligent man as distinguished from the intelligent animal presents to himself what is going to happen. The animal may act in such a way as to insure its food tomorrow. A squirrel hides nuts, but we do not hold that the squirrel has a picture of what is going to happen. The young squirrel is born in the summer time and has no directions from other forms, but it will start hiding nuts as well as the older ones. Such action shows that experience could not direct the activity of the specific form. The provident man, however, does definitely pursue a certain course, pictures a certain situation, and directs his own conduct with reference to it. The squirrel follows certain blind impulses, and the carrying-out of its impulses leads to the same result that the storing of grain does for the provident man. It is this picture, however, of what the future is to be as determining our present conduct that is the characteristic of human intelligence—the future as present in terms of ideas. (Mead, 1934;119)

The future and the past are therefore social objects to the actor. A memory is applied to the present; the imagined consequences of an act are considered. Like all else, the past and future changes as we change our uses for them in the present.

The focus of symbolic interactionism remains the present. "The past and the future do not exist in themselves, but are the past and the future of a particular present. The past is a different past for every particular present; a new present means a new past and a new future" (Tillman, 1970;537). Memory brings "the past into the present," and imagination brings "the future into the present" (p. 541).

ACTION AND MOTIVES

According to the symbolic interactionist, individuals are goal directed. We are constantly determining lines of action toward objects in keeping with our goals. Goals are not static, and therefore lines of action are constantly shifting. Whatever is done at a given moment must be understood as having developed over a period of time, with a number of factors contributing to the direction of action at different points, with goals in mind shifting, objects being rede-

---

*Reprinted from *Mind, Self and Society* by George Herbert Mead by permission of The University of Chicago Press. Copyright © 1934 by The University of Chicago. All rights reserved.

fined, and other people's acts affecting direction. Action is to be explained not by deep-seated stable motives but by shifting goals and definitions of the situation.

The distinction between motives and goals is a subtle but very important one. If we imagine human action as being the result of individual *motives,* there is a tendency to see action as determined *by an internal state,* preceding action, stable over time, having little to do with either the definition of the situation encountered or with interaction in the situation. A motive is a trait that the individual carries to the situation that causes action. The human is conceptualized as possessing a stable internal state that causes action. Action is said to *spring from* motives. To ask about motives normally assumes a constant underlying cause that drives the direction of an individual's action over time. Although such causes do exist and people often use them to explain behaviors, normally their importance is exaggerated.

Goals are emphasized in symbolic interactionism, and as soon as they are brought into the analysis, a rational process is seen as taking place; the human is conceptualized as defining and redefining situations in relation to those goals. The situation itself becomes central to what we do rather than the motives we might bring to it. A goal is something that the human being *defines,* and thus human action is thought to be governed by definition, interaction, and ongoing decision making. Situations are worked out in relation to the goals we define, and because action is ongoing, our goals and definitions are constantly being defined and redefined.

Symbolic interactionists, however, regard motives as important in a different sense. They are important in the same sense that past and future are—we define them as important in situations, and so we act as though they are important. Whatever the actual role of motives (and in most cases that role is probably minor), humans *impute* motives—we explain one another's actions through assigning motives. Motives are the *stated reasons* for an act, the *verbalized cause* of human action that assumes intentions on the part of the actor. "You kept my money because you wanted to cheat me, because you wanted to take advantage of my weakness in order to get rich"; or "You treated me to lunch because you need me for your friend"; or "You saved that man from drowning because you are a loving person and were doing a courageous thing in light of the danger facing you." Whatever the many complex actual reasons for our action taking a certain direction, the explanation we find easiest to give involves deep-seated motives. Motives, however, are *oversimplified explanations.* They become important in the sense that what we *say* or *think* is the reason for our act or the acts of others makes a difference in what we do. Motives are attempts by people to summarize and make some sense out of complex acts. They are labels, summary statements, of reasons we give that an act occurs. The losing baseball coach cries out: "We lost because you did not try hard enough. You did not want to win this game badly enough. You lack desire." It is difficult to imagine anyone disagreeing with this interpretation; it is also difficult to discover other possible reasons for the loss. Lack of desire is the easiest explanation; it is the only thing that can be easily changed; it is the easiest thing that individuals can control. And, finally, it is something that the coach can always find evidence for. It is indeed a very useful explanation (Fine, 1987;64).

Dennis Brissett and Charles Edgley (1975) define motives as communications used "to justify or rationalize the conduct of the actors . . . [and] enable certain interactions to persist" (p. 6). Both Max Weber (1947) and C. Wright Mills (1940) describe motives in this same vein: Motives are verbalized explanations of behavior, and as such serve to explain, rationalize, or condemn one's own acts or the acts of others. To Mills motives are "vocabularies" that an actor uses to justify or explain action. Marvin Scott and Stanford Lyman (1968) call such motives "accounts," reasons we give for why we do what we do. Sometimes accounts are believed by the actor, and sometimes they are given because they are useful but not believed. The point is that motives are not really important except and until there is a reason for us to create them, a necessity to describe cause to self or others.

One reason, then, that we impute motives is that we are better able to separate the good guys from the bad guys. There are, to all of us, acceptable and unacceptable motives. When we observe others and impute unacceptable motives to them, we may withdraw from interaction or feel justified in punishing them. Or if we examine our own acts and find our motives questionable, we may change what we do. We may act toward others in order to give the impression that our motives are honorable, and they, we may assume, do the same in their acts. Motives are important, therefore, for understanding how people come to explain and rationalize one another's acts and their own acts in a relatively simple way. In symbolic interactionism it is this *definition* of self and others that is an important variable in each situation. Our labels of each other, although oversimplified, lead us to smile at the other, put the other in prison, go out on a date with the other, marry the other, vote for the other, or make fun of the other.

Our vocabulary of motives is used to explain our own acts, too. We *justify* our acts when we admit to doing them but claim that they are not bad. We give *excuses* when we admit that our act is bad but refuse to accept full responsibility. Justifications and excuses are retrospective; they are accounts given concerning acts that have already taken place. However, we also give accounts for acts that are about to take place. That is, we make *disclaimers,* accounts that soften our prospective acts when we suspect that others might judge us harshly and attribute identities that we wish to avoid:

> Life is filled with occasions on which individuals find it necessary to engage in acts that undermine the emergent meaning of situations and make probable the destruction of their identities in them. Even if they do not feel constrained to act in such ways, individuals may perceive opportunities—even legitimate ones—in lines of action they know others will take exception to. And on some occasions, individuals may sense the possibility of being typified in ways they would like to avoid, but find themselves without any certain way of anticipating the response.

Under such circumstances as these and others, disclaimers are invoked. (Hewitt and Stokes, 1975;1)

"I suppose that I really shouldn't say this, but . . ." "No offense, but . . ." "I know I am sometimes wrong, but . . ." "I'm not really a male chauvinist, but . . ." What are we doing? We are warning others not to take what we say or do and use it against us. It is one of many ways we try to maintain our identities, avoid rejection by others, clarify motives, and help maintain continuous interaction.

Whether or not a single motive—stated or unstated—is indeed the cause of an isolated act in the stream of action is an empirical question to be investigated. By itself it is almost always an unsatisfactory answer. We define situations we act in; sometimes an underlying motive might play a role. It is, however, the definition of that motive that undoubtedly plays a much larger role.

EMOTIONS AND ACTION

Over the past twenty years symbolic interactionists have increasingly turned their attention to the study of emotions. Emotions are very important in human action and have been neglected for too long. But true to style, the view of the role of emotions changes as the symbolic interactionist examines them.

Most people treat emotions the same way as attitudes, motives, and our past: as the source of action. Action is thought to spring from within the individual. The usual conceptualization of emotion is as an internal response that the individual has little or no control over, and that leads to an overt response. Although this does happen on occasion, emotions have a far more important role in human action.

On the one hand, emotions are biological: Something changes inside the actor—rapid heartbeat, flushed face. On the other hand, emotions, like everything else, are *defined:* We isolate them, give them a name, direct them, *use them.* Just as there is an objective reality "out there" that we learn to identify and define, so there is also an internal reality. Physical changes occur within our bodies at various times in our stream of action. Some are fleeting, and some last for a long time. The bodily change may be in heartbeat, pulse, respiration rate, facial flush, perspiration, or motor activity (Kemper, 1978;47). But the human is able to act back on himself or herself, defining, thinking about, feeling guilty or good about, that bodily change. Indeed, other animals also have bodily changes we might define as emotional states, but it is difficult to imagine other animals defining them, reflecting on them, controlling them, or using them as human beings are able to do.

Human beings not only respond to their environment because of an internal emotional response, but they also *feel* those emotional responses. They give meaning to their bodily changes. "I am angry!" "I am in love." "I am jealous!" "I feel good." "I am sad." To human beings emotions become social objects defined and used in situations. Whatever changes occur inside the individual, the actor must deal with them: Label them, control them, hide them, direct them, use them to achieve goals, and even try to alter them.

There is a control that the actor exercises over his or her emotions, actions that take place in relation to self. The emotion is not simply a causal response to a stimulus in the situation. The mere existence of physical change may in fact influence an act or even the direction of action over time, but our action toward our own bodily state—what we feel and what we do with that—is more important.

There is, admits Norman Denzin (1984), "nonreflective emotional experience," parts of the body that exist as sensations or states and which do not become part of our stream of consciousness. However, emotions are generally more than this. They are reflective and emotional experiences that become objects to define, consider, and to use in situations (pp. 71, 112–13). The human actor recognizes something happening internally, defines what it is (anger, depression, frustration, happiness), judges it as positive or negative, or expresses it, represses it, or manages it; the actor may store it and in the future recall it. In all of these ways—and undoubtedly others—emotions become social objects used by the actor; they involve "reflection, feeling, cognition, and interpretation," some being "purely private, others public or collective" (p. 5).

Humans express their emotions, and in that sense they use emotions in the same way they use all objects. We feel angry; we express that anger in a situation. We love someone, and we use that love toward the other in our action. We feel sorrow, and we express it. We feel hatred toward a group of racists, and we use that feeling in our speech and acts toward the group.

Humans also repress their emotions. In this sense emotions become social objects that we think should not be expressed. Gary Alan Fine (1987;87), for example, in his study of Little League baseball teams, points out the central importance that emotional control has for the boys, the parents, and the coaches. It is important not only to learn how to play baseball, but also to repress inappropriate feelings (e.g., laughing at another's pain or getting angry at the other team's winning), to control aggression, to hide fears, to keep from crying. In their study of medical doctors, Robert Coombs and Pauline Powers (1975) found repression of feeling. The doctor "cannot take death and dying too personally." The doctor

> is expected to retain composure, no matter how dramatic or tragic the death scene might be. Rationality and clearness of judgment in moments of grave peril must characterize his every action. The physician who loses coolness and presence of mind also loses the confidence of patients and staff. Clearly, a doctor sobbing over a favorite patient is no doctor at all. (P. 251)

Yet, for those doctors who were interviewed, emotion was felt internally but not expressed. One interviewer in the study reported: "Everybody I've talked to so far is having a horrible time dealing with death and dying; and it isn't just on a professional level, but personally too" (p. 264).

Humans are active in situations, and perhaps nothing makes this more clear than the fact that we also *manage* emotions in situations. We create them;

we make ourselves feel. Arlie Hochschild calls this "emotion work." We try to get psyched up for our classes, we try to feel good in order to have fun on a date, we try to feel sympathetic when others are depressed, we try to feel grateful when someone helps us, we try to fight the guilt we feel when we do something wrong. In a study by Hochschild (1983), students were asked to describe an event where they experienced a deep emotion. Their reports were filled with such phrases as "I psyched myself up; I squashed my anger down; I tried hard not to feel disappointed; I forced myself to have a good time; I mustered up some gratitude; I put a damper on my love for her; I snapped myself out of the depression" (p. 39). All of these are descriptions of people trying to take charge of their internal states—trying to manage what is taking place inside their bodies.

Emotions are therefore social objects, used in situations by the active, problem-solving human being. And because they are social objects, they too are learned in interaction with others. We learn to isolate physical changes within us, to label them, to judge them, to manage them, to repress them, to express them, and even to produce them. "They are learned in social relationships, initially in the primary group of the family" (Denzin, 1984;52). We are taught to be polite in expressing our emotions: "I'm sorry"; "Thank you"; "I feel bad about your misfortune." Emotions "are embodied 'self-feelings' of people," learned from culture (Power, 1985;215).

Emotions, motives, past, future, other people in situations, significant others, reference groups, knowledge, symbols, and self—all of these are social objects, shared in interaction, used in situations by the actor to guide decision making and action.

ACTION AND CHOICE

It is significant how symbolic interactionists treat emotions. Most social scientists treat them as shapers of actions, causes of human action. Symbolic interactionists treat emotions as part of what the *active human being uses* in situations. The actor is in charge of which direction his or her stream of action takes.

In the end action means *choice* to the symbolic interactionist, at least to some degree. Humans *act* and do not *react;* they *use* their environment and do not simply *respond* to it. Humans define their world, and then they redefine it again and again. They consider their past and balance their future options. Action becomes a complex interplay of both overt and covert activity, a result of interpreting and controlling the direction of the stream of action. Mead (1934) states that ideas are "possibilities of overt responses which we test out implicitly in the central nervous system and then reject in favor of those which we do in fact act upon or carry into effect. The process of intelligent conduct is essentially a process of selection from among various alternatives; intelligence is largely a matter of selectivity" (p. 99). All this means active thinking, choice, self-direction. It is, to Mead, "delayed response," holding back action, that makes possible definition, deliberation, and choice:

The central nervous system, in short, enables the individual to exercise conscious control over his behavior. It is the possibility of delayed response which principally differentiates reflective conduct from non-reflective conduct in which the response is always immediate. (P. 117)

Action is conscious control, selection, deliberation, holding back, self-direction, self-control, reflection. Action is here described as individuals *actively* determining their own direction. The human is regarded here as one of the most important causes of his or her own action through interaction with self. Freedom is indeed one of the key elements in Mead's thought. William Desmonde (1957), interpreting Mead, writes:

Through man's capacity to readjust his developing acts to his anticipations of the future, he achieves freedom. The knowledge of what is necessary enables us to make an appropriate adjustment to that reality when it eventuates. We are not bound by the past, but can utilize the past to prepare for the future. (P. 39)

And Bernard Meltzer (1972) casually points out: "Needless to say, this view contradicts the stimulus-response conception of human behavior" (p. 20).

SUMMARY

This chapter is an attempt to tie in everything from earlier chapters. Social objects, symbols, self, mind, and taking the role of the other play themselves out in our understanding of social action. Human action is highly complex, and this chapter has tried to emphasize the following points.

1. Humans engage in a continous stream of action, both overt and covert, influenced by ongoing decisions along that stream, which are influenced in turn by definition, social interaction, and interaction with self. Cause is continuous decision making arising from continuous definition. Action has a history that is directional. Directions in life change because of many decision, many definitions, many actions we take.
2. In order to understand this stream of action humans will normally separate that stream into separate acts. An act is a segment within our stream, given a name, and given significance. An act becomes a social object to us as we isolate and define it according to our goals in the present.
3. Action results from our definition of the situation. Action is directed toward the goals and objects we determine to be important. By seeing action as arising from social interaction, interaction with self, and definition, an emphasis is placed on cause in the present rather than in the past. Emphasis is placed on the decisions made in the present by the actor, rather than by objects in the outside environment pushing the actor one way or another.
4. What other perspectives treat as simple cause of action—such as past, motives, emotion, other people, society—symbolic interactionists treat

as social objects, part of our definition of the situation. Although all of these may sometimes contribute to action and although habit too may enter in, humans are thought here to be in control through their ongoing definition of the situation and through their ongoing organization of their own goals.

Human action, of course, often involves other people. Other people become social objects to us, and we become social objects to them. This is the link between human action and human social interaction. Where people organize their action with one another in mind we have an instance of social interaction. This is the important topic we will examine in Chapter 10.

REFERENCES

BALL, DONALD
  1972   "The Definition of the Situation." *Journal for the Theory of Social Behavior* 2:24–36.
BLUMER, HERBERT
  1953   "Psychological Import of the Human Group." In Muzafer Sherif and M. O. Wilson, eds., *Group Relations at the Crossroads*, pp. 185–202. New York: Harper & Row.
  1966   "Sociological Implications of the Thought of George Herbert Mead." *American Journal of Sociology* 71:535–44. By permission of The University of Chicago Press. Copyright © 1966 by The University of Chicago.
  1969   *Symbolic Interactionism: Perspective and Method.* Englewood Cliffs, N.J.: Prentice Hall. Copyright © 1969. Reprinted by permission of Prentice Hall, Inc.
  1981   "Conversation with Thomas J. Morrioni and Harvey A. Farberman." *Symbolic Interaction* 4:9–22.
BRISSETT, DENNIS, AND CHARLES EDGLEY, EDS.
  1975   *Life as Theater.* Chicago: Aldine.
COOMBS, ROBERT, AND PAULINE S. POWERS
  1975   "Socialization for Death: The Physician's Role." *Urban Life* 5:250–71.
DAVIS, FRED
  1984   "Decade Labeling: The Play of Collective Memory and Narrative Plot." *Symbolic Interaction* 7:15–24.
DENZIN, NORMAN K.
  1984   *On Understanding Emotion.* San Francisco: Jossey-Bass.
DESMONDE, WILLIAM H.
  1957   "George Herbert Mead and Freud: American Social Psychology and Psychoanalysis." In Benjamin Nelson, ed., *Psychoanalysis and the Future*, pp. 31–50. New York: Psychological Association for Psychoanalysis.
DEWEY, JOHN
  1922   *Human Nature and Conduct.* New York: Modern Library.
FINE, GARY ALAN
  1987   *With the Boys: Little League Baseball and Preadolescent Culture.* Chicago: University of Chicago Press.
HEWITT, JOHN P., AND RANDALL STOKES
  1975   "Disclaimers." *American Sociological Review* 40:1–11.

HOCHSCHILD, ARLIE RUSSELL
      1983   *The Managed Heart.* Berkeley: University of California Press.

KEMPER, THEODORE D.
      1978   *A Social Interactional Theory of Emotions.* New York: Wiley.

McCALL, GEORGE J., AND J. L. SIMMONS
      1966   *Identities and Interactions.* New York: Free Press. Reprinted with permission of The Free Press, an imprint of Simon & Schuster. Copyright © 1966 by The Free Press.

MEAD, GEORGE HERBERT
      1934   *Mind, Self and Society.* Chicago: University of Chicago Press. Reprinted by permission of The University of Chicago. Copyright © 1934 by The University of Chicago. All rights reserved.

      1936   *Movements of Thought in the 19th Century.* Ed. Merritt H. Moore. Chicago: University of Chicago Press.

MELTZER, BERNARD N.
      1972   *The Social Psychology of George Herbert Mead.* Kalamazoo: Center for Sociological Research, Western Michigan University.

MILLS, C. WRIGHT
      1940   "Situated Action and the Vocabulary of Motives." *American Sociological Review* 6:904–13.

POWER, MARTHA BAUMAN
      1985   "The Ritualization of Emotional Conduct in Early Childhood." *Symbolic Interaction* 6:213–27.

SCOTT, MARVIN E., AND STANFORD M. LYMAN
      1968   "Accounts." *American Sociological Review* 33:46–62.

SHIBUTANI, TAMOTSU
      1961   *Society and Personality: An Interactionist Approach to Social Psychology,* Englewood Cliffs, N.J.: Prentice Hall. Copyright © 1961. Reprinted by permission of Prentice Hall, Inc.

STONE, GREGORY P., AND HARVEY A. FARBERMAN
      1970   *Social Psychology through Symbolic Interaction.* Lexington, Mass.: Ginn.

THOMAS, WILLIAM I., AND DOROTHY THOMAS
      1928   *The Child in America.* New York: Knopf.

TILLMAN, MARY KATHERINE
      1970   "Temporality and Role-taking in G. H. Mead." *Social Research* 37:533–46.

TROYER, WILLIAM LEWIS
      1946   "Mead's Social and Functional Theory of Mind." *American Sociological Review* 11:198–202.

WARRINER, CHARLES K.
      1970   *The Emergence of Society.* Homewood, Ill.: Dorsey Press.

WEBER, MAX
      1947   *Theory of Social and Economic Organization.* Trans. Talcott Parsons and A.M. Henderson. Glencoe, Ill.: Free Press.

10

Social Interaction

Everything we have discussed arises *from* social interaction: social objects, symbols, self, mind, decisions, change in our stream of action, perspectives, reality, definitions of the situation, and role taking. As we will see in Chapter 11, society too arises from interaction.

Everything we have discussed *is part of* interaction. When we interact we become social objects to one another; we use symbols; we direct self, engage in mind/covert action, make decisions, change directions, share perspectives, define reality, define the situation, and role take. Understanding the nature of interaction must recognize the existence of all of these activities.

SOCIAL ACTION

Social action is the name sociologists usually give to actions that in some way take account of other actors. Action is social when we consider others. Our acts are guided by others and their acts. Others make a difference to what we do in situations. Others are somehow used by the actor; *others are social objects.* I talk to you, listen to you, wink at you, ignore you, impress you, make love to you, greet you—in all these ways and many others I am engaging in social action because you are a social object to me in the situation. When we try to influence others or convince them of our views, or when we share something with others, help them or hurt them, love them or reject them, aid them or try to destroy them, we are social actors. Almost everything we do, we do in part in relation to others—they have become social objects to us in the situation. Herbert Blumer (1953) simply calls this "taking others into account":

> In my judgment, the most important feature of human association is that the participants *take each other into account.* . . . Taking another person into account means being aware of him, identifying him in some way, making some judgment or appraisal of him, identifying the meaning of his action, trying to find out what he has on his mind or trying to figure out what he intends to do. Such awareness of another person in this sense taking him and his acts into consideration becomes the occasion for orienting oneself and for the direction of one's own conduct. (P. 194)

Social action means that what the actor does involves another person or persons. It means that action is guided by what others do in the situation. If I dress for others as well as for myself, that is social action. If I throw a ball at others, that is social action. If I remain quiet in order not to disturb others in the library, this is social action. If I walk down the street with others in mind, and if my action is guided by that—if their presence makes a difference to my action—then my walking is social action.

Sometimes when we are social actors we consider the acts of others, act, and that's it. Much more often when we are social actors, *our acts are meant to communicate*. Almost all social action is *symbolic* to some extent. Talking to others is obviously social and symbolic action, but so too is almost all action that others see. My acts communicate to others that I am a good person, intelligent, kind, male, strong, or that I am bored, in a hurry, or really excited. Social action tells people who we are and what we think—our ideas, perspectives, wants, intentions, goals, morals, background, strengths, and dislikes.

Social action therefore means that other people are very important to what we do. It means that they are social objects and therefore guide our action; it also means that what we do in their presence is normally an attempt to communicate to them. Human beings are social and symbolic actors through and through:

> Inclinations, impulses, wishes and feelings may have to be restrained in the light of what one takes into account and in the light of how one judges or interprets what one takes into account. The presence of the other and his developing acts become occasions for the orientation of one's own act and thus provide the incidents of experience which lead one as he is guiding his own action to check himself at this point or that point, to withhold expression of given feelings and to recognize that certain wishes must be held in abeyance. (Blumer, 1953;197)

THE MEANING OF SOCIAL INTERACTION

Mutual Social Action

What does social action have to do with social interaction? Interaction is built on social action. Just as I take you into account as I act, so do you take me into account as you act. Just as I symbolically act toward you, so too do you interpret that act and symbolically act toward me. *Interaction means actors take one another into account, communicate, and interpret one another as they go along:*

> What are some examples of social interaction? A conversation, a knife fight, a chess game, love-making. None of these things can be done by one. It takes two to tango, just as it takes two bodies to produce gravitational attraction or two electrons to produce electro-static repulsion. None of these things can be viewed simply as a result of two independent units simultaneously unwinding their self-determined lines of action. The action of one unit is dependent upon the action of the other, *and vice versa*. . . . There must be mutual influence. . . . (McCall and Simmons, 1966;48–49)[*]

[*]Reprinted from *Identities and Interactions* by George J. McCall and J. L. Simmons, by permission of The Free Press, an imprint of Simon & Schuster. Copyright © 1966 by The Free Press.

I act; you consider my act, and you act; I consider your act, and I act; you consider my act, and you act. This give-and-take process is what is meant by interaction. The acts of each actor become social objects that the other considers as he or she acts. We never know what we will do next in our stream of action, in part because it will depend on what the other does. The actions that take place between actors in interaction become important objects used to guide what actors do. Interaction means that streams of action cross, each influencing the other, neither one determined by the unalterable decisions of one.

Games are interaction in slow motion. When I move a chess piece, I may have a plan. However, after I act, you make a decision and you act (based on your definition of my act). Now that you have moved, I must move again—this time based on my original plan *and* on my interpretation of your move. So it is in real life: What we each do depends in part on what others in the situation do. If I begin a conversation with you, the things you say in relation to me become important to me as I form what I want to say as we go along. If I want to sell something to you, what I say and do will depend on your actions—I must adjust to you, and you must adjust to me. We can say the same for two world leaders in a meeting, a public debate, two people on a date, a discussion group, a committee, a gang making plans, or a number of musicians trying to play together for the first time.

When social interaction enters into our understanding of the human being, we can truly begin to uncover the importance of our social life for everything we do and are. Interaction becomes the basic starting point for understanding groups and societies. What people do is heavily influenced by what action unfolds over time as they try out their acts in situations, then altering plans and acts on the basis of what others do—or, more exactly, on their definition of what others do. As we act back and forth our goals change, and our definitions and ultimately the decisions and directions we go. All depends on the give-and-take of social interaction that involves the ongoing definition of one another's actions. Factors outside the situation may play a role in what we do, but they are almost always tempered, altered, even ignored by the actors who are busy defining and redefining one another's action taking place in the situation itself.

Social interaction is complex. It is not like rats responding to one another. It is, instead, action that is (1) *symbolic* and (2) involves continuously by *taking the role of the other*. We intentionally communicate to one another and we constantly interpret one another's actions by taking the perspective of the other.

Social Interaction Is Symbolic

Almost all social interaction is symbolic; thus, we get to the meaning of "symbolic interactionism": *the study of human beings interacting symbolically with one another and with themselves, and in the process of that symbolic interaction making decisions and directing their streams of action.*

When we say that social interaction is symbolic we mean that the acts of each actor have meaning to the actor doing them and are acts normally interpreted by those with whom the actor acts toward. Of course, this means that each actor is symbolically interacting with self as he or she acts toward the other and watches the other. "This process of interaction," Blumer (1969) writes, "consists of making indications to others of what to do and in interpreting the indications as made by others" (p. 20).

"We modify our lines of action," George McCall and J. L. Simmons (1966) point out, "on the basis of what we perceive alter's implications to be with respect to our manifest and latent plans of action" (p. 136). I determine a line of action, then act overtly. The other (alter) acts overtly toward me, and I interpret what that act means (represents) in light of my own act. I alter my line of action slightly or to a great extent. The other must do the same in acting toward me. The conceptualization of actors constantly shifting what they do in relation to an interpretation of what others do is a highly complex view of the human being. We interpret the other and we communicate to the other, and the other, in turn, must interpret, communicate, and alter his or her action. This is a constant, never-ending process.

Human social interaction is symbolic through and through. It is not the interaction of billiard balls or ants or baseballs and bats or teeth or birds or bees. When you push me out of line, I interpret your act, and then I act toward you. When I push you back, you, in turn, interpret my act. We may end up in a fist fight or in a conversation about the movie we are about to see or in an argument with several people around us who do not care for our playing. In fact, we may very well end up very differently from the way we meant to end up: A shove that was meant as a joke could end up being interpreted as too strong for a joke. That was the point we made in the chapters on symbols: Our acts in relation to each other are symbolic—we intend to communicate, and we often interpret others' acts as intentional communication. When it is in fact intentional, George Herbert Mead calls the act a symbol or a "significant gesture," an act that has meaning to both the actor and to the other. Other animals gesture, and the gesture can act as a stimulus leading to a response, but the "conversation of gestures" between other animals is not significant in that it is without symbolic meaning; the doer does not understand the meaning of what he or she does. Thinking is not part of the action.

Symbolic interaction is complex, and when we try to understand it as the cause of human action it becomes even more complex. Yet the truth of its importance seems obvious when we remember the words of Erving Goffman (1983):

> In sum, then, whenever we come into contact with another through the mails, over the telephone, in face-to-face talk, or even merely through immediate co-presence, we find ourselves with one central obligation: to render our behavior understandably relevant to what the other can come to perceive is going on. Whatever else, our activity must be addressed to the other's mind, that is, to the other's capacity to read our words and actions for evidence of our feelings, thoughts, and intent. (P. 51)

Our actions "must be addressed to the other's mind." We intend our acts for others, we intend that they represent something about us. And others watch us, and, if they are to act appropriately, they must see those acts as representations and interpret what in the world is going on in the situation. This is all very complex and central to all human interaction. *Social interaction is symbolic social interaction.*

Social Interaction Involves Role Taking

Because interaction is symbolic, role taking is involved for both communicating and interpreting. Adjusting acts in relation to one another involves understanding the actions from the perspective of the other. We come to learn about the other and expect things from the other through role taking; the other, in turn, comes to know us, what we are doing, and what to expect from us.

Part of role taking in interaction is emotional. We not only understand the other but attempt to feel like the other. Norman Denzin (1984) describes this as emotional intersubjectivity: two parents having the same feelings toward a dead child, one actor taking pleasure in another's pain, emotional contagion at a rock concert, and two actors developing a long-term love relationship (pp. 146–56). Susan Shott (1979) reminds us how often the emotions we feel are a result of taking the role of others in interaction: shame, guilt, embarrassment, pride, vanity, and empathy, for example.

This ability to role take in interaction together with the fact that interaction is symbolic makes human interaction very complex and never perfectly predictable. It means that now

> It has become possible for a human actor to direct his actions according to the potential responses of his partners in interaction. Human action is oriented in accordance with behavioural expectations; since the same capacity is, in principle, at the disposal of one's partner in an interaction, a shared, and binding, pattern of reciprocal behavioral expectations is the precondition of collective activity. (Joas, 1985;115–16)

Social interaction is therefore accompanied by all kinds of covert interaction, including taking the role of the other, thinking about one's own communication, interpreting the acts of others, as well as considering both the expectations and the directions of others.

THE GENERAL IMPORTANCE OF SOCIAL INTERACTION

It is important to remember what social interaction is as we have described it here: actors engaged in mutual social action (taking one another into account), symbolically communicating, taking the role of one another, and interpreting one another's acts. Such interaction means that action will inevitably build up as the actors go along, adjusting their acts to the ongoing acts of one another over time.

It is impossible to exaggerate the role of social interaction in all that we do, think, and are. Everything described in this book relates back to interaction. The title of this perspective is "symbolic interactionism." Therefore, it is imperative that we consider at this time the different ways social interaction enters into human life. It is probably best to break this down into four general topics:

1. Social interaction creates our qualities as human beings.
2. Social interaction is an important cause of what the individual does in situations.
3. Social interaction forms our identities.
4. Social interaction creates society.

SOCIAL INTERACTION FORMS OUR BASIC HUMAN QUALITIES

What are we? What are we really? What is human nature? What are we as a species in nature? It is enjoyable and challenging to debate these questions, and sometimes we even find out something that helps us understand ourselves. This book has emphasized over and over again that what we really are is not to be found in our biology or in instinct; it is, instead, to be found in certain other qualities: our abilities to define and use our environment as social objects, to create and use symbols, to act back on ourselves, to point things out to ourselves about our environment, and to role take. *Such abilities all are dependent on social interaction.* Human nature, writes Charles Cooley (1909;30), is not something we are born with; instead, it arises in social interaction. As others act toward us and communicate symbolically, so we begin to act back toward them symbolically, and each of us adjusts action accordingly, and each develops all the qualities that make us human beings. Let me briefly remind you how each of our qualities arise from social interaction.

Social interaction, first of all, *creates the social objects we use,* and therefore *alters our relationship with our environment.* We learn about what exists, we learn to call those things names, and we come to understand them. We talk about our environment to one another and point out things to one another. Things take on meaning—stand for a line of action—as a result of this interaction process. We come to share what we know about objects; they thus become social objects. "Symbolic interactionism sees meanings as social products, as creations that are formed in and through the defining activities of people as they interact" (Blumer, 1969;5). Instead of responding to our environment, we are able to understand it and use it to achieve our own goals in the particular situation. We develop an active relationship toward our environment. So, too, do we develop *perspectives* which we then use to define reality. Because we share perspectives in social interaction, reality is altered considerably; we now see reality through a social construction. Social interaction is therefore responsible for what we see in the world around us; it therefore becomes basic to how we act in that world.

Second, *social interaction creates human symbols.* In contrast to other animals our communication is not based on what nature provides us, but what we come to learn as we interact with one another. What something represents is decided on by human beings as they communicate with one another. Definitions change; new symbols arise out of old ones; completely new definitions are developed by people in interaction. It is *not* our ability to communicate that distinguishes us from other animals; it is *not* our ability to make sounds; it is, instead, our ability to create, use, and share symbols in social interaction, and to agree among one another what the meaning of those symbols are.

Third, *interaction creates and defines self.* We come to see ourselves as objects owing to social interaction. As we interact with significant others and in our reference groups, we become aware of ourselves as objects, we come to see, assess, judge self, and create identities.

Fourth, *interaction creates and influences mind.* Mind is covert symbolic action toward the self. Both symbols and self arise from social interaction.

Fifth, *interaction creates and influences our role-taking ability.* Role taking first arises out of interaction with significant others. How we role take, how well we role take, and how well we are able to understand others, depend on interaction.

As we have seen, a central point in the whole symbolic interactionist perspective is the idea that human beings are "by their very nature" definers: symbol users; self-aware, mind-using, role-taking beings. These are not qualities that we simply possess; these are our most central qualities. And these qualities are not given to us in nature, but only through social interaction. Our very humanity arises out of our social interaction.

SOCIAL INTERACTION IS AN IMPORTANT CAUSE OF HUMAN ACTION

Social interaction is a cause in its own right. It is not simply other people that matter; it is *interaction* with those people. Others do not simply cause our action; instead, others act, we interpret their acts, we adjust our acts to theirs, and they act again (after interpreting and adjusting their acts to ours). What we do at any point in our interaction depends in part on what others do; more importantly, it depends on our definition of what others do. What they do, in turn, depends on their interpretation of what we do. No one knows where we all will end up. It depends on the continuous alignment of acts in relation to one another. Parents do not simply socialize their children; children interpret what is going on and in turn actually socialize their parents. Instructors teach classes, but if there is interaction, students alter the instructors' directions too.

Put simply, human beings in interacting with one another have to take account of what each . . . is doing or is about to do; they are forced to direct their own conduct or handle their situations in terms of what they take into account. Thus, the activities of others enter as positive factors in the formation of their own conduct; in the face of the actions of others one may abandon an intention on purpose, revise it, check or suspend it, intensify it, or replace it. . . . One has to *fit* one's own line of activity in some manner to the actions of others. The actions of others have to be taken into account and cannot be regarded as merely an arena for the expression of what one is disposed to do or sets out to do. (Blumer, 1969;8)

I act. . . . You act. . . . I act. . . . You act. I act with you in mind. . . . You act with me in mind. We each interpret the acts of the other and form our action accordingly. Wherever we each begin in our social interaction does not determine where we end up. Our actions depend on one another. Two children try to persuade each other who gets the piece of cake with the most frosting. Back and forth they go, until they get into a shouting match, then into a fist fight. One hurts the other, and both are punished for something that started out so innocently. Who knew that things would end this way? When I first asked Susan for a date, who knew then that interaction over time would lead both of us to alter our streams of action so that we would end up married, interacting for thirty or more years? World War I was clearly caused by the interaction of world leaders each symbolically communicating, interpreting, and adjusting actions to one another until all of Europe found itself in war. I interact with my son, and through that interaction we are both influenced; yet, what he ends up doing in real situations depends also on the interaction that takes place with friends and even strangers as he acts along his stream of action. As a parent, I do not simply *form* him; instead his action changes in social interaction with a lot of people besides just me, and what he ends up doing depends on much more than how I have "shaped him."

Our streams of action have long histories, and at almost every point there is social interaction, which results in decision making and the altering of our action. It is not that I commit murder because something happened to me fifteen years ago, or that I got a college degree because I became interested in school at the age of six, or that I have a job teaching school because that is what my father did. Each decision along the stream of action is influenced by a long history of decision making, and each decision in that history must be understood as influenced by the ongoing give-and-take of social interaction. It is important to step outside of the traditional perspectives most of us use in order to see action as caused by more than single predispositional factors within the individual or simply by what other people do to us in a particular situation.

The central point [is] that human interaction is a positive shaping process in its own right. The participants in it have to build up their respective lines of conduct by constant interpretation of each other's ongoing lines of action. (Blumer, 1966;538)

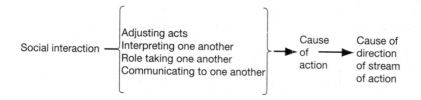

FIGURE 10-1

Almost every isolated act taken by almost every human being would have been at least slightly different if others had acted differently to previous acts. It is not simply who we are that matters; it is not simply who we are around that matters. What matters most is the interaction that unfolds between us and them (see Figure 10-1).

An exciting, classic, and clear illustration of the centrality of interaction to decision making and action is this description by a college student in a sociology text that I read as a college freshman (from *The Gang* by Frederic M. Thrasher, 1936). It is fascinating as well as illustrative, and it will probably have more than a passing significance for understanding events in your own life:

> We three college students—Mac, Art, and Tom—were rooming together while attending V_____ University, one of the oldest colleges in the South. On the day of our crime all three of us spent over three hours in the library—really working. That was on Sunday and our crime was committed at 1:30 that night (or rather Monday morning).
>
> The conversation began with a remark about the numerous recent bank failures in the state, probably stimulated by one of us glancing at a map of the state. It then shifted to discussion of a local bank that had closed its doors the day before. Tom, who worked at the post-office occasionally as special mail clerk, happened to mention that a sack containing a large amount of money had been received at the post-office that afternoon, consigned to a local bank that feared a run.
>
> The conversation then turned to the careless way in which the money was handled at the office—a plain canvas sack thrown into an open safe. We discussed the ease with which a thief could get into the building and steal the money. Tom drew a plan showing the desk at which the only clerk worked and the location of the only gun in the office. At first the conversation was entirely confined to how easily criminals might manage to steal the money. Somehow it shifted to a personal basis: as to how easily we might get the money. This shift came so naturally that even the next morning we were unable to decide when and by whom the first remark had been made.
>
> A possible plan was discussed as to how we might steal the package. Tom could go to the office and gain admittance on the pretense of looking for an important letter. Then Art and I, masked and armed, could rush in, tie Tom and the clerk, and make off with the package. We had lost sight of the fact that the package contained money. We were simply discussing the possibility of playing an exciting

prank with no thought of actually committing it. We had played many harmless pranks and had discussed them in much the same way before; but the knowledge that there was danger in the prank made it a subject to linger over.

After about an hour and a half of talk, I started to take off my shoes. As I unlaced them, I thought of how it looked as if I were the one to kill our interesting project. I foolishly said something to the effect that if Tom was going down town, I thought I would write a letter that was already overdue. Tom was anxiously awaiting a letter that should be in that night. He suggested that I go down also as it was a very decent night. I consented and Art decided to join us. I sat down and wrote the letter—meanwhile we continued our talk about the money package. My letter finished, something seemed to change. We found further inaction impossible: we had either to rob the post-office or go to bed. Tom brought out his two guns; I hunted up a couple of regular plain handkerchiefs, and Art added some rope to the assortment. At the time we were still individually and collectively playing a game with ourselves. Each of us expected one of the other two to give the thing the horse laugh and suggest going to bed and letting the letters wait till morning. But it seemed that we forgot everything—our position in school, our families and friends, the danger to us and to our folks. We all made our preparations more or less mechanically. Our minds were in a daze.

Putting on our regular overcoats and caps, we left the rooms quietly. On the way down town we passed the night patrolman without any really serious qualms. Tom entered the post-office as was his usual custom, being a subclerk, and Art and I crept up to the rear door. Tom appeared at a window with his hat, a signal that there were no reasons why our plan would not be effective. At the door, in full illumination of light, we arranged our handkerchiefs over our faces and took our guns out of our pockets. We were ready.

"Have you enough guts to go through with this thing?" I asked, turning to Art, who was behind me.

"If you have," he answered.

Frankly I felt that I had gone far enough, but for some unknown reason I did not throw out a remark that would have ended it all then and there. And Art didn't. He later said that he was just too scared to suggest anything. We were both, it seems, in a sort of daze.

Tom opened the door and we followed our plan out to the end. There was no active resistance by the regular night man.

Then after we left the office with thousands of dollars in our hands we did not realize all that it meant. Our first words were not about getting the money. They were about the fact that our prank (and it was still that to us) had been successful. When we reached our rooms, having hidden the money in an abandoned dredger, the seriousness of the thing began to penetrate our minds. For an hour or so we lay quietly and finally settled on a plan that seemed safe in returning the money without making our identity known. Then I went to sleep. (Pp. 300–303)[*]

Definition by the narrator, action, definition by the others, action, definition and action by the narrator again—here is action building up among people, each of their streams of action being influenced by the ongoing inter-

[*]Reprinted from *The Gang* by Frederic M. Thrasher by permission of The University of Chicago Press and William E. Girton. Copyright © 1927 by The University of Chicago. All rights reserved.

action. The example is perhaps dramatic, but it illustrates what we all do in almost every situation. We act in ways that were unintended at first, in ways that others might assume were intended right from the start. However, the act of robbing the post office must be understood in terms of the history of decisions made by actors as they take each other into account. Why did you do that? Are you immoral? Are you stupid? Are you evil? Are you a criminal at heart? Did your poverty or your riches lead to that? We constantly ask such questions about ourselves and others. We look for easy answers—that was his choice, the environment caused it, his personality is that way—but we must look to the interaction with self and others for the reasons we act the way we do. "The direction taken by a person's conduct is seen as something that is constructed in the reciprocal give and take of interdependent men and women who are adjusting to one another" (Shibutani, 1961;23).

Of course, this explanation of what we all do does not ignore the fact that we are much more than a glob of nothing when we act in a situation. We are individuals, and each of us brings important qualities to the situation from our past. However, instead of arguing as most social scientists do, that these are traits that cause what we do, the symbolic interactionist defines these as social objects *we use* in the situation. We enter situations with knowledge, self, identities, symbols, a past, a view of the future, goals, significant others, reference groups, perspectives, various skills, and so on. We draw upon all of these things—and many others—to define the situation and act. These things are not causes, but our use for them in our definition and decision making is. Then—as others act back in the situation—their acts become additional social objects for us to consider. Figure 10–2 illustrates this complex interrelationship between what the actor brings to the situation and what happens in social interaction (see page 162).

The dynamic nature of interaction and definition is lost on the printed page. We can capture only the very basics. Definitions and interpretations of the acts of other people are rapidly developed in interaction with self. Where there is time for deliberation, such as in games or in dealing with serious problems, all of the steps are evident. However, in most situations the process is very rapid and accompanies overt action.

SOCIAL INTERACTION SHAPES IDENTITIES

One of the most important qualities that we all develop over time is some idea of who in the world we are—our identity. Identity is really a process; who we are is an ongoing development. Indeed, we actually have many identities, some important one day, others important the next. Recall that identities are the way we identify ourselves and present ourselves in situations. Our identities matter in what we do; they matter in what we try to communicate to others; and they matter to others. They are highly complex, but at the heart of identity is social interaction, for it is through social interaction that identities are formed, maintained, and changed. It is important to understand identity

FIGURE 10–2

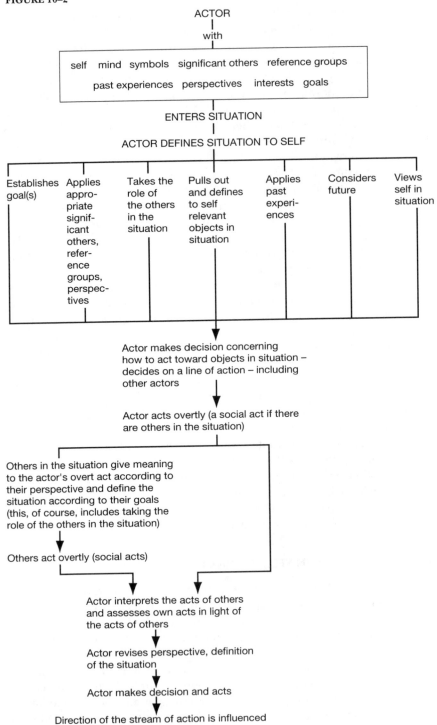

ACTOR
|
with

| self   mind   symbols   significant others   reference groups |
| past experiences   perspectives   interests   goals |

ENTERS SITUATION
|
ACTOR DEFINES SITUATION TO SELF

| Establishes goal(s) | Applies appropriate significant others, reference groups, perspectives | Takes the role of the others in the situation | Pulls out and defines to self relevant objects in situation | Applies past experiences | Considers future | Views self in situation |

Actor makes decision concerning how to act toward objects in situation – decides on a line of action – including other actors

Actor acts overtly (a social act if there are others in the situation)

Others in the situation give meaning to the actor's overt act according to their perspective and define the situation according to their goals (this, of course, includes taking the role of the others in the situation)

Others act overtly (social acts)

Actor interprets the acts of others and assesses own acts in light of the acts of others

Actor revises perspective, definition of the situation

Actor makes decision and acts

Direction of the stream of action is influenced

formation as a negotiation process which unfolds as we interact: "This is who I am"—"No; this is who you are"—"Wrong! This is who I am"—"No way! This is who you are." This negotiation process involves actors doing two things simultaneously: (1) continuously labeling others and attributing identities to them, and (2) continuously announcing to others the identity that they think they are. Out of this ongoing process, people's identities emerge and are reaffirmed. It is through the acts of others that we are recognized for who we are; it is through our acts that others are recognized for who they are.

We Label One Another in Social Interaction

We define who others are and what they want as we interact. We attribute identities to them, and these identities become important for how we act in relation to them. We label them based on what they do or say or how they are dressed or what we have heard. We label them according to what they announce their identity to be. Our label calls forth appropriate action for us. We sometimes stereotype others; that is, we apply a negative label to them based on sketchy information and we refuse to change the label as we interact. More often, we tentatively label those with whom we interact and during interaction come to revise our definition of them many times over. The label we apply may be easy for us in some situations, difficult in others:

> For example, if we walk into a theater and find a man in nonmilitary uniform standing expectantly at the door, we know automatically that he is a ticket taker and that we must present to him valid tickets if we wish to continue into the theater. The ticket-taker is not so labeled, nor is his uniform particularly distinctive, yet we do not have to ask why he is blocking our entrance, because the situation itself is so standardized in our culture that it provides sufficient clues as to the mutual implications of the persons involved. (McCall and Simmons, 1966;128)

It is relatively easy to distinguish men from women; it is usually easy to label someone as very elderly or very young; we may label some people black and some white; and we can usually tell who is married and who single. Situations are often standardized and identities easy to define: A lecture class has an instructor, graduate assistants, students; a football game has a quarterback, referees, cheerleaders, and so on. But very often labeling other people in interaction is far more complicated, based on subtle, not clearly delineated, clues, and usually subject to a great deal of alteration as we interact:

> This clarity of circumstance does not obtain in every human encounter or even in the majority of them. In fact, it is most likely to occur in precisely such routine and superficial interactions as the exchange of a ticket for entrance to the theater. And even then, the interaction may "spill over" from the specified into other exchanges and responses if the ticket-taker has a curious haircut, is an attractive girl, or is the son of one's insurance man. (McCall and Simmons, 1966;128)

Who people are depends on interaction, definition, and redefinition, what Peter Berger and Thomas Luckmann (1966) refer to as a negotiation process (p. 31). We label others and describe to ourselves what qualities they probably possess based on our labels. We interpret their acts based on such labels and imagined qualities, but usually we alter this as we act back and forth. Each actor's acts are social objects to be interpreted, leading to definition and renewed labeling. We develop an ongoing adjustment of actions back and forth. We do not simply know now what we are going to do next, because *it depends* in part on what others do, how we interpret that, and whether or not the identities we attributed earlier are confirmed. We may jump to conclusions before they are warranted, or we may be very careful before we identify the other, but always the definition of the other as an object, a social object, is part of our social interaction.

We Attempt to Shape Identities in Social Interaction

Our definition of the other often influences his or her definition of self. As I act toward you as a student, so you are influenced to think of yourself and feel *as a student.* As people salute you or degrade who you are in their actions, so we begin to recognize who we are in relation to others. Robert Merton (1957;421) described the "self-fulfilling prophecy": Acting as though something were true of the other, and even though it may not be, the other, in turn, thinks of self in these terms and acts in a way that is consistent with the label. We call students "dumb," children "bad," little girls "cute," women "emotional," men "aggressive," teachers "wise," homosexuals "sick." The labels define something as real, action is taken according to that definition, and others in the interaction are influenced to believe in the label and act accordingly, in such a way as to fulfill the definition. This process, of course, is never inevitable, because definitions can be made, labels applied, but the other's action can fail to conform to the definition and help create a new definition.

One way of influencing people's actions is to cast them into a role that we want so that they think of themselves in that manner and behave in the way we want. E. A. Weinstein and P. Deutschberger (1963) call this "altercasting." "You are a good Christian person; Christian people do not swear." "You are a man; men do not cry." "You are a woman; women are supposed to care for their families." Casting others into identities that make sense to us and aid our plans in interaction is controlling the situation to some extent. I cast you into an inferior status (socioeconomic class, occupation, looks, or intelligence), and then I influence our interaction. "People like you are supposed to believe people like me." I shame you in front of others, embarrass you, purposely degrade you. Or I may tell you that you are a sweet person, an intelligent human being, a sensitive lover—again, in part to define the situation for you and to help control the direction of the interaction.

Of course, you may not believe my definition of you in the situation, and you may declare an identity different from my definition. We will in the end negotiate an identity. However, power—based on intelligence, wealth, control of employment, grades, and so on—will play a role in whose definition wins in the long run.

Sometimes it is not important if you believe me or not. If I can convince others who you are, I influence their definition of you and thus their action toward you, and ultimately your interaction with them. In a court of law I define you as a liar; to a friend I call you a cheat; to a business associate I define you as a bright rising star. You are someone who people label, and the labels that arise in interaction with me and with others become important for interaction.

The process of degradation is perhaps an extreme example, but it is an excellent one and highly appropriate here. Harold Garfinkel (1956) describes how one can be effective in degrading someone in public. Degradation he defines as a situation "whereby the public identity of an actor is transformed into something looked on as lower in the local scheme of social types" (p. 402). He carefully and insightfully lists the important ingredients of successful degradation of the other:

1. The event—say, an act of copying someone's exam—must appear to stand out from the everyday ordinary situation. The actor to be denounced must also be made to appear to stand out from other people.
2. Both the event and the actor must be typed—they must be treated as part of a type of event and actor. Thus, the event is *cheating* and the actor is a *cheater*. The listeners must constantly be reminded of this, and there should be an attempt always to contrast such types with the opposite types: honesty and a moral person.
3. The denouncer must carefully identify himself or herself with the listeners and with the community. The denunciation is not his or hers alone but conforms to what all reasonable human beings believe. Similarly, the denouncer must show that the denunciation does not arise from harm done to him or her, but from an identification with the rules of the community itself. It is as a member of the community—not as an individual—that he or she has suffered. "We all suffer when there is cheating. The whole system of education is denounced. There can be no fair grading where cheaters are not punished."
4. The one who is denounced must appear to be distanced from everyone else who supports the rules of the group. He or she must be made strange. "We all want to succeed in college. But we are not cheats! Here is a cheat." (Adapted from Garfinkel, 1956;422–23)

Garfinkel concludes:

These are the conditions that must be fulfilled for a successful denunciation. If they are absent, the denunciation will fail. Regardless of the situation when the denouncer enters, if he [or she] is to succeed in degrading the other [actor], it is necessary to introduce these features. (P. 423)

To denunciate successfully is to influence the direction of interaction by influencing the labels that others attribute to the actor and the acts that they therefore initiate. It can, of course, influence the actor's view of self, influencing his or her actions in relation to others. Sometimes this may mean accepting the label and continuing to act according to it; sometimes this may mean altering directions in order to prove the label wrong. There are many examples of this in our lives: in courts of law, in school, in families, and among friends. Even presidential candidates are not immune—witness, for example, the case of Gary Hart, forced to remove himself from the race for president because of a successful denunciation based on what he called an innocent encounter with a woman. When he reentered the race, no matter how hard he tried, the harm of the denunciation could not be shaken.

Thus, as we interact with others we label them. We tell them who we think they are. We act toward them as if they are . . . a man . . . a professor . . . a husband . . . a moral person . . . an educated scholar. Our acts become a symbolic statement by us. Such acts by an assortment of people usually have some impact on who the actor thinks he or she is. In one situation one may be defined one way, in another a very different way, but over time a consistency emerges—an identity is formed. And as we take on that identity, we increasingly act consistently with it. The more we become someone, the more we act accordingly; the more we act accordingly, the more likely others will see us for what we have become; the more others see and label us in this manner, the more we will continue to become that someone.

We Shape Our Own Identities in Social Interaction

We are not helpless in social interaction. Remember that others do not simply influence us, but that we consider their actions, we define and interpret them, and we make our decisions through mind action. We are active participants in our identity formation.

When we act around others, we make an attempt to present ourselves according to the identities we claim for ourselves. My self label—identity—influences what Goffman calls my *presentation of self to others*. We may announce our identity in an obvious or subtle way; we may dress to kill, put on a smile, paint our office the "in" colors, or look tough. Gregory Stone (1962;100) describes dress as important for telling others who we are, announcing our identities. He points out that our appearance is a substitute for our past and present action, and tells others what to expect from us. Clothing tells others our proposals in the situation. Alison Lurie (1981) makes this same point in *The Language of Clothes:*

> More generally, the idea that even when we say nothing our clothes are talking noisily to everyone who sees us, telling them who we are, where we come from, what we like to do in bed and a dozen other intimate things, may be unsettling. To wear what "everyone else" is wearing is no solution to the problem, any more than it would be to say what everyone else is saying. We all know people who try

to do this; but even if their imitation of "everyone" is successful, their clothes do not shut up; rather they broadcast without stopping the information that this is a timid and conventional man or woman, and possibly an untrustworthy one. We can lie in the language of dress, or try to tell the truth; but unless we are naked and bald it is impossible to be silent. (P. 261)

One of the very best descriptions of how we each try to influence others' views of us is Goffman's (1959) description at the beginning of *Presentation of Self in Everyday Life*. Goffman's analysis begins with a simple idea: When we interact, we know that what we say and do makes a difference to others, that others do indeed figure us out and act toward us accordingly; therefore, we make efforts to give off acts that influence others to think of us in the way that we want; in a real sense interaction is a stage where we all act out parts that we choose to present to others. In other words, we take an active role in telling others who we are, and we control our actions in order to give off the image that we want:

> Regardless of the particular objective which the individual has in mind and of his motive for having this objective, it will be in his interests to control the conduct of the others, especially their responsive treatment of him. This control is achieved largely by influencing the definition of the situation which the others come to formulate, and he can influence this definition by expressing himself in such a way as to give them the kind of impression that will lead them to act voluntarily in accordance with his own plan. Thus, when an individual appears in the presence of others, there will usually be some reason for him to mobilize his activity so that it will convey an impression to others which it is in his interests to convey. (p. 4)

The presentation of self in situations reminds us once again that human beings are symbol users. We try to communicate messages to others. In the case of identity, we control our actions so that what we do represents our identity to others. In fact it even goes further than our actions: Our friends, cars, religious objects, neighbors, clothes, and hair tell others what we want them to know about us, the identity we wish them to see. Those running for political office must be especially careful in this regard. Jesse Jackson found it difficult to overcome the burden of friendship with Louis Farrakhan. A person running for governor in Michigan would find it difficult to drive a Japanese-made car. Even our spouses matter in our presentation of self to others:

> As performers giving off impressions of public morality and fitness for office, public figures try to maintain the idea that they are indeed fulfilling the standards of civic conventionality, by which they are to be judged. At the same time, the activity of "engineering" convincing impressions of those standards makes them "merchants of morality." . . . The public wife appears on that stage . . . to nurture impressions of that "steady moral light." (Gillespie, 1980;119, 123)

The work of Goffman reminds us that creating identity is an active negotiation process between who others tell us we are and our continuous attempts to present who we think we are to others.

Social interaction then takes on further importance now. It not only is the basis of our human nature; it not only shapes how we act in situations; but it is also the negotiation process through which we create one another's identities.

SOCIAL INTERACTION CREATES SOCIETY

Interaction is also responsible for society. It is through it that society is formed, reaffirmed, and altered, and it is through the absence of continuous interaction that society ceases to exist. Society depends on individuals continuously interacting with one another and with themselves. It is to this important topic of *society* that we now turn in Chapter 11.

SUMMARY

It should be obvious by now how central social interaction is to the human being. This whole symbolic interactionist perspective comes together with the introduction of this concept. Let us briefly put together the central ideas concerning social interaction—its meaning and its importance:

1. Human beings are social symbolic actors. We take others into account as we act; we symbolically communicate in our actions; we interpret one another's actions.
2. Social interaction is simply mutual social action that involves symbolic communication and interpretation of one another's acts. Social interaction also involves role taking and organizing our acts as we take one another into account.
3. Social interaction creates our qualities as human beings: social objects, symbols, self, mind, and our ability to take the role of the other.
4. Social interaction is a cause of action in its own right. What we do in a situation depends on our interpretation of other people's actions; their action depends on their interpretation of ours. Action unfolds over time.
5. Social interaction shapes our identities. It is not others who create who we are, and it is not simply who we "really are" inside. Instead, identity results from a negotiation process that arises in social interaction. We label others in interaction; we attempt to shape the identities of others in interaction; we tell others who we think we are in social interaction. Through it all we come to think of our self as something; an identity is formed. And our action is now influenced by who in the world we think we are.
6. Finally, social interaction creates society.

REFERENCES

BERGER, PETER L., AND THOMAS LUCKMANN
   1966   *The Social Construction of Reality.* New York: Doubleday.

BLUMER, HERBERT
> 1953 "Psychological Import of the Human Group." In Muzafer Sherif and M. O. Wilson, eds., *Group Relations at the Crossroads,* pp. 185–202. New York: Harper & Row.
>
> 1962 "Society as Symbolic Interaction." In Arnold Rose, ed., *Human Behavior and Social Processes,* pp. 179–92. Boston: Houghton Mifflin Co.
>
> 1966 "Sociological Implications of the Thought of George Herbert Mead." *American Journal of Sociology* 71:535–44. By permission of The University of Chicago Press. Copyright © 1966 by The University of Chicago.
>
> 1969 *Symbolic Interactionism: Perspective and Method.* Englewood Cliffs, N.J.: Prentice Hall. Copyright © 1969. Reprinted by permission of Prentice Hall, Inc.

COOLEY, CHARLES HORTON
> 1909 *Social Organization,* 1962 ed. New York: Schocken Books.

CRITTENDEN, KATHLEEN S.
> 1983 "Sociological Aspects of Attribution." *Annual Review of Sociology* 9:425–46.

DENZIN, NORMAN K.
> 1984 "Toward a Phenomenology of Domestic, Family Violence." *American Journal of Sociology* 90:483–513.

FELSON, RICHARD B.
> 1978 "Aggression as Impression Management." *Social Psychology* 41:205–213.

GARFINKEL, HAROLD
> 1956 "Conditions of Successful Degradation Ceremonies." *American Journal of Sociology* 61:420–24.

GILLESPIE, JOANNA
> 1980 "The Phenomenon of the Public Wife: An Exercise in Goffman's Impression Management." *Symbolic Interaction* 3:109–26.

GOFFMAN, ERVING
> 1959 *The Presentation of Self in Everyday Life.* Garden City, N.Y.: Doubleday.
>
> 1983 "The Interaction Order." *American Sociological Review* 48:1–17.

JOAS, HANS
> 1985 *G. H. Mead.* Trans. Raymond Meyer. Cambridge, Mass.: MIT Press.

LURIE, ALISON
> 1981 *The Language of Clothes.* Random House.

MCCALL, GEORGE J., AND J. L. SIMMONS
> 1966 *Identities and Interactions.* New York: Free Press. Reprinted with permission of The Free Press, an imprint of Simon & Schuster. Copyright © 1966 by The Free Press.

MERTON, ROBERT K.
> 1957 *Social Theory and Social Structure.* New York: Free Press.

SHIBUTANI, TAMOTSU
> 1961 *Society and Personality: An Interactionist Approach to Social Psychology.* Englewood Cliffs, N.J.: Prentice Hall. Copyright © 1961. Reprinted by permission of Prentice Hall.

SHOTT, SUSAN
> 1979 "Emotion and Social Life: A Symbolic Interactionist Analysis." *American Journal of Sociology* 84:1317–34.

STONE, GREGORY P.
> 1962 "Appearance and the Self." In Arnold Rose, ed., *Human Behavior and Social Processes,* pp. 86–118. Boston: Houghton Mifflin.

THOMAS, WILLIAM I., AND DOROTHY THOMAS
  1928   *The Child in America.* New York: Knopf.

THRASHER, FREDERIC M.
  1936   *The Gang.* Chicago: University of Chicago Press. By permission of The
          University of Chicago Press and William E. Girton. Copyright © 1927 by
          The University of Chicago. All rights reserved.

WEINSTEIN, E. A., AND P. DEUTSCHBERGER
  1963   "Some Dimensions of Altercasting." *Sociometry* 26:454–66.

11

Society

Sociology was defined as the "science of society" by the French philosopher Auguste Comte in the early nineteenth century. Although sociologists may differ on what exactly should be the emphasis in what they study, all seem to agree that society must enter into the analysis somewhere, that one goal must be to understand the nature of society as well as the interrelationship between the individual and society. Therefore, it is imperative for a social psychology that has relevance to sociology to consider society.

Comte divided the study of society into statics (structure) and dynamics (change). Throughout the history of sociology, thinkers have clustered around two poles, some emphasizing structure, others dynamics; some describing the permanence of society's controls, some emphasizing the ever-changing nature of society and even shying away from terms such as "structure" and "society."

Those who have emphasized structure have tended to examine the historical reality of society: Society is a set of forces that exert themselves on the individual. Society is a set of institutions, stratification systems, and cultural patterns into which individuals are born and are socialized, playing roles according to scripts laid down by others, living and dead. Society has a permanence that shapes each individual. Society socializes the individual; the individual internalizes society. The major criticism of this view is that it is a highly deterministic perspective that leaves little room to conceptualize the active person who defines and changes society. It shows how we all are shaped by society, but it does not show how the individual is able to shape society; it does not see how society is always being formed and shaped through interaction.

The second view of society is one that emphasizes a dynamic, changing nature and de-emphasizes structure and the historical development of institutions, stratification systems, and cultural patterns. It focuses instead on change, on individuals interacting—influenced by the past, but also defining that past—developing new definitions of the present, and shaping society. Society is described as a process; society is individuals who interact. The criticism of this view is that it tends to overlook the power of society, the deterministic nature of institutions, of structure, and of cultural patterns. And a second important criticism is that it focuses too much on interacting individuals constantly redefining society, changing society: It becomes a wonder that society is able to exist at all and maintain its structure with the constant self-direction that takes place.

Both perspectives of society are useful, and although some theorists attempt to integrate them, it is difficult to do, and most end up emphasizing one or the other view. Most sociologists fall on the side of society as structure, society as historical, society as permanent, society as determining, although they will sometimes attempt to look at the dynamics of human interaction and change. The symbolic interactionists, probably more than any other school in sociology, conceptualize society in the dynamic sense: as individuals in interaction with one another, defining and altering the direction of one another's acts. Certain qualities are necessarily emphasized, whereas others are ignored. "Human society might best be regarded as an on-going process, a *becoming* rather than a *being*. Society might be viewed most fruitfully as a succession of events, a flow of gestural interchanges among people" (Shibutani, 1961;174). Symbolic interactionists recognize that society has a history and exists as a somewhat stable entity, but they are not able to give this side its due, simply because the focus is on interaction and change.

The purpose of this chapter is to examine society from the perspective of symbolic interactionism. You will find that society is a central concept of this book, that it integrates all the other concepts, and that the resulting definition makes good sense and helps us understand the nature of the human being.

GROUPS, ORGANIZATIONS, SOCIAL WORLDS, AND SOCIETIES

There is, in symbolic interactionism, no reason for a distinction between types of organization. Each dyad, each group, each organization, each interaction situation, each social world, even the most temporary, is a society, or at least a society in an early stage of development. Even the crowd, where interaction is considered "primitive," is the beginning of society. Through studying the crowd we can come to understand the nature of society, for some of the same dynamics that characterize the crowd characterize all organization.

Crowds, groups, organizations, communities, and societies all are made up of individuals who interact. Society—all group life—is defined here as *individuals in interaction*, doing the kinds of things discussed in earlier chapters: role taking, communicating, interpreting one another, adjusting their acts to one another, directing and controlling self, sharing perspectives. The terms "group," "society," "organization," and "social world" will be used interchangeably—we will regard all groups as societies. In other contexts, it may be useful to distinguish them, but for purposes of understanding the nature of organization from a symbolic interactionist perspective, it is not necessary.

SOCIETY IS SYMBOLIC INTERACTION

In Chapter 3 the ideas of Tamotsu Shibutani were introduced, and his article "Reference Groups as Perspectives" was analyzed extensively. Shibutani emphasizes that "social worlds" are made up of individuals who communicate with symbols, who come to share a perspective in interaction. He describes these social worlds as lacking geographical unity, held together primarily by this communication. The readers of a professional journal form a social world, as do the elderly, preadolescents, fantasy game players, and the gay community. Gary Fine (1987) studied the social world of preadolescent boys, whom he describes as living in a social world with a culture of their own, driven by a desire to be and act like men and to separate themselves from the worlds of girls and younger children. What makes them a social world is their interaction, communication, and shared reality (p. 185).

The fact that a social world needs no geographic unity but instead is tied by symbolic interaction is significant here. A social world is like all societies: It is made up of people interacting and communicating with symbols.

Society is ongoing social interaction. Social interaction means, first of all, that actors take one another's acts into account, and they decide on action dependent on that fact. A group is made up of individuals whose acts matter to one another. They consider one another: Their acts "are intertwined," "joint," "fitted together," "interdependent." This does not mean that they imitate one another, or that they necessarily do the same things, but at least each individual's acts matter to the others (Blumer, 1969;109). A group or society, then, is made up of social actors who act back and forth and form their acts in relation to one another. Herbert Blumer (1966) refers to this as "joint action" and points out that it ranges "from a simple collaboration of two individuals to a complex alignment of the acts of huge organizations or institutions" (p. 540). An employer and an employee each may have his or her own reasons for taking the other into account, each has something different at stake, but they are involved in joint action—ongoing coordinated interaction:

> Such alignment may take place for any number of reasons, depending on the situations calling for joint action, and need not involve, or spring from, the sharing of common values. The participants may fit their acts to one another in orderly joint actions on the basis of compromise, out of duress, because they may use one another in achieving their respective ends, because it is the sensible thing to do, or out of sheer necessity. . . . In very large measure, society becomes the formation of workable relations. (Blumer, 1966;544)*

Society, then, is interacting individuals. A family unit, the First Baptist Church, the crowd at a football game, two people who meet at Sam's bar—to the extent that each one of these examples is characterized by individuals who act with one another in mind, by individuals who take account of one another

*Reprinted from "Sociological Implications of the Thought of George Herbert Mead" by Herbert Blumer in *The American Journal of Sociology* by permission of The University of Chicago Press. Copyright © 1966 by The University of Chicago. All rights reserved.

as they act—to that extent we call it a society. Sometimes a society has only a short existence, but more often a much longer life. The United States is a society to the extent that we can identify interaction among those who live within its borders. To the extent that such interaction is segregated, then to that extent we might identify many separate societies instead of one larger one.

Society, however, is more than just interaction; it is *symbolic* interaction. It involves communication and interpretation by the actors. Blumer (1969) points out:

> Whether the collectivity be an army engaged in a campaign, a corporation seeking to expand its operations, or a nation trying to correct an unfavorable balance of trade, it needs to construct its action through an interpretation of what is happening in its area of operation. The interpretative process takes place by participants making indications to one another, not merely each to himself. Joint or collective action is an outcome of such a process of interpretive interaction. (P. 16)

It is through *understanding* the act from the other person's perspective that society is made possible. It is through *communicating* to others what one is doing, what one believes, and what one is about to do that society is able to exist. It is through *socializing others* through symbolic acts that interaction continues over time. *Cooperation* depends on symbols, actors communicating and interpreting one another's acts as they go along:

> It is only as men use their capacity to symbol as a tool of communication that they create the essential ingredient of society. . . . It is at this point that society comes into being for they can agree upon what their acts, themselves as actors, and other events shall mean to them *together.* . . .
>
> Communication involves a totally new phenomenon, that of a *collective* meaning. Although this collective meaning exists in the separate minds of the individual actors its content is defined by their communication and by the implicit and explicit agreements that this is the meaning that things shall have for them *in their interaction.* (Warriner, 1970;133)

Society, then, is individuals interacting over time: acting with one another in mind, adjusting their acts to one another as they go along, symbolically communicating and interpreting one another's acts.

SOCIETY IS COOPERATIVE SYMBOLIC INTERACTION

Society involves *individuals engaging in cooperative action.* Blumer's description of "joint action" is really cooperative interaction. Almost all cases of interaction are cases of cooperative problem solving, but some are not. Enemies who are eternally hostile to one another may take one another into account and may communicate, may even understand one another very clearly, may even act alike, but will not constitute a society, because their action is not characterized by a cooperative effort to deal with a situation.

When two enemies are threatened, they may join forces, and they begin to be a society. The United States is a society to the extent that people cooperate in dealing with situations. Cooperation may involve having common goals, but not necessarily. Cooperation does not depend on the same goals, but on the fact that interaction is such that actors can use one another's resources to act effectively in situations encountered, to deal with problems, major or minor. Society exists as long as people work together in spite of their personal differences. Society is more a matter of interdependence where individuals help one another resolve problems each faces, rather than a situation where actors have the same goals. People may have different things at stake—for example, a student may want to graduate, a teacher may want to teach something vital—yet the interaction can be cooperative problem solving, and the people thus qualify as a group or society.

Individuals interact. *When they interact cooperatively, a society is formed.*

Individuals act in situations, and their action is aimed at working out problems, major or minor, in the situation. *When individuals act cooperatively to solve problems in situations, a society is formed.*

The meaning of cooperative social interaction has been investigated at the University of Iowa under the direction of Carl Couch. Although this research has focused on interaction between two actors, it has attempted to understand the nature of all cooperation, or more exactly, how actors in social situations work together to complete a task.*

Typically, a problem situation is set up in a laboratory, and people must decide to ignore that situation or to join forces and deal with it. Their actions are videotaped and analyzed. The critical question is: "What exactly takes place between people for them to participate in a cooperative act?" The research looks at cooperation that lasts for a few moments; society, of course, is ongoing interaction, but the process involved is basically the same. There are five processes that must occur, and these are identical to what is meant here by cooperation:

1. *Ongoing communication:* For cooperation to take place, actors must be "copresent." That is, actors must be together in a situation where there is opportunity to communicate, where each is available for the other as both a subject and an object of communication. Cooperation depends on the ability of the actors to exchange ideas, requests, and orders about how each is to deal with the situation at hand. Communication may be vocal but also can be writing, eye movements, or gestures. From interaction between two people to interaction in large societies, cooperation depends on people communicating as they go along.

---

*The remainder of this section was written cooperatively with Professor Joel Powell, a graduate of the University of Iowa. It also relies heavily on Dan E. Miller, Robert A. Hintz, Jr., and Carl J. Couch, in "The Elements and Structure of Openings," *Constructing Social Life,* pp. 1-24, Champaign, Ill.: Stipes, 1975.

2. *Mutual role taking:* Actors must be "mutually responsive." That is, actors must be in the position for taking each other into account over time. We must be in the position of observing the acts of the other and making a good guess concerning the future acts of the other in order to know what we should do. Those who do not note what others are doing cannot cooperate. In fact, it is also important for each actor to recognize that the other is also taking him or her into account.

3. *Defining the others as social objects:* Actors must develop "congruent functional identities." That is, they must recognize who the other is in the situation—a learner, a fullback, a single woman interested in going on a date—and these identities must be important to the goals of the actor in that situation. In turn, the actor's identity must be seen to be useful for the others too. Cooperation involves each actor recognizing that the other actor has an identity that is useful for completing the task that they are both facing.

4. *Defining social objects together:* Actors must develop a "shared focus of attention." That is, in interaction an object in the situation must become important to each actor. An object is shared, around which people organize their actions: a scream from another room, hostages, a topic of conversation, the opportunity to make money, a piece of music to perform.

5. *Developing goals in interaction:* Actors must develop goals that are either the same or complementary. A shared goal or cluster of goals emerges: to win a game, to help someone in need, to negotiate a contract, to study for an exam, to plan a business.

Cooperation means, then that people communicate (are copresent) and take one another's roles on an ongoing basis (are mutually responsive); they regard one another as important in their actions (regard one another has having congruent functional identities), they generally agree on what is important in their environment (have shared focus of attention); and they develop common or complementary goals. Without any one of these, the interaction becomes something other than cooperation and society is no more. If they are no longer copresent and cannot communicate or role take, then they cannot know what to do in relation to one another. If they do not see one another as necessary partners in order to achieve their goals, then they do not find it important to act in accordance with one another. If they do not come to share a definition of objects in their environment, they cannot coordinate their actions in relation to those objects, and if they develop goals that are in conflict with others then it is not until such goals can be made the same or complementary that cooperation exists.

Let us suppose, for example, that a number of people decide to have a party. For them to cooperate effectively they must somehow perform all of these five processes. That is, they must decide when to get together in order to organize the party: either now, on the telephone next week, or at lunch on Monday (they must decide when they are going to communicate; when they plan to be copresent). Even if they decide to delegate the planning to one person, they must be copresent to do this. They must communicate to and understand one another in terms of what each wants at the party (menu, guests, time, place, and so on). They must also take the role of the others, becoming sensitive to and taking into account each individual's desire (in effect, they must become mutually responsive). As they interact they must recognize that at this point in time each is a participant in planning, and that each will be expected to participate in carrying out assigned tasks. Each becomes a partner in the future: "It is *our* party" (each is an important social object; each takes on a congruent functional identity). In social interaction the actors might discuss bad parties, cool people, good music, but the discussion continues to focus on the plan (a common focus of attention; a shared social object). Of course, a shared goal continues to be reaffirmed (having a good party). All go away, continue to work, communicate as to how things are going, continue to take one another's work into account, alter their plan as they go along, and even redefine the goal.

So it is in every instance of cooperative social interaction: negotiation over hostages, planning a wedding, starting a business, playing checkers, conserving energy, teaching and learning sociology in the classroom, studying together for an exam, dancing, giving emergency care in a hospital, and fighting a war. There is communication, taking others into account, recognizing one another as useful in dealing with situations, defining objects in the situation in a similar way, and developing similar or complementary goals. All are examples of societies being formed; all are examples of cooperative symbolic interaction.

Interaction that does not involve cooperation is not society. In fact, actors can be copresent, mutually responsive, but lack either congruent functional identities, a shared focus, or complementary goals. For example, violent conflict is interaction that stands in marked contrast to what society is. Violent interaction normally disrupts society rather than maintains it. Some of us love, marry, and form a family group that ends up riddled with violent conflict. Over time such violence may become the primary way that actors relate to one another:

> If not checked, it [violence] turns back on itself and destroys its participants and their relationships with one another. . . . The family becomes a network of violent, interacting individuals. No one trusts anyone else. They have collectively passed through that thin wall that divides a "normal" family from a "deviant," "different," violent family. They become outsiders to one another. An emotional climate of violence attaches itself to the family. They are participants in a progressively differentiated system of negative symbolic interaction. The actions and utterances of each member call forth violent and violence-repressed reactions on the part of every other member. The potentiality for violence becomes the veil through which all thought and action in the family is first screened. (Denzin, 1984;490)

Here there is interaction, here actors communicate symbolically and align their acts, but here there are negative emotions, an inability to cooperate, a lack of trust, and alienation that undermine a societal order. "The course of daily interaction between the family members becomes problematic and unpredictable. . . . Situations get out of control, and the actions each member takes become consequential for all future dealings they have with each other" (p. 494). So, too, does violent interaction between nations or groups within nations stand in marked contrast to the cooperation necessary for society.

Two qualities are therefore central to society: symbolic interaction and cooperation. There is one more: *culture.*

SOCIETY IS SYMBOLIC COOPERATIVE INTERACTION THAT DEVELOPS CULTURE

Culture Is a Shared Perspective

Over time cooperative symbolic interaction creates culture. Every society has a culture; culture helps create continuity over time and is taken on by the actors as guides to action. Individuals enter situations with all kinds of tools to guide them as they interact with others, but the longer they interact with those others, the more likely something new will enter into their guides for action— the emerging culture of the group:

> A group finds itself sharing a common situation and common problems. Various members of the group experiment with possible solutions to those problems and report their experiences to their fellows. In the course of their collective discussion, the members of the group arrive at a definition of the situation, its problems and possibilities, and develop a consensus as to the most appropriate and efficient ways of behaving. This consensus thenceforth constrains the activities of individual members of the group, who will probably act on it, given the opportunity. (Becker, 1982;520)

Culture means the "consensus" of the group, the agreements, the shared understandings, the shared language and knowledge, and the rules that are supposed to govern action.

In Chapter 3 we introduced the ideas of Shibutani (1955), who described culture as the *shared perspective* of a society or reference group. He called culture a group's perspective or frame of reference it takes toward reality. Each person who takes on the perspective

> perceives, thinks, forms judgments, and controls himself according to the frame of reference of the group in which he is participating. Since he defines objects, other people, the world, and himself from the perspective that he shares with others, he can visualize his proposed line of action from this generalized standpoint, anticipate the reactions of others, inhibit undesirable impulses, and thus guide his conduct. The socialized person is a society in miniature; he sets the same standards of conduct for himself as he sets for others, and he judges himself in the same terms. He can define situations properly and meet his obligations, even in the absence of other people, because, as already noted, his perspective always takes into account the expectations of others. Thus, it is the ability to define situations from the same standpoint as others that makes personal controls possible. (P. 564)

Culture Is a Generalized Other

The culture of society becomes the guide for the individual's definition and action. In his work, George Herbert Mead used the term "generalized other" to describe the shared culture of the group. Both "perspective" and "generalized other" capture the meaning of what culture is. In fact, it is easiest to understand culture if we divide it up into both of these. A culture is a society's perspective *and* generalized other. Whereas "perspective" implies that culture means a shared reality, "generalized other" places the emphasis on a culture as a *shared body of rules*. A generalized other is the law that must be obeyed; it is the system; it is the conscience of the group that individuals are expected to follow in social interaction. Peter L. Berger and Thomas Luckmann (1966) give an excellent description of the emergence of a generalized other:

> Primary socialization creates in the child's consciousness a progressive abstraction from the roles and attitudes of specific others to roles and attitudes in *general*. For example, in the internalization of norms there is a progression from "Mummy is angry with me *now*" to "Mummy is angry with me *whenever* I spill the soup." As additional significant others (father, grandmother, older sister, and so on) support the mother's negative attitude toward soup-spilling, the generality of the norm is subjectively extended. The decisive step comes when the child recognizes that *everybody* is against soup-spilling, and the norm is generalized to "One does not spill soup"—"one" being himself as a part of a generality that includes, in principle, *all* society insofar as it is significant to the child. This abstraction from the roles and attitudes of concrete significant others is called the generalized other. Its formation within consciousness means that the individual now identifies not only with concrete others but with a generality of others, that is, with a society. (P. 132)

It is this generalized other that the individual learns in interaction, and it is this generalized other that the individual comes to use to direct, control, and judge the self; it is the generalized other that becomes the individual's moral guide. As the individual develops his or her individual qualities—self and mind—a social being who controls self in line with others is being developed. Self and society emerge together. Maturity of self means a recognition by the individual that one's own needs, one's own goals, one's own ideas must be worked out to some extent by considering the rules of the wider community.

Lonnie Athens (1986;376-79) applies the concept of "generalized other" to an understanding of violent offenders. He describes four types of people: the pacifist, the marginally violent person, the violent person, and the ultra-violent person. These types are different from one another in the generalized other they assume in situations within which they act. The pacifist, for example, has an antiviolent generalized other—one that "provides him or her with pronounced and categorical support for never acting violently toward other persons." Contrast this with the ultraviolent person: one who has a generalized other that "provides him or her with pronounced and categorical support for acting violently toward other persons even when it is not required to defend him or herself or an intimate or to deal with extreme provocation." The other two types are, of course, in between these two extremes. The point, however, is that our generalized others are guides to how we deal with situations—they set our limits, they inform us as to how best to deal with problems—and they arise from our society. Generalized others support or discourage violence by the individual.

The generalized other is the moral system that the individual internalizes, makes his or her own. Continuous interaction depends on individuals who *share* a generalized other, who share a set of rules to some minimal extent. Society—cooperative symbolic interaction—demands a body of rules that people agree to use to direct their action.

Culture then is (1) *a shared perspective* through which individuals in interaction define reality and (2) *a generalized other* through which individuals in interaction control their own acts. Culture arises in symbolic interaction; it is a central quality of any society; it becomes an important social object to individuals who continue to cooperate in that society; it guides their thinking and their self-control.

Culture Maintains Society

The product of symbolic interaction—culture—becomes important for the continuation of society. It is because people come to share and use a perspective and a generalized other that a continuing society is possible.

A *shared perspective* is necessary for understanding one another in order to accomplish difficult tasks. Charles Warriner (1970) writes that people are able to act with others because they "come to share notions as to what they will do. And they can come to share such notions (expectations) only through the communications involved in interaction" (p. 98). A shared perspective is necessary (at least to some extent) in order to perceive one's own place in the interaction. A shared perspective is important for ongoing communication, which in turn, is central to cooperation:

> Group life is organized around communication. Communication . . . signifies shared meanings. . . . The members are able to participate in various coordinated activities because they share a common terminology. Groups form around points of agreement, and then new classifications arise on the basis of further shared experience. (Strauss, 1959;148–49)

A *generalized other* is necessary for self-control and self-direction, which make action consistent with what others are doing, allowing the action to go in an agreed-upon direction established in interaction rather than according to the whims of each individual. We can afford to act alone without a generalized other when our actions do not need to be coordinated with anyone else's; however, once others are needed for cooperation a generalized other needs to enter into what we do.

Society continues, therefore, at least in part because individuals share a culture from which they define reality and control their actions. "Human society rests upon a basis of *consensus*, i.e., the sharing of meanings in the form of common understandings and expectations" (Meltzer, 1972;13-14).

A study by Linda Smircich (1983) of the executive staff in an insurance company illustrates the central place of cultural consensus in maintaining organization. Her article is entitled "Organizations as Shared Meanings," and her conclusion is that organization gets things done on a day-to-day basis through "the development of shared meanings for events, objects, words and people" and through the development of "a sense of commonality of experience that facilitates their coordinated action" (p. 55). In this particular organization the dominant cultural belief was that differences, problems, and conflict were not to be brought out in the open. People knew that the way to maintain the smooth operation of the organization was to maintain a surface conformity. The executive staff also shared a belief as to why this had to be the case: The president wants things that way. This emerging culture gave the executive staff "a sense of commonality and unity to their experience. These beliefs contributed to coordinated, albeit restrained, interaction and an aura of passivity among the staff members" (pp. 57–58). The Monday morning staff meeting, important to the president, was ritual to the executive staff who saw it as "empty formality," where nothing of substance was ever done. The emerging perspective was used by members to control their own acts and to cooperate to achieve goals in the organization.

Sometimes a consensus does not emerge in interaction, and society is impossible. In *The Derelicts of Company K*, Shibutani (1978) specifically examines the problem of demoralization in groups—how groups fall apart and individuals are not able to cooperatively problem solve. His focus was on the morale of Company K, a unit stationed in Minneapolis at the end of World War II. Here is a description of individuals without commitment to a generalized other, a refusal to internalize rules, individuals without self-control in line with cooperative problem solving:

> Company K had all the symptoms of a demoralized group. The most common form of resistance was evasion of duties, but opposition often went well beyond mere recalcitrance. Shouting obscenities and insults from ranks was commonplace. Violence erupted, and a brief reign of terror developed. Local officials, though held personally accountable for the accomplishment of military objectives, found it impossible to maintain order; at times the men became so unruly that the officers simply left them to their own resources. (P. 8)

Shibutani described more examples of demoralization and lack of unity: going AWOL, walking off work details, fighting with and embarrassing supervisors, and refusing to salute. One officer who was particularly disliked ended his lecture with: "You must obey orders regardless of how stupid or absurd they may seem." The entire company burst out in laughter (p. 123). This is the nightmare of organization that fails to work because there is no commitment to a shared culture both as a generalized other and as a perspective that individuals are willing to use as guides to action.

Culture Is Ever Changing

There is a paradox, writes Howard Becker (1982): "On the one hand, culture persists and antedates the participation of particular people in it: indeed, culture can be said to shape the outlooks of people who participate in it." On the other hand, however, everything is always changing: Cultural understandings "have to be reviewed and remade continually, and in the remaking they change." This is not a true paradox, Becker continues, as "the understandings last *because* they change to deal with new situations" (pp. 522–23). Societies deal with an ever-changing environment. Culture is communicated, tried out, applied, and altered by cooperative individuals in real situations. Like anything else, if it works there is reason to continuously use it; if it does not work exactly right, then it is altered. Culture represents the stability of the group, yet stability cannot be complete, because situations always involve some adjustment on the part of the cooperative group. Society is a complex interplay of consensus and change, carried on through ongoing interaction or communication:

> . . . Consensus is rarely complete even for purposes of a relatively simple enterprise. It is partial; there are almost invariably areas of uncertainty, and it is about these that most of the interchanges take place. With each gesture the uncertainties are successively minimized or eliminated, enabling each person to contribute his share and to enjoy greater confidence in the responses of others. In most situations, then, communication is a continuing process. Men who are acting together try to develop and maintain mutual orientations to facilitate the coordination of their respective efforts, and the interplay must continue until the task is accomplished. The concept of *communication* refers to that interchange of gestures through which consensus is developed, sustained, or broken. (Shibutani, 1961;140-41)

Culture arises in and is changed in interaction as people put forth the particular meanings and ideas that they believe in. Interaction validates past culture, and it revises what is known. It involves conflict and negotiation where actors compete—it is "almost like a battle over whose and which definitions prevail as the basis for future interaction" (Stryker, 1980;57).

The battle is negotiation. Culture is negotiated. What is negotiation? Negotiation means that something among actors emerges out of the acts of all to one another. Each does not get his or her own way exactly, but instead the input by each affects the net result to some extent. Ideas, rules, direction of the group, direction of the individuals—all are negotiated in interaction.

In one simple example, Fine (1987) reports an episode in a Little League baseball game. Of course, there is one rule book that all are supposed to follow. The book tells all that one needs to know. Yet, in specific games, rules must be interpreted to fit the situation, and that interpretation is a result, in part, of negotiation. In one instance, a pitch was thrown that was the most important pitch of the whole game. The batter moved in order to get away from getting hit. However, he actually moved his head into the strike zone and was hit. Should he take his base or was he out? One coach came running out of the dugout. The umpire declared: "I don't know what it is, I've never had a kid get hit in the head like that before." The umpire decided to go over to the other coach for advice and then declared that the batter should continue batting. The first coach then ran out, the fans began screaming foul play, and then the umpire declared the boy out: "He intentionally put his head in the strike zone." Actually, there were several rules covering this situation, but none of them dealt with it exactly. "Even a finely attuned set of rules requires interpretation, and this process of interpretation allows negotiation by the coaches" (p. 23).

A role is also a set of rules, and it, too, is governed by negotiation. Traditionally, roles have been treated as an objective reality confronting the individual entering into organization. Role is normally defined as a set of expectations—or script—that tell the individual what to do. The symbolic interactionist sees this view as overly structured: The fact is that roles are fluid, vague, contradictory. They should be seen as a general outline. Actors shape their own roles to an extent, to meet their own goals. Roles are thus social objects that we learn in interaction and alter according to our definition of the situation. We announce to others what it is we are doing—playing a certain role—but this is an active human being doing that, and we do it until it is not useful to us anymore. We change how we play it when we see that what we are doing does not work or when others tell us through their actions that it is unsatisfactory. How we make our roles, in the end, is through a continuous negotiation process, rather than passively entering into a role and doing what others tell us:

> Actors will behave as though they and others with whom they interact are in particular roles as long as the assumption works by providing a stable and effective framework for interaction. They test the assumption by continuously assessing one another's behavior, checking whether that behavior verifies or validates the occupancy of a position by corresponding to expectations and by demonstrating consistency. (Stryker, 1981;20)

Peter Manning (1977) analyzes two police departments and finds the same negotiating process taking place: Actors use rules as loosely defined guidelines and individuals make ongoing decisions based on a number of factors besides formal rules.

All aspects of culture are negotiated. What sociologists sometimes call social structure—class, power, roles, and authority, for example—like all other rules that are part of culture, may exist and exert themselves on the individual, yet are also defined and used by the individual.

Both the external existence of rules and the definitions matter. All organized life is ordered—guided by rules—yet that order is renewed, altered, acted out time and time again as people in real-life situations interact. It is an exaggeration to say that each rule that is part of culture is negotiated all of the time, yet it is equally an exaggeration to say that rules are fixed for people to follow and obey. All orders are negotiated; acts of people in interaction determine the patterns that prevail (Fine, 1984;240–43).

Society—social interaction, symbolic communication, and cooperation—creates culture. Culture becomes important for ongoing social interaction. Culture is used by the actors to guide their own action. Culture is ever changing and negotiated.

THE INDIVIDUAL EXISTS WITHIN MANY SOCIETIES

Society then can be defined *as any instance of ongoing social interaction that is characterized by cooperation among actors and that creates a shared culture.* The culture is something that becomes an important social object for the individual's view of reality and for the rules he or she uses to control self. In turn, this agreement to use the culture becomes an important reason people can continue to cooper-

FIGURE 11–1

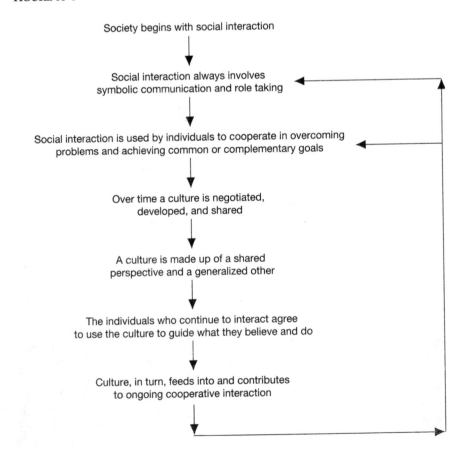

Society begins with social interaction

Social interaction always involves
symbolic communication and role taking

Social interaction is used by individuals to cooperate in overcoming
problems and achieving common or complementary goals

Over time a culture is negotiated,
developed, and shared

A culture is made up of a shared
perspective and a generalized other

The individuals who continue to interact agree
to use the culture to guide what they believe and do

Culture, in turn, feeds into and contributes
to ongoing cooperative interaction

ate. Without social interaction society ceases to exist. Where cooperation is replaced by social conflict there is no society. And without a culture used by the participants in social interaction, society becomes individuals thinking and acting without concern for the whole, and ongoing cooperative interaction cannot continue. We might try to conceptualize society as shown in Figure 11–1.

Sociologists continuously debate the relative importance of a society such as the United States and a society such as a Little League baseball team or an individual family group. It is, first of all, important to regard all societies—from the very largest to the very smallest—as sharing certain qualities, and this point has been emphasized throughout this discussion. All organized life is characterized by ongoing symbolic interaction, cooperative problem solving, and shared culture. I can be a consultant invited to evaluate a business organization or a university, or I can be a social worker who must try to help a community organize itself, or I can be a family counselor whose job it is to help people lead a more cooperative family life. In each case we are examining a society, and in each case it is social interaction, symbolic communication, role taking, cooperative problem solving, and culture that must be evaluated and improved for the society to work. If I am asked about what types of problems are made difficult by having a segregated America I can point to problems of unity that break down where ongoing social interaction, symbolic communication, role taking, cooperative problem solving, and shared culture are no longer in evidence. We can examine the Soviet Union or Lebanon or Yugoslavia to try to identify why these societies are having difficulty surviving, and our answers will focus on these same qualities.

It is when we look at all of these as societies that we can appreciate how many societies we enter all our lives. We are all part of many societies, very diverse, each with its own social interaction, cooperation, and culture. The society that matters to me the most on a day-to-day basis is my family. Here is the society where I try to achieve my goals cooperatively, through ongoing social interaction with those who share with me a common culture. However, I also live within the United States and that too is a society with people interacting, communicating, cooperating, and using a common culture. It works as a society because these qualities exist. When or where they do not, the United States is not working well. We all exist in other societies too: Minneapolis, Augsburg College, the art department, and a bunch of friends who hang out together at Bud's Pool Hall. Our action is guided by our interaction in all of these, we achieve our goals through all of these, and we learn a culture from which we take a perspective and a body of rules to follow.

Some of our societies are very small and some are very large and spread out. Each of the smaller ones exists within larger ones. The larger ones may have an impact on the smaller ones in many possible ways (for example, it may be important to the larger cultures that smaller societies develop). Norman Denzin (1978) investigated the American liquor industry. It is made up of tiers of organization: distilling, producing, rectifying, wholesaling, retailing, and drinking. He found that the larger culture of the industry affected all the interaction within the various tiers and between those tiers. The larger culture was characterized by informal wheeling and dealing, often illegal, and this affected interaction throughout the industry:

> This industry engages in corrupt, semi-legal and illegal behaviors [and] these behaviors have roots that predate prohibition and the Eighteenth Amendment. . . . We have identified—on the part of all or some of the participants in the liquor world—misrepresentations of financial statements, manipulations of stock holdings, commercial and personal bribery of public officials, misrepresentation of funds and products, and at times clear-cut instances of conflict of interest. The liquor industry, as Al Capone suggested, is a "legitimate racket." (P. 110)

Harvey Farberman (1975) found that this same pattern existed in the automobile industry. The rules at the top affected the interaction throughout the industry. He found that the price policies of top managers affected the way everyone—wholesalers, retailers, and customers—interacted with one another. That interaction was "criminogenic," involving illegal aspects consistent with the larger culture.

Smaller societies may also have an impact on the larger automobilie. If they work effectively, they can alter the rules or influence the larger society to include their goals and interests. They can disrupt the cooperative problem solving in society, and they can influence the larger society to change how people act and think there. They can separate themselves from the larger society, or they can be seen as too different or threatening to be allowed to interact in the larger society. Their differences can bring diversity to the larger society and new creative ways to achieve goals and solve problems.

Often, the larger encourages and even forms the smaller (a business may encourage an office to develop its own society or a university may encourage a department to), and often the smaller works to reinforce cooperation in the larger (learning rules in school may ultimately be very important for encouraging the individual to follow the rules of the larger society). Societies can become highly integrated with other societies or they can be increasingly separated or forcefully segregated. However, if you link everything back to social interaction, you will understand the essence of ongoing society: Where interaction is made easy, society will be much easier to accomplish; where it is lost somehow so will society be lost.

Society, as any sociologist would argue, is therefore highly complex. We live in many. Our interaction links us to others and simultaneously separates us from others. Sometimes one society matters to us; at other times a very different society matters. Larger societies affect the smaller, and sometimes smaller societies have an impact on the larger. Sometimes societies exist for a long time, and sometimes they exist as momentary instances of social interaction. Each society, because of social interaction, will be unique and separated from others, yet where there is interaction among people from different societies, a larger society will be added. Every society begins wherever people interact; every society can be understood by examining that interaction (including symbolic communication and role taking), the way people cooperate in that inter-action, and the elements of and importance of the culture that arises.

THE ACTIVE HUMAN BEING IN SOCIETY

We are born into societies that have been around for a long time. We enter into interaction that has gone on between other individuals for a long time. America was here before we were born and will probably be here after we are dead. We interact with other Americans, with our family, with the Joneses, and with the workers at General Motors. It is correct to see each of these as instances of social interaction: Each is a society where people cooperate, solve problems together, communicate, and share rules and perspectives. It is also important, however, to recognize that each has a history, a stream of action where people have interacted and worked together over time. Each situation people face together is not a brand-new society but is influenced by interaction that has gone on before. People have interacted in America for a long time, and through that interaction, a generalized other and perspective have developed among them, ever changing, but also to some extent retaining some consistency over generations. The culture, continuously shared and con-tinuously being redefined, leads those who interact to define one another, self, and the world outside in somewhat the same way as those who interacted earlier.

But that which has the longest history is actively defined by real live thinking actors. Lest we forget: Every human society is made up of actors with selves, minds, and the ability to take one another's roles. This means that soci-ety cannot simply stamp out its members, but that people are active in society: They shape it. They *use* the culture to deal with their own problems and reach their personal goals. It becomes a social object to them rather than simply a force causing behavior. And new situations arise that demand new definitions, new kinds of problem solving, and the culture is transformed by the acts of people back and forth in social interaction. Society may exist over time, but at all times what has developed is evaluated, negotiated, and changed.

You will not find the essence of human society in the study of ants or bees or even other primates. That is because the societies that we form are formed with actors who possess selves and engage in ongoing mind action. That makes human society problem solving just like the actors who make it up. It is not by instinct or simple imitation that society continues but by symbolic interaction by beings with self and mind.

Blumer makes this point over and over: *Human society is made up of actors with selves.* Social interaction is not something out there that stamps itself on the individual, nor is culture. Instead, "human association is a moving process in which the participants note and gauge each other's actions," where they organize their action in relation to one another, and where they inhibit them-selves, encourage themselves, and guide themselves as action unfolds over time (Blumer, 1953;197). Self-control is not passive control; it is individuals considering others and actively directing themselves in relation to those others. Cooperation is accomplished through controlling self in line with others for the purpose of achieving a goal. Each works with the others; all coordinate their activities, dealing with the environment together. Human society is not humans blindly imitating one another, but instead it is humans who actively direct themselves to cooperate:

> Human society is an on-going process in which each participant is continually checking his own behavior in response to real or anticipated reactions of other people. Coordination is possible because each person controls himself from within, and it is self-consciousness that makes such voluntary conduct possible. Concerted action depends upon the voluntary contributions of the individual participants, but since each person forms a self-image from the standpoint of the perspective shared in the group, such self-criticism serves to integrate the contribution of each into an organized social pattern. (Shibutani, 1961;92-93)

And Mead also reminds us that human society is unique: *It is made up of actors who engage in mind action.* Society means cooperative problem solving. As they act, humans must think about that which they do. They consider their own acts in relation to others, and they role take the other's acts. Mind enables the actor to figure out situations, to evaluate the acts of others, to determine ways to deal with the problems at hand, to turn on society "and thus in a degree, to reconstruct and modify in terms of his [or her] self the general pattern of social or group behavior in terms of which his [or her] self was originally constituted" (Mead, 1934;263). Rules do not exist "out there" determining what we all do. Interpretation of that reality—like all reality—occurs in interaction with self and others. Rules are social objects *used* by actors in situations to control their action.

So it is that symbolic interactionism departs from the general view of society that is so often a part of the discipline of sociology. Society does shape us: It gives us our selves, symbols, mind, our ability to role take, our social objects, our culture. Yet human beings—possessing self and mind—act back on society and shape it, putting forth ideas, actions, directions that arise from within and that influence the direction of others in the ongoing cooperative order.

Yes, we are socialized to accept the culture. But in our acts we turn on our socializers and we act in directions we choose. People are not robots, Shibutani (1978) reminds us in *The Derelicts of Company K.* The soldiers' refusal to obey was a reaction to an authority perceived to be unjust. It was not in their interests to obey, and they caused problems for the army (p. 436).

Whereas most theories of society almost dare us to show how it is possible for freedom and creativity to exist, the symbolic interactionist shows that freedom and creativity arise *from* society, not in spite of it. In truth, society does make us as we interact with others. But with what society provides—symbols, self, mind, role-taking ability—we turn around and make society.

SUMMARY

To the symbolic interactionist, society is always developing as people interact. Society is said to have the following qualities:

1. It is characterized by social symbolic interaction. Actors take one another into account as they act, they intentionally communicate, and they interpret one another's acts.
2. It is characterized by a certain type of interaction: cooperation. Society is cooperative problem solving.
3. It possesses culture, a shared perspective and a body of rules that facilitate social interaction and cooperation.

Every instance of social symbolic interaction that is cooperative and develops culture is a society, from very small groups to very large entities. Each individual is a member of many societies, each playing a role in his or her definition of reality and self-control.

Like everything else in the symbolic interactionist perspective, human society is thought to be something created, defined, altered, and used by actors who are active beings, who possess selves, and engage in mind action.

REFERENCES

ATHENS, LONNIE
    1986   "Types of Violent Persons." *Studies in Symbolic Interaction* 7:367–89.
BECKER, HOWARD S.
    1982   "Culture: A Sociological View." *Yale Review* 71:513–27.
BERGER, PETER L., AND THOMAS LUCKMANN
    1966   *The Social Construction of Reality.* New York: Doubleday.
BLUMER, HERBERT
    1953   "Psychological Import of the Human Group." In Muzafer Sherif and M. O. Wilson, eds., *Group Relations at the Crossroads*, pp. 185–202. New York: Harper & Row.

    1966   "Sociological Implications of the Thought of George Herbert Mead." *American Journal of Sociology* 71:535–44. By permission of The University of Chicago Press. Copyright © 1966 by The University of Chicago. All rights reserved.

    1969   *Symbolic Interactionism: Perspective and Method.* Englewood Cliffs, N.J.: Prentice Hall. Copyright © 1969. Reprinted by permission of Prentice Hall, Inc.
DENZIN, NORMAN K.
    1978   "Crime and the American Liquor Industry." *Studies in Symbolic Interaction* 1:87–118.

    1984   "Toward a Phenomenology of Domestic Family Violence." *American Journal of Sociology* 90:483–513.
FARBERMAN, HARVEY
    1975   "A Criminogenic Market Structure: The Automobile Industry." *The Sociological Quarterly* 16:438–57.

FINE, GARY ALAN
    1984   "Negotiated Orders and Organizational Cultures." *Annual Review of Sociology* 10:239–62.

    1987   *With the Boys: Little League Baseball and Preadolescent Culture.* Chicago: University of Chicago Press.

MANNING, PETER
    1977   *Police Work.* Cambridge, Mass.: MIT Press.

MEAD, GEORGE HERBERT
    1934   *Mind, Self and Society.* Chicago: University of Chicago Press. Reprinted by permission of The University of Chicago Press. Copyright © 1934 by the University of Chicago. All rights reserved.

    1936   *Movements of Thought in the 19th Century.* Ed. Merritt H. Moore. Chicago: University of Chicago Press.

    1938   *The Philosophy of the Act.* Ed. Merritt H. Moore. Chicago: University of Chicago Press.

MELTZER, BERNARD N.
    1972   *The Social Psychology of George Herbert Mead.* Kalamazoo: Center for Sociological Research, Western Michigan University.

MILLER, DAN E., ROBERT A. HINTZ, JR., AND CARL J. COUCH
    1975   "The Elements and Structure of Openings." In *Constructing Social Life,* pp. 1–24. Champaign, Ill.: Stipes.

SHIBUTANI, TAMOTSU
    1955   "Reference Groups as Perspectives." *American Journal of Sociology* 60:562–69.

    1961   *Society and Personality: An Interactionist Approach to Social Psychology.* Englewood Cliffs, N.J.: Prentice Hall. Copyright © 1961. Reprinted by permission of Prentice Hall, Inc.

    1978   *The Derelicts of Company K: A Sociological Study of Demoralization.* San Francisco: Jossey–Bass.

SMIRCICH, LINDA
    1983   "Organizations as Shared Meanings." In Louis R. Pondy et al., ed., *Organizational Symbolism,* pp. 55–65. Greenwich, Conn.: JAI Press.

STRAUSS, ANSELM
    1959   *Mirrors and Masks.* New York: Free Press.

STRYKER, SHELDON
    1980   *Symbolic Interactionism.* Menlo Park, Calif.: Benjamin/Cummings.

    1981   "Symbolic Interactionism: Themes and Variations." In Morris Rosenberg and Ralph Turner, eds., *Social Psychology,* pp. 1–29. New York: Basic Books.

WARRINER, CHARLES K.
    1970   *The Emergence of Society.* Homewood, Ill.: Dorsey Press.

12

Erving Goffman

Written by Spencer Cahill, University of South Florida*

GOFFMAN AND SYMBOLIC INTERACTIONISM

No introduction to symbolic interactionism would be complete without some discussion of Erving Goffman's contributions to the perspective. Both before and since his unexpected death in 1982, Goffman's many books and essays have influenced not only symbolic interactionists but also sociologists more generally and, perhaps less extensively but still notably, cultural anthropologists and psychologists. The tradition of thought now known as symbolic interactionism also undoubtedly influenced Goffman but probably not as much as he has influenced it.

When Goffman came to the University of Chicago as a graduate student in the late 1940s, the legacy of George Herbert Mead, Charles Horton Cooley, and other forerunners of symbolic interactionism still loomed large. Professors there at the time, like Herbert Blumer and Everett Hughes, as well as many of Goffman's fellow graduate students, later became known as important figures in the history of symbolic interactionism. Goffman, too, is often called a symbolic interactionist, but he strongly objected to that label (Goffman, 1988). Although Goffman did address many of the same topics as symbolic interactionists, he drew at least as much inspiration and guidance from the ideas of the early French sociologist Emile Durkheim and the British anthropologist A. R. Radcliffe-Brown as from those of Mead or Cooley.

Goffman's abiding concern was with what he came to call "the interaction order" (Goffman, 1983)—the structure, process, and products of social interaction. Goffman's approach to the study of social interaction is often called *dramaturgical,* meaning that he viewed social life as something like a staged drama. Although that is an important aspect of Goffman's general perspective, there is an equally if not more important component. Goffman also viewed interaction as something like a religious ceremony *filled with ritual observances.* For Goffman, these two characteristics of social interaction—drama and ritual—are complementary, and both are implicated in the *collaborative manufacture of selves.*

*Revised by Joel Charon for purposes of style.

Like most symbolic interactionists, Goffman gives "self" a prominent place in his writings. His focus is not the self-concept carried by an actor from situation to situation but the socially situated self developed in and governing specific interactions. According to Goffman (1959;253), the self is "something of collaborative manufacture" that must be produced anew on each and every occasion of social interaction. It is both the product of the drama of interaction and the object of the interpersonal rituals that Goffman analyzes.

These three themes—drama, self, and ritual—form the core of Goffman's perspective, and these will be briefly introduced in the description that follows. It should be noted that all three are central to the morality that is the foundation for all society, and each, in turn, exists in and is influenced by a larger social context, which Goffman calls the "social environment."

DRAMA IN INTERACTION

Impressions and Performance

Goffman's (1959) analysis of the dramatic processes of social interaction begins with a rather simple observation:

> When an individual enters the presence of others they commonly seek to acquire information about him or to bring into play information about him already possessed. They will be interested in his general socio-economic status, his conception of self, his trustworthiness, etc. Although some of this information seems to be sought as an end in itself, there are usually quite practical reasons for acquiring it. Information about the individual helps to define the situation, enabling others to know in advance what he will expect of them and what they may expect of him. (P. 1)

Even with those we know well, when they act in a situation we must determine their current mood, their view of us, and which of their many social identities they consider relevant at the moment. We need to acquire even more information about those with whom we are not acquainted in order to know how to treat and what to expect from them. Yet we rarely ask one another to supply such information, but instead depend on an individual's "front" or appearance, manner, and the setting where we meet to define the situation (pp. 22–30).

Although we are forming impressions of others on the basis of such readily apparent expressions of self, we are aware that they are doing the same with us, and we act accordingly. The way we act and dress for a job interview is different from the way we act and dress for a party. Through our appearance and manner or "personal front" (Goffman, 1959;24), we manage others' impressions of us, influence their definitions of situations, and affect their conduct. Goffman (p. 24) aptly describes the activity that serves to influence others in these ways as a "performance." Some of our performances may be thoroughly calculated to evoke a particular response; others may be less calculated and much easier to do because they seem more natural to us or more "authentic." In either case, we must dramatically convince others that we are who and what we want them to consider us to be:

> Whether an honest performer wishes to convey the truth or whether a dishonest performer wishes to convey a falsehood, both must take care to enliven their performance with appropriate expressions, exclude from their performances expressions that might discredit the impression fostered and take care lest the audience impute unintended meanings. (P. 66)

Whenever we interact with others, we are not only performers but an audience for their performances as well. Each participant in social interaction expresses a self and forms an impression of each of the other participants based on their appearance and manner, and the setting of the interaction. In most cases, they quickly arrive at what Goffman (1959;10) describes as a "working consensus" about definitions of one another and the situation that then guides their interaction. Like stage actors, social actors enact roles, assume characters, and play through scenes when engaged in interaction with one another. Although Goffman (pp. 254–55) acknowledges that these dramas of everyday social life are somewhat more fateful than theatrical productions for those who enact and witness them, he points out that both kinds of drama involve use of the same techniques. Social actors like theatrical actors rely on costume, makeup, body carriage, dialect, props, and other dramatic devices to produce a shared experience and sense of reality.

Goffman points to the way we commonly divide social settings as evidence of the staged character of everyday social life. In his words, most social settings consist of a front region—or frontstage—where a performance is given and a back region—or backstage—"where the impression fostered by the performance is knowingly contradicted" (p. 112). To protect the vital secrets of shows visible there, the backstage is generally separated from the frontstage by barriers to perception, and audiences' access to that region is restricted. Thus, in the backstage kitchen of most restaurants food is placed back on plates after falling on the floor and staff ridicule customers. It is well out of sight and hearing from the frontstage dining area, where the impression of careful food preparation and polite service is dramatically fostered.

Of course, audiences are aware that performers are likely to present themselves and the social entities they represent in a favorable light. Thus, they often look for evidence of deception. They may try to overhear or catch a glimpse of what is happening backstage. More often, they check aspects of performances that are easily controlled by actors against supposedly less controllable and controlled aspects like the tightness of a smile. This is a common method of evaluating the honesty of performances perfected by parents who always know when their children are lying.

On the other hand, performers may exploit the dramatic effect of seemingly automatic expressions for their own purposes. That is, they may actually control expressions that appear spontaneous and uncontrolled. The verbal discharges of internal states that Goffman (1981a) calls "response cries" provide examples. The "strain grunts" we sometimes emit when exerting ourselves may be purposefully enacted to dramatize for the benefit of some audience the effort we are expending (p. 104). Similarly, revulsion sounds like "Eeuw," which dramatically demonstrate the limits of our tolerance, may sometimes be premeditated to foster the impression that we are the kind of person who is disgusted by certain sights and smells.

Goffman (1961b;107) recognized that individuals do not always or even usually expressively "embrace" their formal roles in a situation. He describes numerous instances of individuals expressing "distance" from social roles and the images of self they imply. For example, a teacher may mention a popular song or recount a personally embarrassing incident indicating that she is not as different from the other members of the class as her official role in the classroom implies. And students may listen to her lecture with a bored look or disdainful smirk dramatizing their lack of enthusiasm for their current role.

However, Goffman (1961b;139) argues that individuals thereby free themselves from social roles and projected definitions of self, not to be free, but because other social roles and identities have a hold on them. Goffman empirically illustrates this with the example of physicians who distance themselves from the role of surgeon while performing operations. They sometimes announce their identity as fishermen by telling of a recent fishing trip, proudly claim the identity of family man by recounting some story of domestic life, and demonstrate their identity as a sexually vital male by flirting with nurses. Goffman (1961b;144) argued that such expressive "dances of social identification" or constant changes of dramatic "footing" (Goffman, 1981a) are evidence of individuals' multiple social identifications and how they manage those competing commitments. We may take an individual's graceful gliding in and out of social roles and identities as indicating his or her "real" or "true" self, but that is as much a dramatic effect as any of his or her specific role identities.

Performance Teams

In addition to dramatically enacting roles and characters, social actors also attempt to manage others' impressions of the groups, establishments, and organizations that they represent. The members and personnel of such social units often constitute what Goffman (1959;79) calls "performance teams" that cooperate in "staging a single routine." For example, family members often cooperate in staging shows of domestic bliss and respectability. Similarly, pilots and flight attendants sometimes cooperate in staging shows of calm confidence and competence under life-threatening circumstances. Staging such routines takes teamwork. The team members often rehearse their lines in audiences' absence, provide one another stage directions through such subtle cues as a raised eyebrow or kick under the table, and otherwise support one another's individual performances.

Goffman emphasizes that the routine staged by a performance team is precariously dependent on the loyalty of each of its members. The show of domestic bliss and hospitality being carefully staged by a husband and wife can be quickly spoiled by their child, unschooled in the arts of impression management, who tells the houseguests how mad Mommy was with Daddy for inviting them. Like this child, every member of a performance team usually possesses some information that can give away the team's show because maintaining a fostered impression almost always involves concealing or playing down certain facts. As Goffman (1959) notes, "since we are all participants on teams we must carry within ourselves the sweet guilt of conspirators" (p. 105). To have a job, to be a member of a family or virtually any other social entity is to be part of a dramatic conspiracy to control the information that is available to others and their definitions of situations.

To Goffman, therefore, human beings act on a stage; they perform for others; they impress and they are impressed. They are both actors and audiences. And they often form a cooperative performance team that works to present a united front to others. We know we do this; others know we do this; we know that others know we do this. Life is drama, and to understand interaction, self, or society this must be considered.

Reaction to Goffman's Dramaturgical View

Although Goffman is not embraced by all symbolic interactionists, his dramaturgical view does represent a view of the human being that is attractive to many. The attractiveness is in the fact that he makes the human actor into an active being who has some control over what takes place in interaction. To perform is to control how others define and treat you. It is not simply to respond to what others do. Although we are performing actors, we use that to our advantage in real situations; and, as the play begins to change because of the performances of others, we change. Together we dramatically construct one another's self and the social situations in which we act.

Although Goffman's dramaturgical analysis of social life has inspired emulation by other sociologists (e.g., Brisset and Edgley, 1990), it has also provoked considerable criticism. Critics of Goffman's dramaturgical view argue that his analysis of social life verges on a kind of perverse cynicism. They contend human beings are not mere performers. This is too much of an exaggeration that reduces individuals to little more than superficial hypocrites. In the words of one reviewer:

> You come away . . . seeing artifice and histrionics everywhere. But Mr. Goffman's moral is very sad, because his skepticism is . . . unrelieved . . . he seems to say we can't assemble authentic characters out of the bits of business that actors show. (Numberg, 1981;11)

Along similar lines, other critics accuse Goffman of reading "a Machiavellian kind of manipulation into human interaction" (Karp and Yoels, 1986;80) and of depicting social life as little more than a continuous con game (Cuzzort, 1969;173–92).

Although Goffman did focus attention on the trickery and pretense of everyday social life, he did not see contrivance and chicanery everywhere as many of his critics suggest. Instead, Goffman (1959;66) wrote that we are both honest and dishonest social performers: We sometimes express who we truly believe we are, and sometimes we try to present an image of self that benefits us but is false. However, what is important is that honest and dishonest performances are still performances and have the same general characteristics. Goffman therefore reasoned that we could "profitably study performances that are quite false to learn about ones that are quite honest" (p. 66). By concentrating on how easily dramaturgical techniques could be exploited for self-serving and unsavory purposes, Goffman shows not how often but how seldom individuals take unfair advantage of the dramatic character of social interaction and reality.

Rather than reading a kind of Machiavellian manipulation into human interaction, Goffman emphasizes its intrinsically cooperative and moral character. That is, he shows us that mutual performance creates the mutually acceptable rules that form the basis of orderly social interaction. I perform for you and present myself in a way I choose. You perform for me and present yourself in a way you choose. Some of this performance is honest, some dishonest. Yet, if there is no clear evidence of deception, we agree to respect each other's performance and treat each other accordingly. Out of this arises the morality that guides our acts and allows for the continuation of our interaction. Goffman leaves little doubt that the drama of interaction is a deeply moral matter.

THE SELF OF SOCIAL INTERACTION

Goffman's View of Self

Like many symbolic interactionists today, Goffman viewed the self as something cooperatively built up on each and every occasion of social interaction. In this respect, he took Mead's (1934;140) characterization of the self as essentially *social* more seriously than did Mead himself. According to Goffman (1967) "the Meadian notion that the individual takes toward himself [or herself], the attitude that others take toward him [or her] seems very much an oversimplification" (pp. 84–85). Rather, the individual "must rely on others to complete the picture" of self that his or her performance merely outlines. Others fill in and sometimes reshape that outline of self through their actions toward the individual. For Goffman, then, a self is not something an individual owns but something others temporarily lend him or her.

Social Control and Self

Goffman (1967) once observed that "societies everywhere, if they are to be societies, must mobilize their members as self-regulating participants in social encounters" (p. 44). The key word here is *self*. Through the respect and regard or lack thereof others show us, they instruct us in what we must and must not do to gain their cooperation in constructing a socially acceptable self. The parent who sharply rebukes a child for creating a public scene and the peers who ridicule him or her for crying when excluded from their play teach the child how to act to present a viable self—a self others will accord him or her. These are the kind of lessons that encourage *self*-regulated participation in social interaction.

Over time, we learn to have feelings attached to the selves that we present to others. We come to care how others see us, and care about the positive social value we effectively claim through our performances, or what Goffman (1967;5–45) called "face." We become attached to the image of hard-working student that earns us the respect of our teachers and family and to the image of class clown that earns us the respect of our peers. Our emotions are thereby mobilized in support of the interaction order that sustains those selves and claims. We are always prepared with informed answers to our teachers' questions and always ready with the humorous quip. And, when we fail to fulfill social expectations, we are embarrassed, turning red-faced and flustered over the projected self we have shattered and the face we have lost (pp. 97–112). The answer that the teacher corrects or the joke that brings frowns rather than laughter results in the burning sensation of shame creeping up the back of our necks.

Goffman (1967;8) suggests that *this emotional attachment to projected selves and face is the most fundamental mechanism of social control leading us to regulate our own conduct*. It deters us from misrepresenting ourselves to others because of the danger of being discovered "in the wrong face" and exposed as a dishonest performer. Similarly, our emotional attachment to face leads us to avoid situations where we would be "out of face" and where others would refuse to recognize and respect the self we present. The straight A student may avoid a notoriously demanding and difficult teacher. An individual who has not learned what fork goes with which course may decline an invitation to an elegant dinner party. And individuals who possess what Goffman (1963b) terms a social "stigma" like a visible disability will often prefer the company of those who share that stigma to strained and uncomfortable interaction with "normals." Like the socially "stigmatized," most of us learn from others' hints and glances and tactful cues what our places are, and generally keep them:

> Social life is an uncluttered, orderly thing because the person voluntarily stays away from the places and topics and times where he is not wanted and where he might be disparaged for going. He cooperates to save his face, finding that there is much to be gained from venturing nothing. (Goffman, 1967;43)

Then again, our emotional attachment to face is also why there is not more deception and chicanery in social interaction.

When individuals reach a working consensus regarding the definition of the situation that will guide their interaction and treatment of one another, they form a moral pact to support one another's fostered impressions of self (Goffman 1959;13). They not only "defend" their own projected self and face but also protect one another's by employing practices like "tactful blindness," politely ignoring one another's slips of the tongue, memory, clothing, and body if at all possible (Goffman, 1967;18). And they have good reasons for doing so. When events or information hopelessly contradicts the impression of self fostered by one of the participants, the definition of the situation that was governing the interaction is shattered. In Goffman's (1967) words, "the minute social system that is brought into being with each encounter" is disorganized, and the participants feel "unruled, unreal and anomic" (p. 135). Lodged in assumptions that no longer hold, all of the participants' projected selves and face are threatened.

Goffman (1971) movingly illustrates what can happen when the collaborative manufacture of selves goes awry with the example of a manic family member. According to Goffman (p. 356), what are considered the mental symptoms of the manic individual in effect involve enactment of a self that other members of his or her family can neither accept nor allow. The life of the entire family is consequently disorganized:

> The individual's failure to encode through deeds and expressive cues, a *workable* definition of himself, one which closely enmeshed others can accord him through the regard they show his person, is to block and trip up and threaten them in almost every movement that they make. The selves that had been the reciprocals of his are undermined. . . . In ceasing to know the sick person, they cease to be sure of themselves. In ceasing to be sure of him and themselves, they can even cease to be sure of their way of knowing . . . for there is no place in possible realities for what is occurring. (P. 390)

The havoc that a manic member brings to a family is only an extreme and extended instance of the trouble any individual who fails to sustain the self that others have accorded him or her can cause. In Goffman's words, the manic "reminds us of what everything is, and that this everything is not very much" (p. 390). That everything is the selves and realities that we collaboratively manufacture and maintain through interaction with others.

We sometimes do gamble with that everything, however. We may challenge our skills as a performer by seeking what Goffman (1967) calls "action" or situations, such as games of skill and daring, where a projected self can easily collapse. We may also test our poise by engaging in what Goffman (pp. 239–58) terms "character contests" like playful or more serious exchanges of insults. Although often harmless, these attempts to gain face at the expense of someone else's face are always risky because we evaluate one another in terms of not only how we handle ourselves but also how we handle one another. Instigators of a character contest can suddenly find that they have gone too far destroying their own faces in the eyes of those whom they had hoped to impress. One strategy for minimizing this risk is to choose a victim for whom the audience will have little sympathy. That is why a man among male companions may verbally harass passing women and an individual among those of similar ethnicity may hurl humiliating insults at someone of another ethnicity. Whatever such an individual may gain through this "aggressive face-work" (pp. 24–25), something of our everything is lost. The mutual protection of projected selves and face that shelters us all is cracked.

As we shall see, Goffman also maintains that an individual's socially situated self and face depends in part on the larger context or environment of interaction. In his words, "an environment . . . is a place where it is easy or difficult to play the ritual game of having a self" (Goffman, 1967;91). For example, some social environments like the back wards of mental hospitals make it nearly impossible for a resident to present a self that others will accept and respect. Other social environments erode what Goffman considered the intrinsic morality of the interaction order by promoting dishonest performances. Although some social environments like a small-town neighborhood may encourage sincere presentations of self, others like secretive governmental bureaucracies and more than a few business organizations encourage individuals to engage in conspiracies of dramaturgical deception.

To Goffman, therefore, self is intimately linked to interaction and society. Selves are cooperatively constructed in interaction, and interaction is influenced by the larger social environment. On the other hand, the dramatic realization of selves in interaction has a distinctive moral character that links individuals to one another and holds society together.

RITUALS OF INTERACTION

The Meaning of Ritual

The brilliance of Goffman is that he focused attention on commonplace elements of social interaction that most of us seldom notice. The following is his description of the common pattern of eye contact between strangers who meet on a city sidewalk or in some other public place:

> What seems to be involved is that one gives to another enough visual notice to demonstrate that one appreciates that the other is present (and that one admits openly to having seen him), while at the next moment withdrawing one's attention from him so as to express that he does not constitute a target of special curiosity or design. (Goffman, 1963a;84)

This fleeting and virtually automatic pattern of social behavior may seem trivial, but Goffman's description suggests that it is not. By quickly glancing at one another and then looking away, strangers mutually establish that they can be trusted to let one another alone. Exceptions prove the rule. When a stranger does stare at us, we usually feel uncomfortable and anxious, if not frightened. Life among strangers in our modern, urbanized society would be one of constant terror without some standard method of establishing mutual trust like the pattern of eye contact Goffman called "civil inattention." In Goffman's

(1967) words, "the gestures we sometimes call empty are perhaps the fullest things of all" (p. 91).

For Goffman, apparently empty gestures, like quickly glancing away from those we do not know, are interpersonal rituals but not simply because they are conventional and performed almost automatically. He also maintained that such conventional and perfunctory acts are expressions of respect and regard for what we value most highly—each individual's "sacred" self (Goffman, 1971;62–63). By avoiding prolonged eye contact with or talking or sitting next to strangers, we express our respect if not reverence for what Goffman (pp. 28–41) called one another's "self territories" and, thereby, for one another. On the other hand, when we unthinkingly blurt out "How 'ya doin'" as we pass an acquaintance even if we are not interested in his or her health, we are showing regard for our relationship to that individual and, thereby, for him or her. These interpersonal rituals attest to our own good will and to how highly we value one another. As Goffman (1967) once observed:

> . . . this secular world is not so irreligious as we might think. Many gods have been done away with, but the individual himself stubbornly remains a deity of considerable importance. He walks with some dignity and is the recipient of many little offerings. (P. 95)

Borrowing a distinction from Durkheim, Goffman (1971;62–65) classifies interpersonal rituals as either positive or negative. Negative interpersonal rituals are those acts through which we avoid intruding upon one another's many self territories. We usually refrain from looking at, talking to, and touching strangers and often treat their possessions similarly. As Goffman (pp. 41–44) notes, we usually treat "markers" of an individual like a jacket draped over the back of a chair or an open notebook on a library table as extensions of their owner, showing those objects the same respect and regard as we would show that individual. If, for example, there are other options, we are as unlikely to sit at a table where there is an open notebook as we are to sit at a table that is occupied by an individual. However, our ritual treatment of those we do know is almost opposite. Rather than briefly glancing at and then looking away from a friend we meet on a city sidewalk, we widen our eyes and raise our eyebrows in a sign of recognition, verbally greet, and sometimes hug or otherwise touch him or her. This is an example of the kind of positive interpersonal rituals that we employ to affirm and signal initiations or extensions of relationships (p. 58). Whereas negative interpersonal rituals express a kind of reverence for the individual's self through the regard shown its inviolable boundaries, positive interpersonal rituals do so by celebrating past, present, or anticipated contact with such a revered object.

The Importance of Ritual

As Goffman (1963a, 1967, 1971) repeatedly argues, our routine observance of such interpersonal rituals or common courtesies demonstrates our commitment to a vast array of shared rules of interpersonal conduct. In an important respect, what we commonly call etiquette is a complex code of ceremonial or ritual prescriptions and proscriptions governing our interactions with one another. That does not mean that we always observe these rules. Rather, they are "enabling conventions" (Goffman, 1983;5) that provide a background of common expectations against which almost anything someone does or does not do is seen by others as meaningful. Because strangers are expected to look away from one another, they can show that they are curious about or interested in further interaction with one another by not doing so. That is why flirtatious or menacing glances are flirtatious or menacing. Because acquaintances are expected to greet one another, friends can express disappointment or anger with one another at the moment through an obvious snub. Because touching is expected between intimates, a lover who recoils from another's touch and angrily snaps "Don't touch me" conveys that all is not right with their relationship. These are all examples of what Goffman (1971;61 fn 54) terms "meaningful nonadherences," and their meaningfulness results from mutually understood but usually unnoticed rules of ritual conduct.

Then there are the many times we violate our shared code of ritual conduct either inadvertently or for good practical reasons. We sometimes accidentally bump into strangers or stop to ask them for directions or the time. We sometimes pass by friends while lost in thought. However, when we commit such ritual offenses and realize that we have done so, we almost always engage in what Goffman (1971;108) called "remedial work of various kinds." Most often we offer potentially offended parties an apology such as "Excuse me" or "I'm sorry." Sometimes we also offer an explanation or account like "Excuse me, but I'm lost" or "Sorry, I was daydreaming." Other times we request the approval of those who might be offended by an act before committing it. For example, before sitting in one of the few empty seats in a crowded theater, we usually ask the stranger sitting in the adjoining seat if he or she minds if we sit there.

Perhaps the best evidence of our commitment to a shared code of ritual conduct is the number of times a day we employ remedial expression like apologies, accounts, and requests. Even when we address someone like a salesclerk who is paid to assist us, we often preface inquiries like whether a particular item in a certain size is in stock with an apologetic "Excuse me." This virtually automatic and tired expression is an abridged form of an elaborate plea for mercy:

> I know that I have violated a ritual expectation, do not take that violation lightly, and beg you to judge me not on the basis of this violation but in terms of the knowledge of and regard for ritual expectations that I am now showing.

In most cases, others graciously grant this implicit request, relieving us of responsibility for our violations of ritual expectations.

According to Goffman (1971;95–187), what usually ensues when ritual expectations are not fulfilled is itself an interpersonal ritual. These remedial interchanges have a standard form projecting an expected sequence of "moves." For example, when an apology is not accepted, we often repeat it in more and more elaborate forms until the potentially offended party accepts it and completes the sequence. When an expected apology is not forthcoming, the offended party may sarcastically say something like "Hey, no problem," emphasizing the offender's failure to offer an expected apology. Of course, the absence of an apology may be a meaningful nonadherance expressing how little respect and regard the offender has for the offended.

We clearly do not consider everyone equally deserving of ritual expressions of respect and regard. We feel little ritual obligation toward those who do not fulfill their own toward us. We also feel similarly about those whose unkept appearance or strange manner suggests that they have little self-respect, pride, or concern for our opinion of them. When we come upon such persons on city sidewalks, we may stare disapprovingly, make disparaging remarks loud enough for them to overhear, or treat them as "nonpersons" not worthy of a glance (Goffman, 1963a;83). In Goffman's (1967;83) words, individuals must show proper "demeanor" to "warrant deferential treatment" or ritual offerings of respect and regard. The demeanor we show through our "deportment, dress, and bearing" conveys to others that we are persons of certain desirable or undesirable qualities and largely determines how much deference they will give us. In simpler terms, how we present ourselves to others influences how they treat us. That dramatic process largely determines the ritual structure of our interactions with others.

Through this analysis, Goffman leads us in yet another direction. He is showing us that ritual acts are an essential part of all of our interaction and are necessary for the continuation of that interaction. Interpersonal rituals are the source of mutual trust, social relationships, and the moral order of society.

THE ENVIRONMENTS OF SOCIAL INTERACTION

Goffman never sees interaction existing in a vacuum. Our performances take place in social environments that influence them. Critics of Goffman often miss this important point. The "false" performances that Goffman studies in order to learn about ones that are quite "honest" occur in social establishments where a great deal of importance is placed on the control of audiences' definitions of the situation. They occur in restaurants, where waiters and waitresses try to foster an impression of personal concern for each and every customer to maximize tips (Goffman, 1959;122), in hospitals where doctors and nurses present a front of professional competence in order to gain patients' cooperation (Goffman, 1961a;340–350), and in funeral homes where the illusion that the deceased is in a deep and tranquil sleep would be shattered if the bereaved witnessed the preparation of the body (Goffman, 1959;44).

The seemingly Machiavellian individuals whom Goffman describes engage in deceptive performances because they act within social establishments that encourage control of others' definition of the situation and conduct. The control of the bereaveds' impression of the deceased in funeral homes and of patients' conduct in hospitals may seem harmless and even desirable, but that is not true of all organizationally encouraged subterfuge, as Goffman (1974) makes clear in his description of undercover police work:

> ... it transforms self-interest into selflessness and insulates a misrepresenter from the immorality of misrepresentation. Insulates as might a game. But here the game engulfs the world and is played against persons who may fail to recognize that they have become players. (P. 175)

Although Goffman argues that social life is built on dramatic artifice, he also clearly points out that dramaturgical deception can have negative consequences. The organization of social establishments and society more generally may encourage social actors to break others' implicit trust that individuals are what they claim to be, undermining the intrinsic morality of the interaction order and the foundation of society. It may also deprive some individuals of any reason to observe that morality.

In a very influential book called *Asylums*, Goffman (1961a) illustrates how social arrangements can pervert the morality of the interaction order in this way with the example of social life in a mental hospital. In his words, the mental patient "starts out with at least a portion of the rights, liberties and satisfactions of the civilian and ends up on a psychiatric ward stripped of almost everything" (p. 148). Cut off from contact with the outside world, patients are subject to the diffuse authority of a small supervisory staff who manage virtually every aspect of their lives. Defined by their very presence in the hospital as very sick, inmates do not get support from the staff nor from one another in their attempts to project a more viable self. Some inmates, with the help of sympathetic members of the staff, do find cracks in the social arrangements of the hospital where they can intermittently have a more viable self (pp. 173–320). Yet such minor victories are small consolation for patients' many defeats. Their only hope of regaining some of the rights, liberties, and satisfactions that they have lost is to accept the hospital's conception of them as ill. They are made to purchase those privileges at the expense of face.

Goffman's (1961a;158) primary point is that "an all embracing conception of the member" is built right into the social arrangements of "total institutions" like prisons, nursing homes, and mental hospitals. For inmates of mental hospitals at least, that conception provides them no defensible line for projecting a viable self and effectively claiming positive social value. Goffman notes that the fate of mental patients has unique interest for exactly this reason:

> ... it can illustrate the possibility that in casting off the raiments of the old self— or in having this cover torn away—the person need not seek a new robe and a new audience before which to cower. Instead he can learn the amoral arts of shamelessness. (P. 169)

Thus, the very social arrangements that are designed to encourage self-regulation and morally responsible conduct may have the opposite effect. Mental patients, prisoners, and inmates of many other total institutions pay in advance for whatever sins they may commit against the intrinsic morality of the interaction order and have never had better reasons for doing so. Shamelessly amoral acts are their only means of expressing outrage over what is being done to them.

Throughout his writings, Goffman shows us how fragile society, interaction, and self are. All three depend on our willing observance of the intrinsic morality of the interaction order. Social arrangements that encourage dramaturgical deception, restrict individuals' control over their presentations of self, and deprive them of social respect and regard undermine that morality threatening our everything. Everything from society to interaction to self ultimately depends on authentic performances, mutual trust, and support of one another's presented self and face.

SUMMARY

Goffman focuses attention on "the interaction order." All is tied to interaction: definitions of reality, self, moral order, and the surrounding social environment. Using his own concepts and emphases, Goffman analyzes what happens as people act in relation to one another. He shows how the actor forms his or her own acts, how individuals cooperatively construct selves, and how through ritual social control becomes the kind of self-control necessary for the continuation of society. His work enriches the perspective of symbolic interactionism and simultaneously shows its links to sociology.

Like both Durkheim and Mead, Goffman (1974) held "society to be first in everyway" (p. 13). All agreed that society is central to forming what the human being is. However, more than either Durkheim or Mead, Goffman spelled out how the intrinsic morality of the interaction order provides the bindings of society. In Goffman's view, the real cornerstones of society include (1) presentation of selves that are consistent with the facts of individuals' social lives, (2) support of one another's projected selves, (3) protection of one another's face, and (4) ritual expressions of respect and regard for one another. Social arrangements that diminish individuals' commitment to these basic moral principles erode the very foundation of society itself.

Regardless of whether one fully accepts Goffman's views, it is virtually impossible to look at the world or oneself the same after reading his insightful analyses of social life. Goffman (1981b) once suggested that the purpose of studying social life is to "cause others to see what they hadn't seen or connect what they hadn't put together" (p. 4). That was Goffman's goal, and a goal his own studies of social life continue to accomplish.

REFERENCES

BRISSETT, DENNIS, AND CHARLES EDGLEY, EDS.

1990 *Life as Theater,* 2nd ed. New York: Aldine de Gruyter.

CUZZORT, R. P.

1969 *Humanity and Modern Sociological Thought.* New York: Holt, Rinehart & Winston.

GOFFMAN, ERVING

1959 *The Presentation of Self in Everyday Life.* Garden City, N.Y.: Doubleday.

1961a *Asylums.* Garden City, N.Y.: Doubleday.

1961b *Encounters.* New York: Bobbs-Merrill.

1963a *Behavior in Public Places.* New York: Free Press.

1963b *Stigma.* Englewood Cliffs, N.J.: Prentice Hall.

1967 *Interaction Ritual.* New York: Random House.

1971 *Relations in Public.* New York: Basic Books.

1974 *Frame Analysis.* New York: Harper & Row.

1981a *Forms of Talk.* Philadelphia: University of Pennsylvania Press.

1981b "Program Committee Encourages Papers on a Range of Methodolgies." *Footnotes* (9 August): 4.

1983 "The Interaction Order." *American Sociological Review* 48:1–17.

1988 "Entretien avec Erving Goffman." In Yves Winkin, ed. and trans., *Les Moments et Leurs Hommes,* pp. 231–38. Paris: Seuil/Minuit.

KARP, DAVID, AND WILLIAM YOELS

1986 *Sociology and Everyday Life.* Itasca, Ill.: F. E. Peacock.

MEAD, GEORGE HERBERT

1934 *Mind, Self and Society.* Chicago: University of Chicago Press. Reprinted by permission of The University of Chicago Press. Copyright © 1934 by The University of Chicago. All rights reserved.

NUMBERG, GEOFFREY

1981 "The Theatricality of Everyday Life." *The New York Times Book Review* (May 10):11.

13

Symbolic Interactionism: A Final Assessment

Take any situation: a dinner party, an athletic event, a club meeting, a meeting of the United Nations, a battle, a family feud, a revolution, a conflict between ethnic groups—look at any of these in depth and one has to be amazed at the complexity of human social life. Every one of these—in fact, all situations—can be approached and analyzed from a number of perspectives, each telling us something more, each unlocking new and enlightening aspects of human beings. The lesson has to be humility: No perspective, no matter how useful, can tell us all there is about any situation. A Marxist perspective sensitizes us to inequality, conflict, power, and economics. A sociological perspective will point us to social structure, roles, social stratification, and institutions. A psychoanalyst reveals to us the subconscious at work in situations, drives, defense mechanisms, personality. Psychological social psychologists tell us how individuals are influenced by one another in situations and how attitudes are formed and changed in situations. It is easy to criticize each of these perspectives. We can say that each one is *incomplete,* each ignores some important aspects of the situation, and each undoubtedly overemphasizes certain things.

This criticism is true, of course, of the symbolic interactionist perspective. When the focus is on interaction, both personality predispositions and social structure fail to be examined in great depth. Unconscious reactions are de-emphasized. The symbolic interactionist emphasizes that humans are dynamic, that they are rational problem solvers, and that society is a process of individuals in interaction—cooperating, role taking, aligning acts, and communicating. The human engages in overt and covert action in the *present*—recalling past, planning for future—and the action that takes place between individuals is an important influence on the direction of individuals and societies. The choice of concentrating on interaction is a bias in the same way that perspectives must concentrate on some things at the expense of others—but this concentration is central to the understanding of what humans do. The symbolic interactionist focuses on concepts few scientists have seriously considered, and thus the perspective has always been a criticism of mainstream social science. Expecting symbolic interactionism to explain everything is erroneous, but, in my opinion, it is correct to say that symbolic interactionism is an exciting and useful perspective for understanding human social life. It has made important contributions to social science, sociology, social psychology, to those who "work with people," and to students interested in understanding themselves and society.

SYMBOLIC INTERACTIONISM AND HUMAN FREEDOM: A REVIEW

Tamotsu Shibutani (1978) finishes his book on *The Derelicts of Company K* with this final appraisal of an army unit that simply did not work:

> Human beings think for themselves. Although some may be prevented from speaking for a time, no one can be forced to believe something that is not plausible to him. Furthermore, it is doubtful that conversations among intimate friends can be controlled. This suggests that high morale . . . can only be offered by those who make the contribution. High morale, like affection and respect, is something that has to be earned. (P. 436)

Here Shibutani is telling us that freedom even enters into refusing or giving allegiance, obeying or disobeying, conforming or refusing to conform, accepting the generalized other or directing yourself away from it. Organized life as well as our own individual streams of action depend on decisions, which are to some extent freely made by actors.

Symbolic interactionism is an attempt to break away from traditional social science and to view the human as maker, doer, actor, and as self-directing. It is an attempt to locate what Kant and other philosophers were looking for: a free spirit, a "soul," individual freedom in humans. It is an attempt to locate the freedom that many say scientific sociologists cannot really find. It is, of course, naive to believe that humans are completely free, but this perspective of symbolic interactionism does focus on human qualities—socially created qualities—that break us out of the determining prison of traditional social science. For a moment, perhaps, it might be beneficial to summarize how symbolic interactionism conceptualizes the "free" person:

1. Many might argue that it is the "I" in the self that is the free person. Indeed the "I" is important, but it is not what this book or what the perspective sees as the real source of human freedom. The "I" tells us that socialization is never complete, that part of us goes untouched by society, that we continuously surprise ourselves in what we do, that we are creative, impulsive, spontaneous. The "I" means that we do engage in action not thought out: This is exciting in the sense that action can be taken, thinking about it can occur afterward, and new ideas about the world can arise, new directions can be taken. I say "no" to my master without thinking, and afterward I realize the possibility of refusing to conform, and "no" becomes a thinking act.

2. It is the "me," however, the socialized self, that is the source of human freedom. By giving the human a self, society gives the individual someone to talk to privately, someone to *direct,* someone to think things out with, someone to use to analyze situations. Mind activity is activity that the actor uses to analyze situations and direct himself or herself to perform a certain way in a situation. This is an active, ongoing process, causing action to go one way, then another, causing the individual to reanalyze situations, to recall past and construct future as action unfolds. Rather than habit or instinct taking us through social situations, it is definition and planning carried out with the self that are central. Here the self, of course, cannot be separated from what we mean by mind. Together these qualities make freedom possible. The self allows us to act back on ourselves; mind is all the covert action that we perform back on ourselves. It is selfhood and the ability to engage in mind action which together give us the ability to make and control our own choices in situations.

3. *Symbols* are also a source of human freedom. With words as tools, the human is able to construct new ideas, new syntheses, new strategies. Give the human words and the ability to remember and combine them, and there is no way to stop new creative thoughts and acts. In a sense, every sentence is an individual creation, every student essay exam and term paper, every speech, and every telephone conversation are new creative efforts by symbol users, synthesizing and analyzing in unique ways. Humans are not sometimes creative, but creative in *all* situations. With this they can use what they learn to develop new ideas, see new relationships, refuse what they have been taught, and go in directions that they themselves choose.

4. Humans are constantly changing, constantly "becoming." We are dynamic, our interactions influence what we do and are. We are not damned (or blessed) with our past as a determining agent; we are not imprisoned by the ideas or traits we have developed long ago. It is always in the present that we actively define what is important. Interaction with others and with self constantly shifts our direction, our action, our definition of the world and self.

The social self, symbols, mind, and the fact that we are forever changing in interaction with others and self, clearly explains how the individual is in control of his or her thoughts and actions to some extent. Humans choose, direct their own lives, and actively use their environment; they are not simply formed and controlled by outside or inside forces.

Freedom, of course, is limited. We act freely, but only within a situation that has parameters. It is the purpose of the social sciences, including symbolic interactionism, to understand these parameters along with the active self-determining nature of the individual. Briefly, some of the parameters that symbolic interactionism suggests are the following:

1. The situation will provide some important constraints on what we can do. We are confronted by situations that we must define, but these situations have an existence in themselves. They have a history independent of us—a war is a reality; others may reject us or love us; a class structure in society may place us within its limits; poverty may limit much of our action and concerns; and others may have more resources and, therefore, more power advantage over us—they may at times coerce us, manipulate us, or persuade us. Central here is the fact that actors constantly define situations for others, and people can and are manipulated by this. It is difficult to ignore the situation that confronts us; it is an important parameter.

2. Action is not always directed by symbolic interaction with the self. Alternatives are nonconscious action and habit. Both of these lead us to respond to stimuli without thinking, without problem solving, without considering past and future, without role taking. There are elements of both in what we do, and to the extent that we rely on these in our action, we are not "free" in the sense that freedom is described above. Some individuals may be highly influenced by nonconscious action and habit, unable to deal effectively with new situations or toward new variables in situations, unable to interact with others, unable to role take, unable to cooperate in dealing with complex situations, or unable to communicate effectively. Their freedom is limited.

3. A society, a social world, may be so important to us that its perspective not only becomes a *guide* to situations, but actually shapes our action, making our definition a habitual response. This may depend on the extent and nature of our exclusive interaction with certain other individuals and our identification with them. A religious cult, an isolated family life, or the world of a prison may be a closed world where interaction between a few may be continuous and intense and where there may be constant sharing of a single perspective and a single generalized other. Freedom, creativity, and adjusting acts to ongoing interaction here will be made more difficult; freedom will be small.

4. Human freedom is always limited by language, by our symbols. We can be free only within our symbolic system. That is why learning a number of perspectives, extending our vocabulary, and exposing ourselves to a number of social situations are essential to liberal education. Increasing the symbols available to us for analyzing situations, for thinking, for seeing things in different ways, for directing our self in new directions is essential.

These limits, or parameters, should not cause us to lose sight of the freedom that is human. Perhaps it is better to call it "our active nature": Humans do not respond to situations but are actively involved in both definition and self-direction in these situations.

SYMBOLIC INTERACTIONISM AND SCIENCE

George Herbert Mead argued forcefully for the understanding of human beings through the study of what they *do*, through their action. Action, according to Mead and to the symbolic interactionist perspective, is always overt *and* covert action, what we do in relation to the other and in relation to ourselves. This may be difficult to study scientifically, because self-action is difficult to measure and difficult to predict. This perspective also seems to go against most of our notions of science because it suggests that there is an important element of human freedom in what we do.

There has always been disagreement over the meaning and purpose of science. All seem to agree that science is a method of discovery that relies on empirically gathered evidence and emphasizes a systematic and objective approach to the accumulation and analysis of evidence. Most social scientists have regarded science as a means of testing hypotheses related to causes of human behavior. This has usually involved defining two or more variables and testing a causal relationship between them. Social scientists, in their attempt to be scientific, have adopted from some natural scientists a certain model of science for studying human behavior. As a result, the symbolic nature of the human being has been neglected; covert-minded activity has been considered "outside of science"; action in the present has been overlooked as a cause; and, in the end, "the definition of the situation" by the actor has not been considered an important element in the situation.

Symbolic interactionists take a different approach to science than most social scientists. Instead of using physics as a model, they are much closer to cultural anthropology, which investigates people through observing them talking and acting in their everyday lives. Symbolic interactionists are closer to those biologists who go off and observe nature in the field rather than in the laboratory, animals in nature rather than in captivity. As a result, there are certain principles of investigation which symbolic interactionists follow that we should briefly describe here.

The central principle of symbolic interactionism is that we can understand what is going on only if we understand what the actors themselves believe about their world. The actor lives and knows his or her world. It is imperative to understand what the actors know, see what they see, understand what they understand. We must understand their vocabulary, their ways of looking, and their sense of what is important. What the researcher must do is interact with the actors, observe and partake in their activities, conduct formal interviews, and try to reconstruct their reality. Always it is imperative to understand from their particular point of view what it was that influenced them to act as they did (Schwartz and Jacobs, 1979;179). Herbert Blumer (1969) clearly makes this point:

> The contention that people act on the basis of the meaning of their objects has profound methodological implications. It signifies immediately that if the scholar wishes to understand the action of people, it is necessary to see their

objects as they see them. Failure to see their objects as they see them, or a substitution of his meaning of the objects for their meanings, is the gravest kind of error that the social scientist can commit. Simply put, people act toward things on the basis of the meaning that these things have for them, not on the basis of the meaning that these things have for the outside scholar. (Pp. 50–51)

It is imperative to understand the definitions actors give their actions, even if this means simply asking them for "retrospective accounts of past actions" (Denzin: 1971;166–167).

Symbolic interactionists believe that it is important to gather data through observing people in real situations. Typical social science research is done in laboratories or through questionnaires. Research on people, however, should describe people in real settings—how they work out real situations. This should not be impressionistic and journalistic, but as careful, critical, systematic, and objective as possible. Experiments and videotapes of more controlled situations may be used to supplement what is learned in the real world, but always the real world must be the central laboratory for understanding human action.

Symbolic interactionists do more than go out and watch people in real-life situations; however, these other techniques often indirectly examine real-life situations. Howard Schwartz and Jerry Jacobs (1979, p. 179) describe *participant observation* and *interviewing actors* as two techniques used to understand the perspectives of groups of actors. *Personal accounts* and *life histories* are two attempts to capture the perspectives of individual actors. *Nonreactive techniques,* such as analyzing nonverbal communication, content in written materials, and audio-visual tapes aim at understanding perspectives and action without direct involvement with the actors themselves.

Symbolic interactionists are critical of traditional social science, its use of scientific methodology for the study of human beings, and its definition of "important causal variables." The way we study humans, as anything else in nature—for instance, bugs, stars, rocks, or rats—must be determined first and foremost *by the nature of the empirical world under study.* We must develop empirical techniques that take into account the central qualities of *human* behavior. Science must understand how humans *define situations,* how they *act in the present* by applying past experiences and future plans, how they *solve problems* confronting them. This means that scientists must recognize that past events alone do not *cause* present action without an active person defining the situation and directing the self in the present. The purpose of symbolic interactionism as a scientific perspective must be to understand the cause of human action. But "cause" is transformed to mean human definition, self-direction, and choice in situations. We must better understand how humans think, solve problems, role take, apply their past, and look to the future in situations. Science for understanding human action must recognize that part of human action is choice, is creative, and is free, and thus, paradoxically, the role of science becomes one of understanding how, and to what extent, freedom plays a role in what we do.

The symbolic interactionist regards a careful description of human interaction to be a central goal of social science. Careful observation of action, description of the important elements involved, and a careful description and redefinition of these elements should be achieved. That does not necessarily mean understanding which variable causes which variable, although the important elements at work in social situations may someday be causally linked. In a sense, a "formal sociology" is one of the goals of the symbolic interactionist, the purpose of which is to isolate and carefully describe such central concepts as conflict, role taking, cooperation, negotiation, problem solving, rehearsal of action and situations, definition of the situation, identity, self-direction, symbol, social objects, embarrassment, appearance, poise, and the like. It is important to see such concepts at work in a number of situations, comparing and contrasting instances of them, clarifying them, describing their role and, where appropriate, their absence. I might observe human action and recognize some important process taking place. Then I describe it: "This is what *negotiation* is; this is what happens when people *negotiate;* this is what people think, what they do; this is what happens to the ongoing interaction and the emerging culture." Then I describe a number of situations where *negotiation* exists and also analyze where it is absent. There are many models for this type of analysis: Anselm Strauss's work on negotiation, Edward Gross and Gregory P. Stone's on embarrassment, and many recent studies cited throughout this text, such as works on emotions, identity, demoralization, vocabulary of motives, violence, rules, disclaimers, and so on.

Blumer described two modes of inquiry that should be used to describe the real world: exploration and inspection. *Exploration* is using any ethical procedure that aids in understanding "what's going on around here." Ideas, concepts, leads, and so on are altered as the observer goes along. Preconceptions are always open to change. One attempts to describe in detail what is happening in a social situation. The purpose is to become acquainted with an area of social life and to develop some focus of interest. *Inspection* is the second step. It involves isolating important elements within the situation, and describing the situation in relation to those elements (e.g., conflict, alienation, domination, and cooperation). Inspection also involves forming descriptive statements about that element in a situation, then applying that to other interaction situations. The procedure of inspection must be "flexible, imaginative, creative, unroutinized" (summary borrowed from Stryker, 1981;10).

The symbolic interactionist in studying the human being believes it is very important to move from mechanical models of causation (characteristic of natural science) to processual models. Mechanical models emphasize single variables inevitably leading to certain outcomes. The job of the traditional social scientist has been "to identify the specific antecedent factors which under certain specified conditions produce specific kinds of observable outcomes" (Athens, 1984;241). Processual models emphasize processes—a string of developing factors—"whose initial stages do not automatically determine their later ones," and therefore "the job of the scientist is to discover the stages which are necessary for a given phenomenon to come into existence and one in existence to sustain itself" (p. 249). For example, becoming deviant is a process, never inevitable because of certain isolated factors, but highly probable when a string of factors come together. Cause is complex, multifaceted, developed over time rather than simple, singular, and isolated.

Symbolic interactionism stands as an important criticism of using traditional scientific methods in social science. The study of attitudes, values, animals in laboratories, and people in experimental situations gives some insight into human behavior, but it is not enough. The symbolic interactionist calls for a different direction, as summarized by Blumer (1969):

> It [symbolic interactionism] believes that this determination of problems, concepts, research techniques, and theoretical schemes should be done by the *direct* examination of the actual empirical social world rather than by working with a simulation of that world, or with a preset model of that world, or with a picture of that world derived from a few scattered observations of it, or with a picture of that world fashioned in advance to meet the dictates of some imported theoretical scheme or of some scheme of "scientific" procedure, or with a picture of the world built up from partial and untested accounts of that world. For symbolic interactionism the nature of the empirical social world is to be discovered, to be dug out by a direct, careful, and probing examination of that world. (P. 48)

SYMBOLIC INTERACTIONISM: SOME REPRESENTATIVE STUDIES

The studies that have been inspired by this approach are too numerous to include here in any systematic way. However, six interesting examples might help give some idea of what can be done.

A Study of Pregnant Drug Users

In the summer of 1993, I heard an excellent paper presented at the American Sociological Association meetings. It was written by three researchers who applied the ideas and methods of symbolic interactionism to studying pregnant drug users. Margaret H. Kearney, Sheigla Murphy, and Marsha Rosenbaum reminded me that it is easier to condemn others than to understand them. It is hard for outsiders to understand how someone who is shortly going to give birth continues to use illegal drugs. It is easy to

> judge them as less than human, as violating our deeply-held expectations for mothers: to protect their unborn at the expense of their own pleasure. We assume that because they don't comply with expected maternal behavior, they must not feel maternal feelings. (p. 2)

Do they understand what they do? Do they care for their unborn child? Do they feel guilty in any way? How are we to answer these questions without investigating definitions of the situation by those caught up in it? This is what Kearney, Murphy, and Rosenbaum did by interviewing 120 pregnant and postpartum women who used illegal drugs at least once a week during pregnancy.

Of all the emotions labeled and described by these women, *guilt* was the most common. The women described guilt as arising from a realization that they were harming another human being whom they were supposed to protect. To these women "guilt was remorse at failing to keep the promises of a relationship" with an unborn child (p. 2). Their actions were not something they made light of. It bothered them, and they defined themselves as failures as mothers or potential mothers. They knew they were pregnant, they knew that taking drugs was harmful, and they also believed they could have refrained from drug use if they had really wanted to. When all three ideas were believed, the result was acute guilt.

Guilt was the central emotion. How was it dealt with? Kearney, Murphy, and Rosenbaum identify five strategies: *using more drugs* so they did not have to think about what they were doing, *using fewer drugs* in order to convince themselves they were trying to deal with the problem, *putting off acknowledging pregnancy* as long as possible, and *seeking reassurance* from others that their baby was okay.

A fifth strategy was to try to *change beliefs that fed their guilt.* The most important belief was probably the idea that drug use was one's own fault, rather than something that arose from poverty or other social conditions. These women blamed themselves for their drug use, "for not being in better circumstances at the time of pregnancy, for not having made better choices in life and for not having the self-control and resolve to leave drugs alone" (p. 10). Although some tried to confront the inaccuracy of this, their efforts were doomed to failure. Instead of seeking help, self-blame for their situation only increased their guilt and their drug use.

There is more to the study than what has been described here. However, the points made are tragic, fascinating, and important as they are. The researchers found out how people felt by asking them, not by interpreting their actions as outsiders. They pulled out from the interviews how these women defined their babies, their own behavior, and their situations. They informed me, the reader, that it is too easy to pass judgment through jumping to conclusions without trying to understand how others actually feel. The authors conclude:

> Guilt was a constant companion for these women when they weren't high on drugs. It arose from reflexivity and was a physical and emotional pain. Guilt was remorse for a loss of self-control that had risked harm to a loved one. . . . Strategies to relieve the pain were directed at reducing reflexivity—by numbing awareness or seeking alternatives to the rhetoric that fueled the guilt. (P. 13)

A Study of Sam's Definition of Pain and Injury

In contrast to Kearney, Murphy, and Rosenbaum, who interviewed a number of women in order to understand how they acted in a particular life situation, Timothy Jon Curry (1993) interviewed a single person by the name of Sam in order to understand how he took on a certain identity over time: the identity of an amateur wrestler. Curry was interested in how Sam's definition of pain and injury changed over his wrestling career.

Curry found that (1) Sam's definition of pain and injury, as well as his identity as a wrestler, arose through social interaction and interaction with self; and that (2) in the early stages of his wrestling career, pain and injury were defined as unimportant and something a *man* must endure, but eventually became something to be avoided and what *good wrestlers* must endure.

To understand someone's career, it is important to ask the actor to reconstruct moments in a stream of action that seem to matter in influencing why he or she took on a certain identity rather than another. Sam reported that his parents always assumed that he would be an athlete, and throughout his precollege years they encouraged his participation and attended all of his events. Whereas his mother would react to injury in a very serious and negative manner, his father reacted as if injuries were normal and part of being an athlete. Sam remembers having to make a choice: "being treated like a baby" or being "rough and tough" (p. 278). Early in his career he defined pain and injury as unimportant, normal, and masculine. This was a way to separate himself from femininity, and also brought him closer to his father. Injury and pain were defined by Sam as things to be endured; serious injury was defined as a threat to both his wrestling career and his relationship with his father.

Sam recalled going to a summer camp where he learned to be "supermotivated." He learned to associate pain with physical growth and athleticism. To practice hard and train until he hurt was defined as good for the soul. He learned that "what is disdained is not injury or pain themselves, but allowing pain or injury to stand in the way of accomplishing a goal" (p. 279).

In his senior year of high school, Sam had a serious knee injury, overcame the pain with a shot of cortisone, and was able to win a tournament. Here he demonstrated to himself that he had truly arrived as a wrestler. Sam used this injury as an important step; he came to believe that in order to succeed he had to protect himself more carefully. Pain and injury took on yet another meaning: For him to become an elite wrestler he had to endure pain yet keep from seriously injuring himself.

In college the presence of trainers at all times and easy access to a sports physician highlighted the constant threat of serious injury. The coach made sure that no one was excused from practice because of injury. If nothing else, they were expected to exercise while others wrestled. Pain and injury were defined as something to be faced directly and overcome, never as something to get in the way of performance. Sam and others, if they were going to become "real" wrestlers, needed to assume this definition of pain and injury.

Through his wrestling life, Sam's definition of pain shifted from a symbol of masculinity to something that must be endured and overcome in order to succeed as a wrestler. To grin and bear it is simply part of what a good wrestler must do, knowing that a serious injury can end a career (p. 286).

Definition of our world, in this case the pain one feels, is central to the whole perspective of symbolic interactionism. Understanding such a definition is best accomplished by asking the one who is actually doing the defining. Understanding the history of our stream of action as well as our changing view of self is to look back and isolate different acts or moments. All of this is highlighted in Curry's study of Sam.

A Study of Identity Formation in a Maximum Security Prison

Identity is also the subject of a study by Thomas J. Schmid and Richard S. Jones (1991). Here the focus is on identity transformation in a maximum security prison. How does one see self in such a situation, and what happens to identities that are formed on the outside that one brings to the situation? This study was the result of one researcher's actual experience at a maximum security prison for men over a one-year period as well as field observation by the second researcher, and interviews with twenty first-time inmates.

The research shows that before their arrival at prison, first-time inmates do not yet possess criminal identities, and they have very little in common. They see other prison inmates as violent "with whom they have nothing in common" (p. 417). They arrive afraid and they arrive convinced that they do not want to change who they are while they are at prison. Part of their strategy is to protect themselves from hostilities, other inmates, and guards, to "resolve not to change, or to be changed, in prison." The researchers describe this process as self-dialogue, probably "the most extensive self-assessment he has ever conducted" (p. 418).

Once in prison each inmate is faced with how others in the prison have come to see themselves. Insulation becomes impossible since he cannot avoid social interaction. As he comes to understand the prison world through social interaction, both his behavior and his identity are influenced. There is an ambivalence: A desire to hold on to the identity brought to the prison and a desire to interact and know what to do in the new situation. He draws a sharp line between the identity he brings which he calls his true identity and the one he develops in the prison world. In a sense he is forced to put aside the identity he brought with him in order to survive. The prison identity is "a false identity created for survival in an artificial world" (p. 421). At first the inmate must control how he presents himself to others, simultaneously hiding what he considers his true identity and acting on the basis of an identity he does not really want to accept. Over time, he becomes used to presenting himself according to his temporary identity and his actions become increasingly habitual. He slowly becomes an "insider."

As the inmate faces release, he must again shift to his old identity, taking on the outsider's view of the prison. He puts aside his prison identity, recalls again the outside world and develops a plan to recapture his suspended identity. An interesting realization confronts him: He has changed in prison much more than he wanted to. He asks himself how permanent his changes are and how outsiders will perceive him when he leaves. He wonders if he can make it, and above all, "he repeatedly confronts the question of who he is, and who he will be in the outside world" (p. 426). This is something that he must do within himself; some factors favor a shift, while others retard it. And, once he leaves it is difficult to completely ignore the changes that have taken place as a result of his experiences:

> To the extent that these men draw upon their prison survival tactics to cope with the hardships of the outside world . . . their prison identities will have become inseparable from their "true"' identities. (P. 428)

Here we have a study that tries to understand how people change identities in interaction with others and in interaction with self. It is not a radical permanent shift, since there is a self-conscious attempt to make the prison identity temporary. The prison identity is important for survival while he is in prison, but never does he give up the identity he came with. There is the expectation that eventually he will go back into the world he was used to, and there is a recognition that his outside identity will once again become important. It is through interviews and field observation that the researcher comes close to capturing the actor's definition of the situation and view of self altered in interaction with others and with self.

A Study of Orthodox Synagogue Life

Samuel Heilman (1976) described life in an orthodox synagogue from a symbolic interactionist perspective. How people interact in such a place is carefully described, always with the purpose of understanding the world from their perspective. Actors do things in relation to one another; they communicate, they interpret, they change actions according to what other people do. Meanings arise in such interaction, and although the outsider might interpret a situation one way, the actors themselves see the situation according to a common perspective, developed over a long period of time. The example of the *schnorrer* (one who lives off the good-will donations of others) is described in this context. What is a *schnorrer* to the people involved in the synagogue, and how do they act toward him? How does he communicate that he is not a beggar but needs financial help? How does he express the fact that he is like everyone in the synagogue except he has had misfortune? How is he successful in getting financial help without demeaning himself? The interaction is critical:

> With the end of the prayers, the schnorrer steps forward toward the *bimah* (the pulpit in the center of the room). He holds in his hand two letters of reference,

which he calls to our attention. They are his credentials. But this money-collector will go beyond the letters; he will tell his story.

He speaks in Yiddish (perhaps because he has seen a copy of the *Jewish Daily Forward* in Velvel's pocket, perhaps because he wants to emphasize his Jewishness, or perhaps because he speaks no English). He explains aloud to all those assembled that he has worked hard all his life, as they have, but he has now come upon hard times, especially because he suffers from "arthritis" (the only English word he uses). In his hand he holds a cane. He has a family to support, as we all do, and if we could give him some financial help, he says, he would be most appreciative.

The man's forthrightness has frozen the participants in their places. No one has sneaked out the door or even tried to leave. No one can claim ignorance of this stranger's needs. He has shined a spotlight on all of us by putting one on himself, knowing that, if he can tap one or two people for money, the rest will feel impelled to give in domino-like fashion. A few of the men begin to take out their wallets, looking at the other's actions. All the donations are bills, and all are handed to Rabbi Housmann. Some members ask Housmann for change—something that could not be done without embarrassment were the money being given directly to the schnorrer.

While Housmann is collecting the money, those who have already given wait and talk. The ritualized giving is evidently not yet complete. Some members complain aloud about the need to give, one man saying, "I don't understand. In these times of social security benefits and all. . . ." But the grumbles are hardly as abusive as those made to beggars, and everyone who grumbles still donates. In response to some complaints about the need for giving, Velvel says, "It's a *mitzvah* (positive and mandatory ritual commandment) to give him (that is, the schnorrer) some money." Giving is a religious responsibility, as important for the donor as for the recipient. The others agree and add, as one man puts it, "God forbid that we should ever need it," a comment never heard in the presence of any other kind of mendicant.

The schnorrer receives the money from Housmann and thanks the people aloud. Then, as the people shuffle out, the schnorrer approaches some directly, shaking their hands and offering words of blessing. Finally, he approaches Harwood and asks for a ride to another synagogue nearby, the next stop on his journey. He gets his ride. (Pp. 117–18)[*]

Always, Heilman points out, there is an attempt to establish a commonness between himself and the potential donors: Dress represents a middle-class status, for example. There is an attempt to shake hands, to converse, and to do what a "guest" rather than a simple beggar might do. The schnorrer always tries to build bonds and feelings of acceptance before he "gives his pitch" because he knows that his only chance of success is to ask only *after* establishing his Jewishness and telling his sad story. No matter how often the schnorrer returns, he does not become a friend and a guest to those in the synagogue, but remains an outsider, "stigmatized by his plea for money" (p. 119).

Heilman's account presents to us a picture of life in one part of our world through firsthand and sensitive observation. No scientist could hope to

---

[*]Reprinted from *Synagogue Life: A Study in Symbolic Interaction* by Samuel Heilman, by permission of The University of Chicago Press. Copyright © 1976 by The University of Chicago. All rights reserved.

capture the many complex aspects of interaction, communication, interpretation, and presentation of self through other types of methodology.

A Study of Little League Baseball

From synagogues we move to Little League baseball, another social world that can best be understood through firsthand observation. Gary Alan Fine (1981) examined teams in four communities for three years. His interest was in seeing how preadolescents develop social skills, skills in presenting themselves to others. Such skills are not learned through a "rote learning of behaviors or of an encyclopedia of practical knowledge" (p. 269). Preadolescents learn social skills through interaction with others, dealing with common situations, learning to fit one's own acts with those of others, learning to take one another's roles, interpreting one another's acts, and so on. Fine reports the following from his field notes:

> Hardy sees Tommy get on the bus and announces loudly, "Tommy sucks." Rod adds: "Tommy's a wuss." In unison Jerry and Rod tell Tommy as he approaches, "You suck." Rod particularly is angry at Tommy. "Harmon can't play because of you. What a fag!" Tommy doesn't respond to the abuse from his older tormentors, but looks dejected and perhaps near tears (which is what Rod and Hardy later tell Harmon). The insults build in stridency and anger as Hardy calls Tommy a "woman." Jerry knocks off his hat, and Rod says, "Give him the faggot award." Finally Jerry takes the baseball cap of Tommy's friend and seatmate and tosses it out the window of the moving bus. (P. 269)

What is the point? Why is this a significant encounter? What appears as cruelty and insults to outsiders is part of a social world where preadolescents learn about one another's expectations, where they learn how to present themselves to others, what limits exist to insults, how to react to insults. In fact, if acts go "too far," as was the case in throwing the hat out the window, one learns how to apologize. Organized baseball teams provide an opportunity for interaction among friends, which teaches the necessary skill for successful interaction. And, because there is a relationship among friends developed over a period of time, people have a history of interaction, and any isolated episode is not likely to be very threatening to self-perception. We feel comfortable around friends; we are more likely to be open; we learn many of the essentials of interaction.

A Study of Bachelorhood and Conversion

The final example is a study by John Darling (1977) of "Bachelorhood and Late Marriage." What happens to the man who seems to be a confirmed bachelor when he suddenly gives that up and decides on marriage? The study concentrates on "interaction": how interaction influences bachelorhood to begin with, then how it alters that status. Forty men were studied. Half were over thirty-five and never married; half married after the age of thirty-five.

Here the research technique used was in-depth interviews, the collecting of life histories from the men.

Almost all of the men reported that "in adolescence they had a great deal of difficulty in peer-group interactions" (p. 47). They entered adulthood without much dating experience, *and* they entered without much pressure from significant others (both parents and friends) to date. If they had friends, the friends usually did not date either. "None of them had parents who asked 'Why aren't you dating like others your age?' " (p. 51). About one-third were very involved in interaction with family, which prevented them from seeking relationships outside the home. There is no one quality that influenced bachelorhood; there is a cluster: "Rather, bachelorhood arises in the context of a web of situations and definitions that make marriage unlikely at various points in the life histories of individuals" (p. 51).

Those who decide on marriage after thirty-five are best described as going through a process of "conversion." They are seekers: The old social world within which they lived their lives was "crumbling," and they were lonely. Friends were marrying, and parents died. A turning point occurred for the late-marrieds that did not really occur for those who did not marry. "Most of the late-marrieds had short courtships; they were at turning points that made them ripe for marriage, and they wasted little time in becoming involved with the woman who happened to be available at the time" (p. 50).

These empirical studies are good examples of the perspective of symbolic interactionism. All attempt to capture interaction, definition, and decision making over a period of time. The actor changes; situations are dynamic; action goes first one way, then another. The human is understood as a highly complex problem solver, defining and redefining directions in which to go in situations.

SYMBOLIC INTERACTIONISM: SOME EXAMPLES
OF APPLICATION

A student in my class on symbolic interactionism asked me: "This is all fine and dandy, but what in the world does this perspective have to do with anything? What is its relevance?" I could not believe that this perspective, so powerful for me, could not be applied by the student. "It's relevant to everything human," I began. "All situations can be described using this perspective—this classroom interaction, for example, race relations, war, a football game, a family, a party . . . ," and I went on and on, patting myself on the back as I proudly announced all the applications that occurred to me at the time. "But I'm going to work with delinquents," was the reply. "How can I use this to help them, to change them, to make them better?" Then I knew that relevance to this student meant changing people—how do we as teachers teach better, how can we alter behavior for the better, change attitudes, make a better world? For me relevance has always meant just plain understanding—how well does Marx understand society, or Freud understand it, or Mead? In fact, the point of the symbolic interactionists seems to be that human beings are not easily manipulated, altered, predictable. I realized that the perspective may aid *my understanding of human complexity* but not necessarily suggest how to successfully change or manipulate others.

Another student who was in business management told me: "The thing that symbolic interactionism taught me was that it is very difficult to manage people any way one chooses; people are active and thinking, and they determine their own directions in interaction with others and with themselves. This is important when I go out into the business world and deal with people." Symbolic interactionism may not yet be relevant to those who want to systematically alter people in a given direction, but it is a very relevant perspective for understanding human social situations. As it does this more and more accurately, prediction and the ability to change people may result (if that is what one chooses to do with knowledge).

The point of the business management student cannot be taken lightly: It is interaction that affects the direction of the individual, and the nature of interaction—overt and covert—is difficult for one to control or direct except in a small number of situations. We can teach our children values, but these values will be effective in directing the child only if they influence the child's interaction and only if they continue to be important in the perspectives he or she shares with others. It seems that the teacher or parent must be prepared to see these values transformed or put aside during interaction with others who become the new significant others or reference groups. The convicted criminal can be put away in a prison community, can learn new values, can take on a different perspective, can have a different "personality," but when the prisoner is released these things will be effective only if *interaction* is influenced, and only if interaction does not lead the individual to define the world in the same way he or she defined it before imprisonment. To change the person is to change his or her interaction, social worlds, reference groups, and perspectives, and thus alter the person's definition of self and situations. Given the nature of modern society this goal seems difficult for one person to set for another.

Symbolic interactionism is a perspective that can be applied to all social situations and can help illuminate them. This goes for two people on a date, for a college classroom, for any game like chess or football, for bringing up children, and for social problems such as crime and inequality. All of these involve interaction as well as interaction within individuals with selves, minds, symbols, perspectives, analyzing, problem solving, cooperating, sharing, communicating, and aligning acts. I have tried to apply this perspective to my world, and I find it full of insights. If it is going to be useful, one must take the concepts and use them to analyze situations. I would like to give briefly some examples of how I have applied this perspective to things that concern me.

An Understanding of Society

Society and morality are very appropriate ways to apply this perspective to something important. Nothing human is as complex to understand as the nature of society, and nothing is as important to society as the relationship between morality and society. It is so easy in this modern age to worship the individual and to be attracted to a perspective (such as symbolic interactionism) that supports the fact that the human being is free and is the creator of society. Most of us want to believe this.

Yet Erving Goffman reminds us that society exists only through an agreement by people to cooperate, to respect one another, and to act according to a generalized body of rules. Only when we agree to support one another's face in interaction, to accept what one presents himself or herself to be, is society possible. In short, society rests on respect for one another, the acceptance of a shared body of rules, and the use of a common perspective that allows all to understand one another. Mead, too, returns again and again to the moral basis for society: Society is possible only through the agreement by individuals to use the morals of society as a generalized other—as a guide—to control action in light of the needs of the whole.

Society seems very tenuous in the symbolic interactionist perspective, almost always on the verge of collapse, always negotiated, always changing, always new. But this is not an inaccurate picture: Society does not continue automatically; every group's existence today is not guaranteed tomorrow. It becomes clearer and clearer that the Soviet Union is not a society anymore. It is really made up of several independent societies—not because that is how it must be, but because interaction, cooperation, and culture have separated the Soviet Union into these separate societies. My group of friends can be lost tomorrow—if we no longer interact, share a culture (including rules we agree to control ourselves by), cooperate (to enjoy ourselves playing poker and tennis), talk out the problems that concern us, discuss world events. The group will be no more when we do not respect one another's identities, and when we are unwilling to adjust our own actions in relation to the other individuals and in relation to the whole.

Symbolic interactionism—a perspective so involved in trying to understand individuals and their ability to act freely in the world—makes an important contribution to sociology and to those who are interested in the human being as a social being because it tells us so much about the nature of *society*.

An Understanding of Racism in Society

Symbolic interactionism also can help us understand social problems in this society and in the world. This is no small matter. The student has a right to expect that perspectives within sociology should contribute to understanding the problems of inequality, poverty, racism, sexism, crime, meaningless work, alienation, violent conflict, mental illness, and other problems that caring people should be concerned with.

To many sociologists the society of the United States is characterized by racial inequality, racial segregation, racial conflict, and racism. Symbolic interactionism offers a fresh approach to understanding this problem.

We begin with the nature of society. People who interact with one another form society. They take one another into account; they communicate, role take, and cooperate. They share an understanding of reality, and they develop a set of rules to live by. At the same time, the development of society through cooperative symbolic interaction will, by its very nature, cut off interaction with those outside that interaction. This is the basis for the racial problems in this society, and it is the basis for similar problems in all societies. The United States has developed a segregated society—thus, in a basic sense it is not one society, but several. The reasons for segregation are several, all embedded in our history: slavery, exploitation, racist institutions, legal and de facto segregation. Today, however, we face conflict arising from that segregation, conflict that can threaten whatever other gains we might have made in our history. Let us briefly examine some of the effects of segregation in our society (or any society).

1. Where interaction creates separate societies, each will develop its own culture, and individuals will be governed by different sets of rules and share a different perspective. Without continuous interaction between people in various societies, actors in each will fail to communicate with and understand the other, and role taking and cooperation between them will be minimized. *Human differences, exaggerated and perpetuated through segregated interaction, are what bring about the creation of two societies in one, two societies that continue to be at odds to the extent that opportunities for interaction and cooperation between them are not available.*

2. If one of these separate societies has more power in the political arena of the nation, its representatives will be in the position to stigmatize the other—that is, its leaders will be able to define the other as less worthy; it will be able to define the other society as having a culture that is unacceptable and even threatening to the dominant culture. *Racism is a philosophy expressed in the public arena that condemns as inferior societies that are different, and racism is action that retains the inferior position and continued segregation of societies.*

3. People in the dominant society through interaction develop a perspective—one that is useful for their understanding of reality. Included is their definition of those in the other society and the reasons for their differences, as well as a justification for the inequality that exists between the other society and the dominant one. *It is through this definition of those who are different as heathens, infidels, savages, slaves, or enemies that one society develops a justification for taking land, enslaving, discriminating, or segregating, or simply refusing to work for equality.* The dominant culture might include such ideas as the others are biologically inferior, the others are not motivated (like we are), the others are

threats to what we stand for, or if the others would only be like the rest of us they could be equal. Many ideas in the dominant society would not be blatantly racist, but the implications might be: "Ours is a society where anyone can be whatever he or she wants to be" (thus, the reason why some people— often minorities—are poor is because they do not work hard enough), or "Our educational system gives equal opportunity to all our citizens" (so those who do not make it do not take the opportunities offered to all).

4. Where interaction is segregated, and all people are unable to develop a shared culture, the others will continue to be seen as different. No matter if real differences do in fact exist, where segregation exists differences will be perceived, exaggerated, not understood, and often condemned. It is almost too much to expect people who form their own culture to be able to see other cultures as equally good. *To the extent that people in the dominant society see their own culture as right and true, others who are different will be defined as threats. To them, this makes destructive actions against the others appear justifiable.*

5. Destructive action against others also seems justifiable if we can somehow make them into objects rather than people. It is easier for us to see those people similar to us as people; people who are different from us—who are part of societies separate from us—we do not understand and cannot easily take their roles. *We do not regularly interact, communicate, and cooperate with them. How much easier it is to see them as objects who do not seem to have equally important problems, concerns, interests.* This not only encourages destructive actions, but it also works against efforts to aid the other.

6. *It is conflict rather than cooperation that characterizes segregated societies.* Without interaction, which includes communication, role taking, and recognizing the mutual identities of actors who are necessary for cooperative action, no shared culture is likely to develop, and the different definitions will continue.

It is difficult to illustrate here all the ways that the symbolic interactionist perspective can be usefully applied to this serious problem, but these six points should be a start. Remember: We can understand social problems such as racism and racial conflict through focusing on interaction, cooperation, communication, culture, and definition, and such an analysis can bring us very far. Symbolic interactionist ideas can be applied to understanding problems between all ethnic groups in society, between people of different classes, between labor and management, and between nations. When interaction is cut off between societies, a perspective cannot be easily shared, the acts of each cannot be understood by the other, and problem solving becomes impossible, aligning acts fail to materialize, and emotion and habitual response replace cooperative symbolic interaction between the groups.

An Understanding of Gender Differences

"Nearly all feminists agree that women have historically been denied the opportunity to construct their own separate identity, their own sense of self-hood and purpose apart from the definitions imposed on them by men" (Ferguson, 1980;128–29).

Who are we? What does it mean to be a woman—or a man? Symbolic interactionists see men and women as they see everything else in nature: These are classifications that we regard as useful—otherwise we would not see people this way. But why is it that this distinction is useful? The answer is that we probably have so defined this classification minimally for purposes of having sex, having children, and socializing children. It has proved useful to us, and so we continue to make it.

In most societies this distinction is a primary one, and the biological distinction has grown to be enlarged to include many of our actions, from color of blankets to power relationships and opportunities in life. We might point out that such distinctions have been especially useful for men, who claim a privileged position in society. The definition of who women are in the world may have originally arisen among men (in interaction with one another), or even between men and women, but over time that definition has influenced the views that women have of themselves. My purpose in life—my reason to be—is an integral part of my definition of myself, and if I see myself as an object to be used by men, as an instrument of reproduction, as a servant to others, then this is how I will act and how I will present myself in my actions to others. Others will continue to see me this way, recognizing my identity, and generally approving it through their actions.

The question of how the individual is socialized, and how we come to take on our identities and define what we are supposed to do is the way the symbolic interactionist tries to understand gender differences. Spencer Cahill (1986) observed children in a nursery specifically to understand the process of "gender identity acquisition": At first children act in ways that have little to do with how sex-appropriate those acts are. As adults begin to distinguish through language which of these acts are male and which are female, the children learn who they are and which types of behavior belong to their identities. Then in play with one another they increasingly try to take on appropriate actions that others have identified, and in interaction with one another reaffirm those identities: "You be the mom!" "No, you should be the mom—you're the girl!"

> Through interactions such as these, children apparently learn that in order to gain recognition as full-fledged persons they must avoid appearing and behaving in ways that contradict, in the eyes of others, their socially bestowed sex identity. Because of children's desire to be recognized as such persons, most children become increasingly concerned with doing so. (P. 300)

Who are these people we call women? Who am I, one who is a woman? This reality, like all else, is defined in interaction, and this, like all else, changes in interaction. What is happening today is that women are increasingly defining who they are in interaction with one another rather than in interaction with men. Women in the United States are increasingly forming their own social worlds, and are claiming that they are something other than what men have traditionally claimed. Women have organized in part to change the dominant definitions of men and women, and have attempted to change how political leaders, media, schools, and families limit people through such definitions. Increasingly, we are finding subtle and powerful ways people define gender, and as a society we are recognizing that men and women are far more socially created categories than biological ones.

Always there is in symbolic interactionism the underlying idea that people are not stamped out by their environment or by their socializers, that regardless of how others define us, there is also the fact that individuals will interact with themselves, develop their own identities apart from others, overcoming in part the power of social interaction. Throughout history many women have been able to do this. Probably people have recognized from the beginning that "I do not necessarily have to be who I have learned from others I am." What has changed in our society is that many people are joining to say this, and the result is an emerging definition that includes real alternatives by which people can guide their lives, and go in directions most would not have chosen in the past.

An Understanding of Dating, Marriage, and Family

Much of our lives takes place in families: We are born into families, and then we date, marry, and form our own families.

Almost all of us share the experience of dating. Symbolic interactionism can easily be applied to understanding what goes on when we date and what dating someone may lead to in our lives.

For many of us, asking someone out for a date is an important problem. We do not know what to say. Some of us give far too much importance to how we ask the question, but we simply do not want to blow it. Of course, for others, this does not seem to be a big problem, since they have developed ways of handling such situations. In symbolic interactionist terms, asking someone for a date is a way that we communicate something about ourselves; the question is far more than simply a bunch of words. My words have meaning and they are meant to communicate: I am interested in you or I need company so please join me *or* I'm really scared *or* I'm cool *or* I like having a good time *or* you are just one person of many I can ask *or* you are really special. Of course, no matter what I try to communicate, you will, in turn, interpret my request, taking my role, trying to understand my intentions and a little about who I am: He's nice, he's interested in me, I wonder what he really wants, he's really nervous, and so on. On the phone we might continue to talk, always role taking, communicating, interpreting, and trying to present a picture to the other of who we are.

We meet, we interpret one another according to dress, looks, acts, speech, the objects we surround ourselves with (my car, your cap). We do this in order to help assure the continuation of the interaction, or in order to get away from the other as fast as possible, or in order to continue to influence the other in a way that we choose. Each time we interact, there is an analysis of meaning, a greater sharing of meaning, and over time there will arise a perspective, along with more and more knowledge of how to align our acts in relation to one another. Kissing and love making are symbolic acts, too. They stand for past experience, future intent, current feelings, and view of self and other. Over time we create our own society, and our society becomes a reference group to each of us—when we are together and when we are apart.

Conflict with parents may occur, perhaps because a new perspective is replacing an older one, or a new reference group is emerging. Interaction with parents may occur less often, and failure to align our acts in relation to our parents or take their role on a regular basis will cause an unwillingness and/or an inability to understand one another's communications. Automatic emotional response to one another may enter into our interaction, followed by reflection, guilt, and/or blame. Cooperation no longer may characterize our interaction.

Over time we may decide to marry the one we have dated for a while, and a short time later we may decide that this is not what we want and go in another direction. Several decisions along our stream of action will have to be made for us to marry. And if we do marry, and if parents still object, once the marriage occurs a new situation to be defined now enters all of our lives. Increasingly, our new family becomes important, and our parents may become more and more apart from our interaction. On the other hand, if we have children, our definition of our own parents may change, and their definition of us and our marriage may also change, and with increasing interaction with parents, the old reference group will be renewed. Over time the husband and wife may even drift farther apart, each becoming increasingly involved in social worlds apart from each other—at work, with friends, and so on—and what once looked like an ideal cooperative society may be undermined. Problems of communication, failure to role take and align action accurately may eventually lead to separation and dissolution of the family.

An Understanding of Childhood Socialization

Symbolic interactionism can be useful for almost every aspect of our lives. One of the problems many of us will face is parenthood. What does it mean to be a good parent?

Symbolic interactionists have a view that is different from many other perspectives of what is important in the socialization of children. Most other perspectives assume the stable view of the human being: We are personalities, we develop traits in childhood, and those traits will be carried by us into adulthood. The symbolic interactionist view looks at the human being as an ever-changing actor, communicating, role taking, cooperating, problem solving along a stream of action. We are all capable of going in many directions. What we value at one point will be different from what we value at another point. What we believe—about the world and about ourselves—will constantly change, as well as our significant others and our reference groups. Does parenthood matter? If so, how?

Parenthood does in fact matter. To begin with, all along we have emphasized that actors are influenced in the directions that they take along their stream of action by decisions they make due in part to interaction with others. All the acts that we perform in relation to our children can have an influence on the directions they go in life—what we do in our lives that they can observe, what we intentionally communicate to them, the words we use to describe them, the identities we give them. Continuous interaction has a good chance of influencing direction. Even though it is unlikely that ongoing interaction will continue to any great extent as they become adults, the directions they were influenced to take through interaction with us at an earlier point in their lives may always remain important.

On top of this, if through interaction we remain significant others to our children, our perspectives will be used by them to define their world. Without interaction, we will probably become less important; if others replace us as significant others, our perspectives will no longer be used. However, if they find our perspective useful or if they continue to regard us as important actors in their lives, then our perspectives will continue to be important to them.

Parenthood is far more complex than simple influence over directions or remaining significant others to our children. If the human being is the kind of actor that the symbolic interactionist claims, then there are certain qualities that parents should encourage in their children, including the following:

1. *The ability to problem solve.* Problem solving is not an inherent faculty; we don't know how to do it without someone teaching us the skills necessary. Children should be encouraged to handle their own situations through a thoughtful approach to figuring out how to realistically handle situations as they occur. Problem solving is an ability to figure out for oneself how to study, how to find a job, how to perform well on a job, how to develop and maintain friendships, how to counsel others who need our advice, and how to approach almost everything we can name. This ability to understand situations and to control them to achieve goals should be an important goal for parents to nurture. Instead of teaching a child how to act in specific situations, the parent must encourage the child to figure out situations in a thoughtful manner.

2. *The ability to communicate, understand others, and role take:* Many of the problems that we all have center on these abilities. Through constantly interacting with children, encouraging them to communicate, sensitiz-

ing them to understanding what others mean, we are teaching our children skills that will matter in situations they encounter.

3. *Giving our children a moral sense:* It is very difficult to assure that the morals we give our children will follow them through life. That depends on ongoing interaction to a great extent. If they continue to use us as their significant others, then our morals will certainly remain important; if they interact with others who reaffirm our morals, then our morals will also remain important. However, there is no guarantee that this will happen, and chances are it will not happen in this society, which is so broken up into smaller societies, into many instances of interaction.

Developing a moral sense, however, is different from handing down a set of morals. A moral sense is simply a recognition that if one is going to live with other people then one should be willing to take on a shared morality, one should be willing to be governed by the rules of the society to some extent, rather than be governed simply by what one wants to accomplish at a particular moment. It means that one should constantly take the role of others and try to understand their needs as well as his or her own, and that to remain together, one must act with them in mind.

Finally, parenting matters for one more reason. The whole symbolic interactionist perspective is premised on the idea that ultimately human beings regularly define their situations and act according to those definitions. Because we live in human society and encounter many diverse situations and other human beings throughout our day, our successes depend in large part on our ability to think in the situations we act in. Causing children to respond emotionally to situations prevents thoughtful problem solving. Failure to teach self-control causes the individual to respond impulsively to situations, usually leading to inappropriate actions and missing goals. The harmful effects of child abuse—physical and emotional—stand in the way of dealing with ongoing situations, according to our definition of them, by causing unconscious response.

All of these principles—and more—are inferred from the perspective of symbolic interactionism, and are important guides for parents. Indeed, many of these principles are found in other perspectives too, and improving role taking, communication, and problem solving remains an important goal in much of the therapy that psychologists and counselors emphasize today.

Symbolic Interactionism: A View of the College Experience

Symbolic interactionism, when applied to my own life as a teacher, is awfully humbling. I started my career hoping to influence students, to get them to look at the world sociologically, humanistically, or through the symbolic interactionist perspective. I hoped to teach something that would remain with students, to make a difference in some important way. I was a teacher, in part, to try to create a better world. I woke up one day when a student stated: "You know, this is all very interesting, this is even relevant to my life, but this classroom is the only place I ever discuss these things or hear anything about them. Outside this classroom there just is not any interest or knowledge about them. I won't remember any of this when the class is all over." I realized then why things are so easily forgotten after a final exam.

A perspective is remembered if it is applied and found to be useful in a number of situations. But this is unlikely to happen unless other people around us also use it regularly and share it in interaction. A perspective is remembered if one has a reference group that shares it, if it is associated with our significant others. The different perspectives gained in the classroom cannot be expected to be remembered and applied—they are forgotten unless they continue to be shared through interaction. College itself can be an important perspective that we remember—it can become a reference group providing a perspective for our present situation—but whatever was gained will be changed considerably as we interact *now* with new people.

Unhappily, for those of us who think we can actually teach something lasting, what will probably happen to our students is this: They might learn the perspective we are trying to teach, barely remember it after the exam, or they may interact with others who share it or take another class that shares it (or may never take another class like it or interact with others who share it). They will probably graduate with little except a dim memory that will, in turn, be transformed as they interact with others in the work world who may share a perspective that contradicts or even ridicules the perspectives learned in college.

Realistically, the classroom experience is part of a long stream of action for each person. A teacher may influence the direction that stream of action takes. He or she may influence the student's desire to interact with others who share an academic, sociological, psychological, or biological perspective or, at least, may influence the student's desire to continue to interact with those who are open to discussing these perspectives intelligently.

Symbolic Interactionism: A Final Look
230at Application

It is impossible to show all the ways that this perspective can be applied because in fact it can be applied to any human experience. It is a refreshing view, for it explains human action in a way that most perspectives miss. The perspective describes everyday situations as well as complex social problems. The perspective is regularly applied in sociology to understanding social deviance in society. It has illuminated the problems of mental health, racism and racial conflict, and substance abuse. It has been applied to understanding society, education, and communication. It serves as an important guide to all of us seeking to understand ourselves and others, and it helps explain how freedom is possible and society necessary.

THE IMPORTANCE OF THE SYMBOLIC
INTERACTIONIST PERSPECTIVE

The symbolic interactionist perspective is important for all *social science*. It is a criticism of social science, calling forth an alteration of direction and a set of new assumptions about human action. It is revolutionary. By emphasizing the active nature of humans, it questions the scientific potential for fully under-standing and predicting human behavior. It asks that we focus on a definition of the situation, which is an active process, impossible to predict exactly, but to some extent understandable through careful and systematic investigation. It questions the attempts to understand human behavior by studying attitudes or values the human chooses on a questionnaire. It sees experiments done with nonsymbolizing animals as limited approaches to the understanding of the human being, and it questions the validity of applying certain accepted scien-tific methods uncritically to the understanding of human action. Symbolic interactionism sees the human as too complex an organism to be studied by such methods. Action is seen as caused not by something from a distant past, but by symbolic interaction between and within individuals. It emphasizes that actions have a long, continuous history, that the cause of any isolated act is not easily located, and that action shifts direction from time to time. In the end, symbolic interactionism calls for social science to see humans from a different perspective, and to adjust its scientific focus and techniques accordingly.

Symbolic interactionism also has much to offer the *disciplines outside of social science*, such as the humanities, communications, and philosophy. The nature of reality, the meaning of the self, the emergence and importance of society, the nature of symbols, the importance of human communication, and the future of humanity all are topics symbolic interactionists share with these other disciplines. Mead seems to relate increasingly to more and more people outside of sociology, and other symbolic interactionists recognize this. Indeed, the Society for the Study of Symbolic Interaction, an active academic organi-zation that meets and discusses research being done and issues of concern for symbolic interactionists, draws from people all over the world and appeals to many who are not sociologists. Ruth Wallace and Alison Wolf (1986) write that symbolic interactionism "can be seen as an alternative perspective providing theoretical tools which are missing in other perspectives." (p. 231) Peter Hall (1981) reminds us that it has become increasingly diverse, has recently gone into new areas of study, and is using new research techniques.

Symbolic interactionism has a number of important implications for *soci-ology* specifically. It is critical of traditional sociology in the same ways it is crit-ical of all social science. But it is also extremely enriching and adds immea-surably to the important insights of this field. For example, it adds to our understanding of the sociology of knowledge; it describes the social nature of reality, how our group life or our society creates our definition of reality, inter-nal or external. It tells us of the power available to those who control symbols, perspectives, and definitions. The perspective can be applied to understand-ing further the "collective consciousness" in Durkheim, the "class consciousness" and "false consciousness" in Marx, the religious perspectives in Weber, and the "forms of interaction" in Simmel, to name only the most obvious ties with sociological theory. Symbolic interactionism has been applied to the theoretical and empirical study of deviance, emphasizing the importance of definition, self-definition, interaction, and power. It has been applied to socialization, collective behavior, and various social problems. Its definition of society is useful because it emphasizes both society's dynamic nature and the kinds of action between individuals necessary for its continuation. It seems to me that symbolic interactionism, more than any other perspective in sociology, clearly describes the intricate interrelationships between the individual and society: Society makes the individual through creation of the self, mind, symbols, generalized other, perspectives, and symbolic role taking. Conversely, it is the human individual who makes human society through active interpretation, self-direction, role taking, aligning his or her own acts with others, and communicating. By regarding the human as so thoroughly social and symbolic, and by describing the complex ways this is so, symbolic interactionism makes a major contribution to the sociological perspective.

It is difficult to know the precise place that symbolic interactionism fills within the more general sociological perspective. On the one hand, it is part of sociology and one of the leading contemporary perspectives. Its insights are sociological; its practitioners are among the leading sociologists. On the other hand, it differs from the work of most sociologists, asking serious questions about many of the directions we have gone. Ruth Wallace and Alison Wolf (1986) emphasize this complexity:

> Symbolic interactionism . . . has experienced a resurgence recently, with the founding of The Society for the Study of Symbolic Interaction and the publication of a new journal, *Symbolic Interaction.* A perspective that places a primary value on subjective meaning and on process as opposed to structure, combined with a methodology that takes great pains to capture the "world of the other" as seen by that other, asks important sociological questions that cannot be answered by mainstream sociology. Symbolic interactionism can be seen as an alternative perspective providing theoretical tools which are missing in other perspectives. It therefore deserves recognition as an approach that makes important and distinctive contributions to sociology. (P. 231)

Peter Hall (1981) approximates my own perception of symbolic interactionism today:

> Symbolic interaction today has greater theoretical and empirical diversity than a decade ago. More attempts have been made to span other theoretical points of view. It has been extended into new areas of study and uses new research techniques. In addition, some interactionists have formally organized themselves into a society, publish a journal, and hold annual meetings. (P. 49)

Even more than this: Besides this journal there is also a *Studies in Symbolic Interaction Annual,* and besides just one annual meeting, there are several, with increasing opportunities for symbolic interactionists to share ideas and research. There are several interactionists on boards of journals and organizations in mainstream sociology, and increasingly sociologists are using symbolic interactionism in their analysis of socialization, culture, society, and social structure. Goffman's dramaturgical sociology is increasingly making its mark, and ethnomethodology—although probably not symbolic interactionist—has much in common with symbolic interactionism and the two of them make analysis of everyday interaction more important in sociology. It may be, as Sheldon Stryker (1980) suggests, that "by being absorbed into sociology at large, symbolic interactionism may disappear, may—in other words—lose by winning!" (p. 8) Yet, it seems that today symbolic interactionism as a unique perspective has become increasingly attractive to sociologists throughout the world, and remains a distinct perspective.

Finally, we must remember that the symbolic interactionist perspective is important to those of us who are *students of human action,* interested in understanding the nature of human life, society, truth, and freedom. That is the appeal the perspective has had for me, and that has been the underlying theme of this book. This perspective contributes to a liberal arts education: It deals intelligently and systematically with some of the most important questions concerning human life.

SUMMARY

Symbolic interactionism is a perspective. Like all other perspectives, it is limited because it must focus on some aspects of reality and ignore or deemphasize others. It is different from all other social scientific perspectives, and is, in part, a criticism of the directions taken by these other perspectives.

Symbolic interactionism questions the determinism that prevails in much of social science. It tries to show that the possibility of freedom exists only through the use of symbols, self, and mind. And instead of blindly asserting that human beings are in fact free, symbolic interactionism shows many of the limits of freedom. Freedom is a complex issue; to symbolic interactionists its existence is possible, but it is always limited.

Symbolic interactionists consider themselves scientists, but their science is based on a methodology that emphasizes interviewing, observing people acting in the real world, and determining how people define the situations they act in. Representative studies described in this chapter included three that interviewed people in various life situations: bachelors, pregnant drug users, and prison inmates. One study interviewed a single person in order to better understand the development of his identity as a wrestler. Two others were based on participant observation: In one study it was synagogue life; in the other it was a Little League baseball team. Always the focus was on *how people defined their world, and how that definition shaped their action.*

Throughout the book I have tried to show how symbolic interactionism is a useful way to understand the real world. It is not simply a perspective to memorize for an exam, but one that can be easily applied. In this final chapter, I was more direct in showing its applications: from understanding society, racism, and gender inequality, to understanding personal situations such as dating, socializing children, and college life.

Finally, it is important to realize that symbolic interactionism is an increasingly influential perspective today: in the academic community, in social science, and in sociology.

REFERENCES

ATHENS, LONNIE H.
    1984   "Blumer's Method of Naturalistic Inquiry: A Critical Examination." *Studies in Symbolic Interaction* 5:241–57.

BLUMER, HERBERT
    1969   *Symbolic Interactionism: Perspective and Method.* Englewood Cliffs, N.J.: Prentice Hall. Copyright © 1969. Reprinted by permission of Prentice Hall, Inc.

CAHILL, SPENCER E.
    1986   "Socialization, Language, and Gender Identity Acquisition." *Sociological Quarterly* 27:295–311.

CURRY, TIMOTHY JON
    1993   "A Little Pain Never Hurt Anyone: Athletic Career Socialization and the Normalization of Sports Injury." *Symbolic Interaction* 16:273–90.

DARLING, JON
    1977   "Bachelorhood and Late Marriage: An Interactionist Interpretation." *Symbolic Interaction* 1:44–55.

DENZIN, NORMAN K.
    1971   "The Logic of Naturalistic Inquiry." *Social Forces* 50:166–82.

FERGUSON, KATHY E.
    1980   *Self, Society, and Womankind.* Westport, Conn.: Greenwood Press.

FINE, GARY ALAN
    1981   "Friends, Impression Management, and Preadolescent Behavior." In Gregory Stone and Harvey Farberman, *Social Psychology through Symbolic Interaction*, eds., 2nd ed., pp. 257–72. Lexington, Mass.: Ginn.

GROSS, EDWARD, AND GREGORY P. STONE
    1964   "Embarrassment and the Analysis of Role Requirements." *American Journal of Sociology* 70:1–15.

HALL, PETER M.
    1981   "Structuring Symbolic Interaction: Communication and Power." *Communication Yearbook* 4:49–60.

HEILMAN, SAMUEL C.
    1976   *Synagogue Life: A Study in Symbolic Interaction.* Chicago: University of Chicago Press. Copyright © 1976 by The University of Chicago. All rights reserved.

KEARNEY, MARGARET H., SHEIGLA MURPHY, AND MARSHA ROSENBAUM
    1993   "At Least I Feel Guilty: Emotions and Reflexivity in Pregnant Drug Users' Accounts." Unpublished paper presented at the American Sociological Association 88th Annual Meeting.

SCHMID, THOMAS J., AND RICHARD S. JONES
    1991   "Suspended Identity: Identity Transformation in a Maximum Security Prison." *Symbolic Interaction* 14:415–32.

SCHWARTZ, HOWARD, AND JERRY JACOBS
    1979   *Qualitative Sociology: A Method to the Madness.* New York: Free Press.

SHIBUTANI, TAMOTSU
    1978   *The Derelicts of Company K.* San Francisco: Jossey-Bass.

STRYKER, SHELDON
    1980   *Symbolic Interactionism.* Menlo Park, Calif.: Benjamin/Cummings.

    1981   "Symbolic Interactionism: Themes and Variations." *Social Psychology,* pp. 1–29. In Morris Rosenberg and Ralph Turner, eds., New York: Basic Books.

WALLACE, RUTH, AND ALISON WOLF
    1986   *Contemporary Sociological Theory.* Englewood Cliffs, N.J.: Prentice Hall.

Index

GOSHEN COLLEGE - GOOD LIBRARY

3 9310 01017439 7